Practitioner Series

W0112550

Springer
London
Berlin
Heidelberg
New York
Barcelona
Hong Kong
Milan
Paris
Singapore
Tokyo

Mary Clarkson

Developing IT Staff

A Practical Approach

 Springer

Mary Clarkson, MBCS, CEng, MITT, BSc, PGD, MSc
Barclaycard, Northampton

British Library Cataloguing in Publication Data
Clarkson, Mary
    Developing IT staff: a practical approach. – (Practitioner series)
    1. Information technology 2. Employees – Training of
    3. Employees – In-service training of
    I. Title
004'. 07155
ISBN 1852334339

Library of Congress Cataloging-in-Publication Data
Clarkson, Mary, 1951–
    Developing IT staff: a practical approach/Mary Clarkson.
        p. cm. – (Practitioner series)
    Includes bibliographical references and index.
    ISBN 1–85233–433–9 (alk. paper)
    1. Information technology. 2. Employees – Training of. I. Title. II. Series.
T58.5.C46 2001
658.3'1245–dc21

2001017047

Practitioner series ISSN 1439–9245

ISBN 1-85233-433-9   Springer-Verlag London Berlin Heidelberg
a member of BertelsmannSpringerScience + Business Media GmbH
http://www.springer.co.uk

Typeset by Florence Production Ltd, Stoodleigh, Devon
Printed and bound by the Atheneum Press Ltd., Gateshead, Tyne & Wear
34/3830-543210 Printed on acid-free paper SPIN 10791996

Dedication

For my father, Bill Davis

You showed us the stars
And inspired us to reach them

Acknowledgements

My special thanks go to several friends and colleagues for their encouragement and support in so many different ways: David Aubrey, Dick Barton, Margaret Black, Dave Burke, Barbara di Cara, Gordon Clark, Jan Cornell, Joanne Fone, Ian Gausden, Neil Gill, Greg Haracz, Katherine Hills, Rosemary Horwood, David Howe, Martin Kearns, Ken Melling, Richard Milner, Brad Stoddard, Bob Taylor, Dave Turnbull and Bill Wright. Thank you all for your contributions to my understanding of and enthusiasm for training in an IT context. Special thanks to those who reviewed draft copies of the manuscript and gave valuable comments. The book has improved as a result, although I take full responsibility for the finished product. A thousand thanks to those wonderful people who have helped in preparing this book: Barbara Whiteman, who volunteered to read the proofs and calmed me down as deadlines approached, and Rebecca Mowat who has been a very patient editor steering the book and its author through to production. Thank you both for your professional wisdom and steadying influence in what has been for me unknown territory. My heartfelt thanks to sons Will and James and husband Ian for sustained enthusiasm, encouragement and quiet support. Your continued interest and delight have made it all worthwhile.

Learning Cycle and Learning Style models in Chapter 1 are reprinted by permission from:
Peter Honey Publications Limited
Ardingly House
10 Linden Avenue
Maidenhead
Berks SL6 6HB
Tel 01628 633946
Fax 01628 633262
Email peterhoney@peterhoney.co.uk
http://www.peterhoney.co.uk
http://www.learningbuzz.com

Course Feedback Form in Chapter 6 is printed by permission from
Institute of IT Training
Institute House
Sir William Lyons Road
University of Warwick Science Park
Coventry CV4 7EZ
http://www.iitt.org.uk

Java is a trademark of Sun Microsystems, Inc. in the United States and other countries.

Lotus Authorised Education Center is a trademark of Lotus Development Corporation.

Microsoft Certified Network Engineer (MCNE), Microsoft Certified Software Engineer (MCSE) and Visual Basic are either registered trademarks or trademarks of Microsoft Corporation in the United States and other countries.

I have followed the usual convention of using third person masculine pronouns to include both male and female persons. I hope you are neither mislead nor offended by this convention, as I use it only to ensure a readable text.

The text contains many examples of individual training needs. For the most part, these examples are amalgamations of several real individual cases, with fictional names. Any resemblance to actual individuals is unintentional and purely coincidental.

Series Editor's Foreword

IT Training is, or should be, a major interest of any IT activity. But where to find out information about the ramifications of IT Training, and in a practical and readable form? Mary Clarkson's book is the answer.

Developing IT Staff: A Practical Approach can be read as a training manual for IT Trainers, or as a reference handbook, or even as a series of vignettes concerning various aspects of IT Training. The book is a model of clear well-structured writing, obviously a follower of Nietzsche's quote:

"It takes less time to learn how to write nobly than how to write lightly and straightforwardly".

The book is primarily aimed at team leaders in IT departments, but should also be useful in helping people who are not team leaders to understand the learning process for themselves. It provides practical guidelines on how the team leader can get people started on their skill development and support them through the learning process. It is exemplified with real examples of life as a technical specialist, and as an IT training manager.

I believe that any IT concern should own this book, be it business, government, education etc. The learning process continues indefinitely. This book assists it.

Ray Paul

Contents

Introduction xvii

1 Background 1
   1.1 Introduction 1
   1.2 Main Points of this Chapter 1
   1.3 Training and Education 1
   1.4 How Adults Learn 2
      1.4.1 Learning by Experience 2
      1.4.2 Learning Cycle 3
      1.4.3 Learning Styles 3
      1.4.4 Conscious Competence 5
   1.5 Stakeholders 5
      1.5.1 Individual 5
      1.5.2 Team Leader 6
      1.5.3 Trainer 6
      1.5.4 Team 6
      1.5.5 Organization 6
      1.5.6 Customers 6
      1.5.7 Involvement 7
   1.6 Team Leader's Role in Training 7
      1.6.1 Develop the Individuals 7
      1.6.2 Contract Staff 7
      1.6.3 Learning Culture 8
      1.6.4 Nurturing 8
   1.7 Summary 8

2 Spotting the Training Need and Getting SMART 9
   2.1 Introduction 9
   2.2 Main Points of this Chapter 9
   2.3 Perceived Training Need 9
   2.4 Checking Out the Real Training Need 10
   2.5 SMART Objectives 14
      2.5.1 Specific 14
      2.5.2 Measurable 14
      2.5.3 Achievable 15
      2.5.4 Realistic 16
      2.5.5 Timely 16
      2.5.6 Balance 17

2.6   Action Plan   17
2.7   Summary   18

3 **Choosing between Training Methods – Short-term Options** .   19
3.1   Introduction   19
3.2   Main Points of this Chapter   19
3.3   Short Taught Course   19
       3.3.1 Description   19
       3.3.2 Main Features   20
       3.3.3 When to Use a Taught Course   21
       3.3.4 Selection Criteria   22
3.4   Self-Study   25
       3.4.1 Description   25
       3.4.2 Main Features of Computer-Based
              Training   25
       3.4.3 When to Use Computer-Based Training   28
       3.4.4 Main Features of Books   29
       3.4.5 Main Features of Training Videos   29
       3.4.6 Main Features of Audio Cassettes   30
       3.4.7 Selection Criteria   30
3.5   On-the-Job Training   32
       3.5.1 Description   32
       3.5.2 Planning   32
       3.5.3 Progress   35
3.6   Summary   40

4 **Choosing between Training Methods – Long-term Options** . .   41
4.1   Introduction   41
4.2   Main Points of this Chapter   41
4.3   Mentoring   41
       4.3.1 Description   41
       4.3.2 Main Features   42
       4.3.3 Choosing a Mentor   44
       4.3.4 Success Factors   45
       4.3.5 Mentoring Schemes   45
4.4   Accreditations   47
       4.4.1 Description   47
       4.4.2 Main Features   48
       4.4.3 Different Purposes   49
       4.4.4 Different Assessment Methods   50
       4.4.5 When to Use Accreditations   51
       4.4.6 Selection Criteria   52
4.5   Higher Education   53
       4.5.1 Description   53
       4.5.2 Main Features   54
       4.5.3 Different Modes of Attendance   56
       4.5.4 Different Teaching Methods   58
       4.5.5 Different Course Structures   59

	4.5.6	When to Use Higher Education	59
	4.5.7	Selection Criteria	60
	4.5.8	Corporate University	62
4.6	Summary		62

5 Learner Support ... 65

5.1	Introduction		65
5.2	Main Points of this Chapter		65
5.3	Pre-Training Support		65
	5.3.1	Pre-Training Briefing	66
5.4	Post-Training Support		71
	5.4.1	Post-Training Debriefing	71
	5.4.2	Reinforcing the Learning	74
5.5	Coaching the Learner		78
	5.5.1	Who Can Coach	78
	5.5.2	What to Discuss	80
	5.5.3	When to Coach	80
	5.5.4	Supporting Long-term Study	81
5.6	Action Groups		81
	5.6.1	Topic-Focused	82
	5.6.2	Role-Focused	82
	5.6.3	Entry-Focused	82
5.7	Summary		84

6 Evaluation: Was It Worth It? ... 85

6.1	Introduction		85
6.2	Main Points of this Chapter		85
6.3	Why Evaluate: What Evaluation is For		85
	6.3.1	Confirm Training Value	86
	6.3.2	Confirm Training Decisions	86
	6.3.3	Confirm Training Estimates	86
	6.3.4	Confirm Training Solutions	87
	6.3.5	The Need to Evaluate	87
6.4	When and How to Evaluate		88
	6.4.1	Short-term Evaluation – Post-Course Questionnaire	88
	6.4.2	Short-term Evaluation – Post-Training Debriefing	90
	6.4.3	Medium-term Evaluation	91
	6.4.4	Long-term Evaluation	94
	6.4.5	Interpreting Evaluation Responses	95
6.5	Remedies When Training Did Not Work		98
	6.5.1	Check the Circumstances	98
	6.5.2	Remedies with External Training	99
	6.5.3	Remedies with Internal Training	99
	6.5.4	Remedies with Learner-Driven Training	100
6.6	Is It Worth Evaluating?		100
6.7	Summary		101

7   **Career Development**   103
    7.1   Introduction   103
    7.2   Main Points of this Chapter   103
    7.3   Experience as a Development Method   103
    7.4   Defining Job Roles   106
    7.5   Moving From Role to Role   109
    7.6   Developing Within a Role   111
    7.7   Support From Professional Societies   112
    7.8   Summary   114

8   **Skill Assessment**   115
    8.1   Introduction   115
    8.2   Main Points of this Chapter   115
    8.3   Technical Testing   115
          8.3.1   Skill Types   116
          8.3.2   Testing Methods   116
          8.3.3   Uses of Technical Testing   118
    8.4   Performance Appraisals   119
          8.4.1   Different Viewpoints   119
          8.4.2   Observations of Performance   120
    8.5   Psychometric Testing   122
          8.5.1   Description   122
          8.5.2   Reasoning Skills   123
          8.5.3   Uses for Psychometric Tests   124
          8.5.4   Room for Improvement   124
    8.6   Assessment Centres and Development Centres   125
    8.7   Summary   127

9   **Soft Skills – Can They Be Taught?**   129
    9.1   Introduction   129
    9.2   Main Points of this Chapter   129
    9.3   What Are Soft Skills?   130
          9.3.1   Definitions   130
          9.3.2   Using Competencies   131
          9.3.3   Room for Improvement   133
    9.4   Which Ones Are Important?   133
    9.5   Developing Soft Skills   135
    9.6   Challenges We Face   139
          9.6.1   Finding a Role Model   139
          9.6.2   Choosing a Training Method   139
          9.6.3   Allowing Change   140
    9.7   Summary   141

10 **Wider Organizational Picture**   143
    10.1   Introduction   143
    10.2   Main Points of this Chapter   143
    10.3   Organizational Structure and Impact on Training . .   144

10.3.1 Traditional Structure 144
10.3.2 Project-Based Structure 146
10.3.3 Matrix Structure 147
10.3.4 Hybrid Structure 149
10.4 About Large Training Programmes. 150
10.4.1 Three Elements 150
10.4.2 Same Skills, Many People 151
10.4.3 Same People, Many Skills 151
10.4.4 Large in Numbers 151
10.4.5 Large in Time 152
10.4.6 Other Training Programmes 152
10.5 Setting Up Large Training Programmes 153
10.5.1 Training Requirements 153
10.5.2 Practical Arrangements 155
10.5.3 Evaluation 158
10.5.4 Large Training Programme 162
10.6 Training in the Smaller IT Department 163
10.7 Summary 164

11 Trainees: New Entrants to IT 165
11.1 Introduction 165
11.2 Main Points of this Chapter 165
11.3 What Trainees Need to Know 166
11.4 How to Develop Trainees 167
11.5 Organizing the Training 169
11.5.1 Training Programme 169
11.5.2 Individual Training Plan 170
11.5.3 Supporting Trainees 170
11.6 Graduate Entrants 170
11.7 Mature Entrants 172
11.8 Encouraging Trainees . . . . , , 174
11.9 Summary 175

12 Into the Future 177
12.1 Introduction 177
12.2 Main Points of this Chapter 177
12.3 Planning for Future Skills 177
12.4 Analysing Future Needs 178
12.5 Carrying Out the Training 181
12.5.1 Building the Training Programme 181
12.5.2 Evaluation of Training Progress 183
12.5.3 Follow-up Training 183
12.6 Supporting Self Development 183
12.7 Does the Future Ever Come? 184
12.8 Summary 185

Bibliography 187

Index 191

Introduction

What is training for the IT professional? It is more than a short course, it is more than reading a book or manual. It is more than a part time degree course. All of these things are good ways of obtaining instruction, but they are not the whole story. Training actually begins the moment you realize there is something you or one of your people cannot do and the learning process continues until you realize the learner is no longer aware of using the new skill in completing tasks.

Team leaders are increasingly tasked with developing the skills of their people. Yet they are commonly given little or no guidance in how to go about this major task. In this book I give some practical guidelines on how the team leader can get people started on their skill development and support them through the learning process. I use real examples from my experiences as a technical specialist and as an IT training manager. As the learning process is not specific to any one company or sector of the industry, so the examples are not specific either.

The book is primarily aimed at team leaders in IT departments wherever they may be, whether their organizations are large or small, whatever industry they find themselves working in. These are the people who are charged with developing the skills of IT professionals in order to exploit technology and provide solutions to business problems. As team leaders, theirs is the challenge to give day-by-day support to the skill development process. This book is for them. It will also help people who are not team leaders to understand the learning process for themselves. When we are told we "own our own development", what does that mean? This book will help you find out. It will also be of interest to IT management and students of IT management, to give them an insight into some of the issues around training and skill development and why supporting the learning process is so important. It may be that the guidelines in this book will also be helpful for team leaders and training managers in other professions, but that I cannot guarantee.

The book is structured in chapters. Chapter 1 gives some background in training theory and the team leader's role in training. Chapters 2 to 5 look at identifying the training need and finding solutions, taking primarily an individual focus. Chapter 6, on evaluation, looks at ways of telling if the chosen solution worked. Chapters 7 to 12 look at wider issues in training and take primarily a team or departmental focus. Each chapter is intended to stand alone if need be, so you can use them as reference. They should also provide a unified whole if read in order.

1. *Background*

1.1 Introduction

How do adults learn new skills? What is the difference between training and education – and is it relevant to us as team leaders? This book gives practical guidelines
to help the team leader to develop the skills of his people. To inform the discussions that follow, this first chapter gives a little background in training theory.
First I look at the differences between training and education and how they are
relevant to the team leader. Next I briefly consider how adults learn new skills and
examine some useful models of learning theory. Then I consider the stakeholders
in training – who they are and what their main concerns might be. Finally I
conclude that the main training task we have as team leaders is to help our people
learn to learn, to develop their understanding from their experiences.

1.2 Main Points of this Chapter

- Training and education
- How adults learn
- Stakeholders
- Team leader's role in training

1.3 Training and Education

Is there a difference between training and education? The dictionary tells us that
to train is to "bring to a desired standard of performance or behaviour by instruction and practice", or to "teach and accustom *to do* a thing". It also tells us that
to educate is to "train or instruct intellectually, morally and socially". (*Pocket
Oxford Dictionary*, 1984) Thus education has a wider scope than training, while
training is essentially practical in focus.

For our purposes of skill development within a work context, the same difference in emphasis is relevant. We think of training as being short-term and focused
on a small set of topics, while education is long-term and gives a broad foundation

across a range of topics. Training gives instruction and practice in the use of tools, whereas education provides the background including the wider context in which the tool is to be used. Training develops specific skills, while education develops a deeper understanding and wider knowledge of why the skills are necessary and when to use them.

When we think of training within the job of an IT professional, we are thinking of the development of a particular skill or small set of related skills. We are often thinking of a specific tool, language, methodology or piece of equipment. We often need to learn sooner rather than later. So we are generally more concerned with training than with education. The main focus for the IT team leader is on short-term training needs and skill development. Very often a skill involves the use of a specific software tool or language, so that the terms "skill" and "tool" become interchangeable.

1.4 How Adults Learn

1.4.1 Learning by Experience

Adults learn by experience. We learn *about* something by reading or hearing about it, but we learn it for ourselves by doing it. We learn by trial and error, by trying something out and seeing what happens, by making mistakes and trying again until we can get it right. We develop skills in the same way. At first while the skill is unfamiliar we have to really think about what we are doing. As we develop the skill we get used to carrying out the actions, and can stop thinking so hard about each step. When we just carry out the actions, without even being aware that we are doing them, then we have learned the skill and it becomes part of the way we do things.

Adults can learn on their own very effectively. Indeed, some people prefer not to make their mistakes in public but try to perfect their skills in a "safe" environment away from the pressures of normal work deadlines. Many people, on the other hand, find that their learning is speeded up if they can learn with someone else. Here they learn to carry out the actions, they try things to see what happens, and then find someone to talk it over with. In these discussions the two learners exchange experiences – what they tried and how it worked – and together work out why it happened that way. They are using two different viewpoints to assess the same results, and can test their conclusions against each other's point of view. The social aspect of learning can be very powerful as it allows people to explore ideas that are different from their own and to see the subject from a new angle – and thus to learn more about it quickly.

Because we as adults learn by experience, we often need to relate anything new to our previous experience and understanding. Thus we learn best from instruction which relates to what we have done or known before. We can learn all about how to carry out the actions, but until we can relate it to a task we've come across before we may find it hard to master. Once we can relate the new topic to a previous one, we can see where it fits. The context and reasons for the topic become clear. We learn not only how to use the skill but also when and why.

1.4.2 Learning Cycle

Our natural tendency to learn by experience can be described as a learning cycle as depicted in Fig. 1.1. (Honey and Mumford, 1992; their work on learning models is based on original models by Kolb, 1984, but using different descriptions). In the first stage of this learning cycle we try something out, take an action, have an experience, see what happens. In the second stage we review the experience, reflect on what happened, see the result of the action. The third stage is the point of making conclusions about the experience, deciding what the results mean, predicting what might happen in slightly different circumstances. The fourth stage has us planning the next experience, the next part of the experiment, working out what to try next. This learning cycle depicts the thought processes we go through as we learn from an experience, even though we do not always go through all the stages consciously or explicitly.

1.4.3 Learning Styles

In fact, different people tend to prefer one stage or another in the cycle. Recognizing this, Honey and Mumford developed a parallel model of learning styles that mirrors the learning cycle; see Fig. 1.2. They also developed a questionnaire which is in common use as a way of identifying an individual's preferred learning style. The learning styles are:

● Activist – those who enjoy taking actions, getting up and doing something, having an experience often for its own sake.

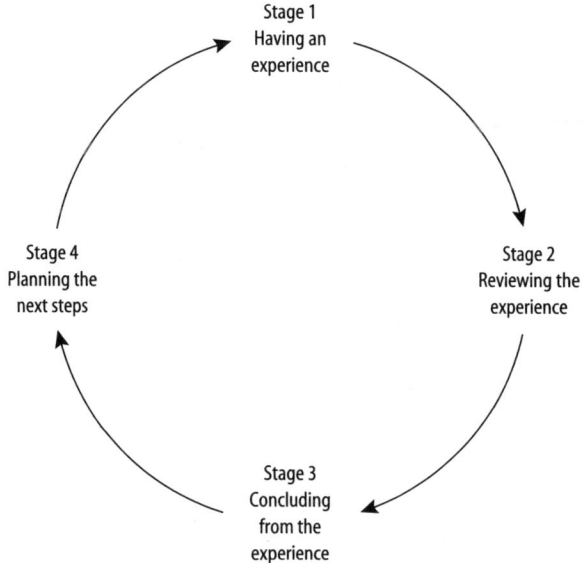

Fig. 1.1 Learning cycle

Source: Honey and Mumford, *The Manual of Learning Styles* 1992, p. 4. Reproduced with permission.

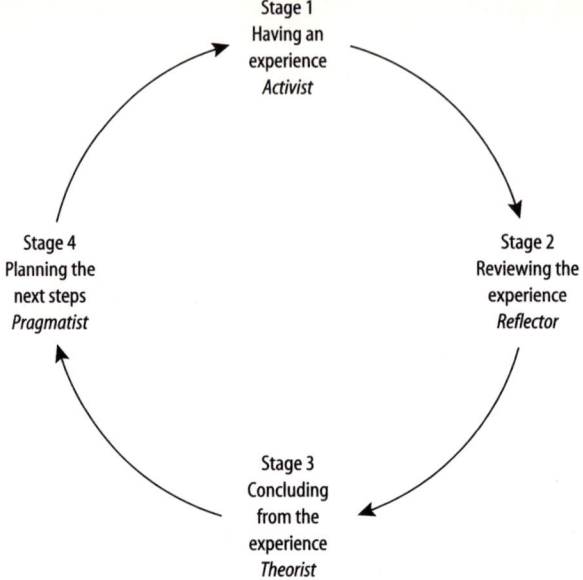

Fig. 1.2 Learning styles

Source: Honey and Mumford, 1992, p. 7. Reproduced with permission.

- Reflector – those who prefer to sit back and think about what they have experienced, reviewing what it might tell them.
- Theorist – those who like to put the results together and make conclusions, work out why what happened did happen and predict whether it would happen in different circumstances.
- Pragmatist – those who like to see how it can be done the next time, get a practical useful result, plan the next steps.

These four learning styles mirror the four stages on the learning cycle. An individual may not prefer just one style but may combine two styles. Someone may be a reflector-theorist for example, wishing to reflect on what he has experienced and also figure out why it happened that way. An individual's learning style will indicate what part(s) of the learning cycle he prefers and will concentrate on most naturally. This does not mean that he cannot do the other stages of the cycle, only that he may have difficulty or reluctance in spending any time on those activities. Thus a reflector will carry out an action then spend a lot of time reflecting on the results; the activist will do the actions but not reflect very long on the outcome – he is ready for the next action!

Both the individual and his team leader should be aware of his preferred learning style, as this will influence the kind of training activity he will enjoy most and gain most from. For example, a reflector will need a training exercise in which he can step back and review what is being learnt or tried; an activist will need to be allowed to learn by doing as actively as possible. Training exercises do not have to precisely match the individual's learning style, as people are adaptable and most can perform adequately at all stages of the cycle. In practice, most training methods do include all four stages of the learning cycle and thus do allow all learning styles to find a comfortable approach to learning.

1.4.4 Conscious Competence

Another interesting model of adult learning contains four steps on the way to unconscious competence (Kalinauckas and King, 1994; Lovell, 1980):

- Unconscious incompetence – when "ignorance is bliss", we don't yet realize that we lack a certain skill. Maybe we don't yet need that skill, maybe we're just blissfully unaware of our shortcomings in that area.
- Conscious incompetence – once we have recognized the skill gap we can start to learn the skill and fill the gap. At this stage, we don't yet have the skill but at least we are aware of the fact and are doing something about it.
- Conscious competence – having learned the basics, in this third step we still have to think about what we are doing when using the skill. "Practice makes perfect", we tell ourselves as we get better at it.
- Unconscious competence – in this final step we have mastered the skill and use it automatically without thinking about it any more. We are no longer consciously aware of the detailed processes of using the skill.

For example, when we start to use a computer keyboard we are in Step One, unaware that there are some keyboard skills we don't yet have. As we start to use the keyboard and try to type quickly we move into Step Two, realizing that there's more to this than meets the eye. If we learn to type properly, we move into Step Three where we have to work hard at hitting the right keys without always looking at what we are doing, and getting it right more and more often. When we have mastered typing skills, then we are in Step Four where we don't have to think about where the keys are but just use them automatically.

An individual can of course be in different steps with different skills, even if he is in one of the steps for his overall role or job.

This Four-Step model can be a useful aid in talking to people about their skill levels, as it asks the individual to relate his performance to the ease with which he carries out the tasks. Is he fluent with the skill, or does he still have to think about each part of the process involved?

1.5 Stakeholders

Who are the stakeholders in the training of IT professionals? There are several interested parties, although some have a relatively small influence on the training process.

1.5.1 Individual

Clearly, the individual learner has an interest in the training he receives. It is his skill set that is being developed, and he will use it not only in the current role but also possibly in future roles. Training has a big impact on the individual learner and he has a large influence on its effectiveness. He has much to gain from the ability to use the new skills as he carries out his work. If he wants to learn, his enthusiasm will carry him through the skill development process.

1.5.2 Team Leader

The learner's team leader (or supervisor or manager) also has an obvious role to play in the development of skills. In many ways training is a partnership between the individual and the team leader, with the team leader providing the opportunity for skill development. The team leader can also impact the effectiveness of the training by the extent to which he supports the individual in the learning process.

1.5.3 Trainer

The trainer or instructor is another clear participant in any training exercise; if a book or other self-study material is to be used, the trainer is the author of the material. The trainer's major impact lies in the material he chooses to present and the way in which he presents it. Good trainers will encourage the learners to go through all the stages of the learning cycle and to consolidate their learning. The trainer may be able to increase the learning by getting the individuals to relate it to their own work context.

1.5.4 Team

The individual is part of a team; these people together form another group of stakeholders. The team shares the workload with the individual; they may have gone through the same learning curve to develop the same skills. They will rely on the individual being able to carry out his tasks without continually asking for help and so will want him to succeed in his skill development. They will also be able to provide support when he returns to the workplace, by patiently answering his questions and helping him learn from his mistakes.

1.5.5 Organization

The organization in which the individual works is a somewhat more remote stake-holder in his training. The organization provides the wherewithal for the training to happen, and provides the environment in which the skill is to be used. Its influence on any one individual's training rarely goes beyond the general setting, although this includes the culture and organizational attitude to learning.

1.5.6 Customers

The individual's customers, whether internal or external, are also interested in his skill development. They need for him to carry out his tasks effectively, in a professional manner. They are more interested in the outcome of the skill development process than in the process itself. Customers tend to notice if the skill development has not yet happened, and they respond with complaints. Rarely are customers conscious of skills applied well. Thus their main influence on training is to raise awareness of training needs.

1.5.7 Involvement

When we make skill development and training decisions, we are not usually consciously thinking of the various stakeholders. Yet they are interested parties and we should not be surprised if sometimes they express that interest. Their viewpoints are valid and their opinions should be respected.

1.6 Team Leader's Role in Training

1.6.1 Develop the Individuals

As team leaders, it is our responsibility to develop all of our people. We need to understand them as individuals. We need to be aware of their different learning styles, their varying rates of learning new things, the different ways in which they react to problems. We as team leaders must recognize the differences and accept them as part of the challenge of leadership. We can work with our people as individuals to realize their potential.

Some individuals are eager to learn new things; others are more reticent about admitting to gaps in their understanding. The reluctant learners need to be reassured that the training need arises not through some failing on their part, but from the fast pace of change in today's technologies.

1.6.2 Contract Staff

In many IT departments, teams include both permanent employees and contract staff. The contractors are brought in for specific pieces of work or to fill highly specialized roles. Most organizations are happy to train their permanent staff, but what about the contractors? We can safely assume that they have the specific skills we hired them for in the first place, and that we do not need to provide training in those areas. But if we ask contractors to develop new skills to carry out their work, for example, a new version of a product they are using, or a new project planning tool we need them to use, then we should expect to support their learning. Contractors are usually keen to keep their skills up to date and are often willing to invest in their own skill development. One option is to provide and pay for the training but not to pay for their time to attend the training. Another option is the opposite, to pay for their time but expect them to meet the actual training costs. Other options include meeting all the costs including their time, or meeting none of the costs, or reaching some agreed compromise.

The important thing is to recognize that contractors are part of the team and deserve our support. They can be encouraged to learn and to help other team members to learn. Very often they have skills they could pass on to other team members, if we made skill transfer part of their responsibilities.

1.6.3 Learning Culture

We also need to understand our people as a group. It is up to us as team leaders to create and maintain an environment of trust in which our people can flourish as individuals supported by each other. They need to be free to learn at their own rates. They also need to be free to express their views and know that they will have the full support of their team members and team leader.

There are many ways to go about developing our people, as we shall see in later chapters. Perhaps the most important thing we can do to create a learning culture is to use our people's talents. By asking for their input frequently and informally, and by listening to their contributions, we create an atmosphere of respect in which our people can develop both their ideas and their skills. (Soat, 1996)

1.6.4 Nurturing

Our main training task as team leaders is to help our people learn to learn. They need to be able to learn from instruction and from their own reading. They need to be able to learn from their own everyday experiences. We need to get our people to talk through what they have learned, helping them pull out the learning points – helping them complete the learning cycle for themselves.

We need to nurture our people, both individually and as a team. Seeing our people gain confidence and respect from knowing that they can do the job well is a hugely rewarding experience.

The most valuable things we can give our people are the ability to learn from mistakes and the ability to pick up new skills quickly. The main requirements are a willingness to learn on the part of the learner and a willingness to nurture on the part of the team leader.

1.7 Summary

In this chapter, I have discussed some of the background theory of training and put it in the context of the IT team leader's role:

- Training and education – training is short-term and skill-focused whereas education is long-term and general.
- How adults learn – four stages of the learning cycle link to four learning styles, describing how adults learn by experience.
- Stakeholders – there are many interested parties in the skill development process.
- Team leader's role in training – as team leaders we can help our people learn to learn.

In Chapter 2 I look at the first step in the skill development process, that of identifying and clarifying the training need.

2. *Spotting the Training Need and Getting SMART*

2.1 Introduction

In this chapter I will look at how to identify the training need – and how to confirm that you have found the *real* training need as opposed to the *perceived* training need. All too often we look at what we think the learner needs and forget to check that that really is what is missing. But we must look beyond the obvious symptoms of a lack of skill and uncover the root causes, be they a lack of skill, lack of time, or lack of communication.

Once the real training need has been identified, it must be checked for SMARTness and turned into an outline action plan that can be monitored and achieved.

2.2 Main Points of this Chapter

- Perceived training need
- Checking out the real training need
- SMART objectives
- Turning the training need into an action plan

2.3 Perceived Training Need

Perceived training needs arise at various points in time. Many companies hold annual development reviews and/or performance appraisals of their staff. If performance has been less than good or if the individual has been struggling to achieve, this may indicate a development need in some part of the skills needed for the task at hand. Or it may be that performance has been fine, and continues to be fine, but the individual wants to develop a new skill or a slightly different aspect of an existing skill. This readiness to move forward is likely to be raised and discussed at a development review. It may be that the individual would like to use existing skills in a broader range of problems, or might be ready to take more responsibility for technical or non-technical aspects of the work. All this leads to a perceived training need.

Another occasion for reviewing training needs arises when an individual moves from one job or assignment to another. Usually this will mean continuing or building on some key aspect of the work but with a difference in some other aspect, a programmer/analyst moving from large mainframe systems to small distributed systems work for example. The change of team triggers a discussion of training needs.

A third discussion point arises when an entire team needs to change skills, for example when a new piece of software is to be introduced, or when a project is just beginning. It is relatively natural to address the problem of new skills at this point, for the entire project team.

Example

Let us suppose that a large project is beginning, call it Project Lightbulb. This will be a re-write of a major core system for the organization, converting from old to new technology to ensure that the information systems will continue to be able to support the business functions into the foreseeable future. What might be the perceived training needs?

Clearly there will be a training need in the new technology itself. All project members will see that – and are likely to be delighted to be "in the fore front". This will be a high profile project using forward-looking techniques and tools. Most of the people on the team will also have their individual training needs from their last review; these are still perceived training needs. It is worth re-examining all these perceived needs together in order to prioritize. As the project progresses, so new members will join the team and they will bring different skills with them, and will have different training needs; they will also need the training on the new technology.

In our large project we will look at some individuals and the training they will need in order to apply the new development tools to their part of the overall work:

Helen – project manager.
David – analyst/designer.
John – programmer/analyst and system builder.
Karen – tester.
Paul – an analyst/programmer who joins late from another project; he can use computer-based training and in-house course notes which have been developed by the time he joins.

2.4 Checking Out the Real Training Need

So far we have the individual discussing training needs with the team leader. We now have to check that the perceived training need is in fact the real training need – it may not be.

There are several ways of doing this and you will probably find yourself using all of them at different times, depending on the nature of the training need and how it has arisen. Sometimes it seems easy, for example when picking up a new skill or tool for a new project. Yet care must still be exercised – not all team members will need the same level of understanding, as they won't all need to use the tool in the same way. Other times the obvious training need is not at all what's required; this is often the case with non-technical skills, when people's perceptions of behaviour (and hence skill level) may be very different.

In many instances, any gap between perceived training need and actual training need can be established by looking more closely at the quality of work being produced. This may highlight that some aspects of the subject are fine but some aspects are not. For example, an individual may be producing poor quality program modules; close examination will reveal whether the problem is with the understanding of program structure (indicating training in program design principles) or statement syntax (indicating training in specific language constructs) or with an unclear specification (in which case the training need may be in challenging ambiguous specifications, indicating a need for assertiveness training). The situation may not be this simple – a training need arises from continued difficulties rather than a single instance, after all. But a pattern will emerge as you delve into some of the detail or look at technical quality review results.

Linked to the quality of the work being produced is the difficulty the individual is having with the tasks being set. This needs to be discussed with the staff member but again it may not confirm the perceived training need. For example, if someone is having trouble getting the work done, it may be simply that the tools are not well-understood, in which case the perceived need for training in the relevant tools is the same as the real training need. However, it may equally be the case that the individual is taking on too many extra tasks or that their enthusiasm for their tasks is not high. Or it may be that the equipment is not up to the job. All these things need to be looked at in finding the real training need. Thus in this example the real training need may be in task and priority management rather than in the tool being used.

Example

Amy, a junior programmer, was working well enough under supervision and was given some more autonomous tasks to do in devising module tests. Performance began to slip and the team leader suspected that Amy needed an advanced course in the language, partly as a refresher and partly to teach her some advanced constructs which she may not have picked up earlier. A closer look at the situation showed that her work was fine but that, without the close supervision she'd had previously as a trainee, she was taking on too many extra activities. Although she was up to the job, she needed coaching in managing her workload and training in time management.

Example

Checking out the training need for people on Project Lightbulb is largely a matter of working out what tasks they will have to perform and finding suitable courses and material on those aspects of the new technology.

Helen, as project manager, will need an overall high-level understanding of the technology and its impact on the software development process. She will need to know what project control facilities exist if any. She should also consider her existing project management techniques; will she need to augment those skills with new ideas?

David's main tasks as an analyst are to analyse the current and likely future business functions and to design suitable system modules, taking into account the chief improvements that the new technology brings. His training need will be in those parts of the new technology that support the analysis and design of system modules. Depending on how comprehensive the new technology is, this may mean learning a new design tool or it may mean learning a whole new design methodology with its attendant new ways of thinking.

John on the other hand, as programmer/analyst, will be building modules in the new system and will need practical skills in using the new technology to support coding, testing and integrating modules and other software components.

Karen, who as tester will be testing the system from a business perspective, will need to be able to use the technology to specify and carry out tests and record and track the results. She will need an understanding of the technology and its user support tools both before and after live implementation.

When discussing a person's real training needs, you will need to probe a bit by asking questions. You could ask about their preferences, in terms of what they like or enjoy about doing the job. Sometimes it helps to look at the job as a whole, other times it's more useful to look at different parts of the job. Is there some aspect of the work they don't really like? Is that the aspect that gives difficulty? Or are they comfortable with all the separate components of the job but the combination just doesn't seem to work? This would often indicate a conflict of priorities.

When discussing the real training need it can be enlightening to look at the individual's learning style, as we saw in Chapter 1. The individual's learning style points to their preferred work style as well. It is often the case that a task or piece of work that is difficult for someone is simply not in line with his preferred method of working. However, you can together redefine the task so that it is in line with the preferred work style, at least to some degree. This will give the individual a solid base to work with and you can then help to build on that foundation and widen their comfort zone with tasks outside their usual *modus operandi*. In this case, the real training need is to learn to operate outside their preferred style sometimes. (This is likely to be uncomfortable and the staff member will need your support and encouragement.)

As an example of clashing work style and task, consider the effects of giving a reflective person tasks that are predominantly activist. The task requires short term, quick decisions to be made all the time. There is little thinking time: there are lots of practical things to be done in short time-scales. These aspects of the task make it uncomfortable for someone who prefers to think things through and needs time to assimilate before making decisions. If the rapid-fire tasks are balanced with ones that are closer to his natural work style, then all will be well, as he will be able to spend most or some of his work time doing what comes naturally. If, however, the work is predominantly unnatural, then some of the tasks could be redefined, at least for a while. At the same time, the team leader can help the individual to get used to making quicker decisions, essentially coaching him in decision-making.

Feedback from colleagues provides another pointer to finding the real training need. It may be that an individual identifies a training need based on their own perception of what needs to be done to improve – and in many cases this will be accurate enough to go ahead and address the problem. Sometimes however this gives a false picture – what is needed is an honest and constructive discussion of performance from other people's points of view. Often this feedback will come from the team leader but it could equally well come from other team members or from internal customers, or for example people on other teams who have a working relationship with the individual. The important thing here is to consider the recipients of the piece of work as well as the work itself, as they will have a view on any needs for improvement.

Example

Peter, an analyst/programmer, was having some difficulty in getting reports produced from a database, in response to user requests. The immediate thought was that a course in the report writing facility was needed. But further discussion with Peter and with the user department revealed an inability to understand the user's real needs in terms of management information. Peter had training and coaching on identifying user requirements and on understanding the business, and the problem was overcome – without further training in the report writing facility.

Example

Michael felt that he had a need for training in stress management. The stress he felt was all at work, there were no problems in his domestic life. His team leader helped him to explore the problem by asking questions like "Where is the stress coming from, is it absolutely everywhere?" "Does the tension come from one particular task? team? set of demands? person?" It turned out that Michael had difficulty with one particular team he was supporting as a technical expert, and that the constant changes in specification, often at a very late phase in the development, were causing him huge amounts of extra work to very tight deadlines, necessitating excessive amounts of weekend work.

Michael agreed that part of his problem was that he was not consulted early enough in the development process. His team leader agreed that the team of experts had to be close to the development teams they supported so they could get involved earlier in the development process. This was not so much a training need for Michael as a process change for the department as a whole. However, Michael also agreed that he had a need to be more assertive and to learn to be influential in his communication style with colleagues on the development teams. He also had to get into the habit of stating what to him was the obvious – notably the extra effort involved for late changes, all of which effort would be charged to the project. His training need thus became, not stress management, but influencing his peers as a technical expert.

2.5 SMART Objectives

Having found the real training need for the individual, we now have to start doing something about it. Occasionally, it happens that identifying a development need alerts the individual to problems he is having – and, as if a light has been switched on, he starts changing his behaviour spontaneously, resulting in the desired improvement. Would that it were always so easy! Usually the individual will need some form of instruction or guidance in some new tool or technique.

We need to be systematic in our approach to meeting the training need. Just as we get the best results from managing our system development projects in an orderly fashion, so too will we get the best results from developing our people in an orderly fashion. We have to be SMART – we have to ensure that the way we meet the training need will be Specific, Measurable, Achievable, Realistic and Timely.

What does this mean in terms of training needs?

2.5.1 Specific

Being specific means being able to articulate the training need and turn it into a set of learning objectives. We need to be clear about what we are trying to achieve with the training. To do this, it helps to write it down, trying to state precisely what the individual should be able to do as a result of the training that he cannot do at present. Sometimes this can be stated abstractly, other times it will need to be illustrated with examples.

Example

Let us suppose that two team members need different kinds of training. Fred needs to learn the language C++ while Charlotte needs to learn presentation skills. How might we be specific?

Fred's learning objectives might be that he needs to be able to code modules and simple programs in C++, using keyboard input, screen output and database file access.

Charlotte's learning objectives might be that she should be able to prepare and deliver presentations to small groups of peers and/or users, for example, presenting an overview of the project and progress so far to the user team.

2.5.2 Measurable

Making a training need measurable means knowing how we will be able to tell when the training has succeeded in meeting the need. How will you know that your team member has met the training need, what behaviour changes will you recognize? It may be difficult to do, but we must be able to describe a way of measuring the outcome of the skill development effort. This might be expressed in clearly definable targets or it might be more of a description of behaviour. It is well worth jotting down a few notes at this early planning stage, to enable an evaluation of the effectiveness of the training later on, after the training has taken place. (This will not help us with the first few training decisions, but will help to sharpen our own skills in creating development plans.)

Example

We will know that Fred has met his training need in C++ when he is able to write and run simple programs quickly and unsupervised. He will be proficient when his programs have few errors on the first run and when he has enough confidence to write them quickly for use in larger suites; and when he is able to use fairly sophisticated user interface constructs.

We will know that Charlotte has met her development need when she has the confidence to prepare a presentation for the user team and field any questions they may raise. She might at that stage be able to give the presentation to a wider or more senior audience, and to field their more difficult questions, but equally this may be a further training need to be addressed at a later date. We can also expect that once she has met the present training need, she will be able to prepare other presentations fairly readily without a lot of coaching from her team leader.

2.5.3 Achievable

A training need or learning objective is achievable when the goals we are setting are capable of being met. To some extent this is a matter of common sense in knowing what is do-able. However, it must be borne in mind that the learner does not have the same background as a more experienced person (who might be setting the objectives). What is easily achievable for one person will be much harder for another. It is a good idea to test the objectives for achievability by stretching them a bit and seeing where they break – is x achievable? Is $x + y$ achievable? Is $x + y + z$ achievable?

Example

If we ask Fred to learn C++ programming when he is already familiar with programming concepts, then we have an achievable target. If however we ask him to learn C++ programming but he currently knows nothing about computer systems, then we are giving an unachievable target – the real training need would include the fundamentals of programming concepts.

By asking Charlotte to learn to prepare and deliver presentations about what she is currently working on and is thus familiar with, we are giving her an achievable target. If we asked her to do her first presentation on a subject she knows nothing about, and to field difficult challenging questions, that would be an unachievable target at this stage. Note that it would be an achievable target at a later stage in her development.

2.5.4 Realistic

Making a learning objective realistic is a matter of putting it into context. Will the individual have the time to devote to developing the new skill? Do we have the resources to support the skill development process? Does the new skill address a requirement of the current job, or is it a nice-to-have that is for long-term development? Is the individual likely to be motivated to develop the skill – does he feel the need is real? Is it practical to ask this person to develop this skill? These are all questions that can be used to test the practicability of this training need. They may result in the training need being modified or even postponed.

Example

Given that Fred is already a programmer but has to call on another team member every time he needs a C++ routine, it is realistic to expect him to learn the language himself. We can give him the time he needs to do this and he has a strong desire to expand his skill set. So it is realistic to ask him to develop this skill.

Charlotte would very much like to be able to prepare and deliver presentations of her project both to the user team and to other user departments who might be interested in a similar application system for their own functions. However, she is heavily involved in the quality review process at the moment, so it might not be realistic to ask her to do very many presentations soon after the training. As she will be able to practise the presentation skills in the quality review meetings, it is still realistic to ask her to develop the skill within the agreed timescale.

2.5.5 Timely

Checking that a training need is timely means checking that the training is carried out just before the new skill is needed. This is often easier said than done, but basically means ensuring that the training is neither too early nor too late to be of use. If the training is too early, there is a danger that the new information will have been forgotten before the individual has a chance to put it into practice and thereby to really learn the new patterns of working. On the other hand, if the training is too late, the individual is likely to have picked up enough of the skill from others to get by. He may well have developed bad habits in the process, which will have to be un-learnt. Or the training may be a waste of time if the individual has already become reasonably proficient before the training is available.

Example

Fred really needs to learn C++ fairly soon as he will get frustrated by always relying on other team members. He should aim to learn C++ as part of his work, using the new skill as he develops it.

Charlotte will need some presentation skills sometime in the next six to nine months but there is no real urgency. Any time in the next nine months will be fine, to fit in with her work and holiday commitments.

2.5.6 Balance

These five elements – specific, measurable, achievable, realistic and timely – are not isolated aspects of the training need. They must be considered as a balanced whole. Achieveability, realism and timeliness go hand-in-hand to a large extent. What is achievable in one timescale may not be realistic in a shorter time frame. There are no hard and fast rules here, the important thing being to consider these three aspects when turning the training need into learning objectives. A couple of quick questions will often do the trick: What are we trying to do here? What else is going on in the individual's work or home life? Can we reasonably expect him to develop this skill at this point in time?

2.6 Action plan

Having identified and confirmed the training need, and turned it into SMART objectives, it remains to construct an action plan. This is likely to be built up from the objectives arising from several training needs for the individual, although not necessarily all at once. The action plan combines the desired timings of the various training needs with other factors such as workload, planned holidays and other constraints arising from team members' commitments. The action plan is also written in conjunction with choosing an appropriate training method, which I discuss in Chapter 3.

Example

A suggested action plan for Fred would be to learn C++ in the next few months while he can still rely on his colleagues for support during the learning. As he is due to be away four months from now, and will be needed as backup during his colleagues' holidays after that, the best option is to action this need sooner rather than later. A tentative action plan, then, would be to have a closer look at some C++ programs, then do a computer-based C++ course, followed by writing some programs to run and test with the help of his colleagues. One of his team-mates would be prepared to set aside some time every week to check his understanding and guide him through some of the types of program the team works on.

Example

Charlotte's action plan is likely to be a little different, as she will be covering for her team-mate's absence for the next few weeks and will be helping out with some conference work and the quality reviews for the next month after that. She is due to go away herself for a while and then has a large project to work on. Taking all things into consideration, she should work on presentation skills sometime in 5–6 months' time. This gives plenty of time for her to begin to talk to others who have learned how to do presentations, to see what the pitfalls may be. The conference work may help her to build self-confidence at dealing with numbers of strange people. She should use any opportunity she has to watch other people's presentations and to see what seems to work and what does not, and in what context.

Example

Michael wants to find an external course that will present some theory about influencing people over whom he has no direct authority, and which provides plenty of opportunity try it out and get feedback on how he is doing. He will then put it into practice when he returns to the office, getting feedback from his team leader (who will try to give him pointers and practical help) and from the development teams he is advising. He will know he has been successful when the developers include him in discussions about the technical aspects early in the design stage.

2.7 Summary

In this chapter we have looked more closely at training needs:

- Perceived training need – training needs arise at regular development reviews, at project changes and at other times during the year.
- Real training need – identifying and confirming the training need shows that the real training need is not always the obvious one; it is always worth a short chat to ensure there are no underlying difficulties.
- SMART objectives – creating learning objectives that are specific, measurable, achievable, realistic and timely is the SMART option; a few minutes spent on the exercise is a useful investment – if you like, it's the "design it first" concept applied to training.
- Action plan – balancing other constraints with the training objectives leads to an outline action plan that can be converted into a development plan.

In the next two chapters I describe various types of solution to the training needs. Chapter 3 considers short-term training methods while Chapter 4 discusses long-term training methods.

3. *Choosing between Training Methods – Short-term Options*

■ ■

3.1 Introduction

There are many different solutions to any training need. A well-known and common solution is the taught course whether internal or external. There is a wide range of other training solutions, each suited to a particular set of circumstances. Much instructional material has been packaged in a self-study format, whether computer-based, audio taped or published in books or notes. Some training needs lend themselves more to a solution on the job, in which the learning and the doing are closely integrated. These three training methods provide a training solution within a short time scale, allowing the delegate to develop the skill over a few weeks or months. In this chapter I will look at some of the key aspects of these training methods from the team leader's point of view, and give some pointers on how to choose between them. In the next chapter I will do the same for longer term training methods.

For each type of training method, I give a description and discuss the main features. I then consider when each method is an appropriate choice and how to choose between them. I also give pointers on selecting the particular training course, self-study material or on-the-job action plan.

3.2 Main Points of this Chapter

- Short taught course
- Self-study
- On-the-job training

■ ■

3.3 Short Taught Course

3.3.1 Description

When one thinks of training, very often it is the short taught course that springs to mind. The general pattern for this training method consists of classroom-based

19

instruction led by an experienced trainer with specialized knowledge of the subject, taking place during normal working hours and lasting up to 10 working days.
Figure 3.1 summarizes the main characteristics of taught courses.

There are a large number of training organizations which provide this type of
training; most can be found on the internet. Most training suppliers are commercial companies but some of the Training and Enterprise Councils (TECs;
SCOTVECs in Scotland) also provide short taught courses; some universities and
colleges also have semi-commercial divisions which provide this type of training
to local industry and individuals.

3.3.2 Main Features

Much of the literature about training and its methods give a lot of attention to
short courses from the trainer's point of view, describing and discussing the design
of courses and how to improve the learning experience for all delegates. But what
are the salient points for the delegate and the team leader, and how much variation
is there? Here I describe each of the main features.

Short and focused – the short course generally concentrates on one topic. It
usually takes place within 1–5 consecutive days in the same week, although courses
of more than one week are not uncommon. The course sessions deal with various
topics within the overall subject while not straying too much from the topic at
hand. Such courses usually include some practical sessions of one kind or another,
encouraging the delegates to gain experience of using the new skill or applying
the topic to a sample situation. Some courses are more "hands-on" than others,
typically those giving instruction on specific tools or techniques.

Away from the work area – short courses take place away from the delegates'
work areas. "External" courses are usually held at a geographically separate training
centre and include delegates from several different organizations or companies.

```
                        Main Features

    Short and focused (1-5 days typical)
    Away from the work area
    Class size varies
          • Small (4-6 delegates) practical classes
          • Medium (12-15 delegates) practical classes
          • Large (20-50 delegates) lecture-style seminars

                        When to Use

    Topic to be learned is focused
    Suitable course exists
    Training place available in right timescale
    Delegate can be available for course attendance
    Training venue accessible to delegate
    Sufficient funds to meet costs
```

Fig. 3.1 Taught course at a glance.

"Internal" courses are usually run by the training division of a large organization and are often held at a central location. Courses can also be held in a separate room within the delegates' "home" building; these "in-house courses" could be run either by an external company brought in for training sessions or by an internal training team providing sessions within their organization.

Class sizes – there is much variation in size of class. Some courses are restricted to four delegates, particularly those requiring highly practical instruction at a PC, while other courses or seminars can have as many as 50 or 60 people listening to what is essentially an extended lecture with break-out discussion sessions. Any of these teaching styles can work, particularly for those delegates who also have the relevant learning style. A lecture delivery can be livened up with vivid anecdotes and mental exercises, suiting the reflectors and theorists in the group. Practical experience in a hands-on session will particularly suit delegates with an activist or pragmatist learning style.

We have seen that a key feature of the short course is the fact that the delegate is taken away from the work environment for the duration. This brings its own pressures both for the delegate (who may be distracted by thoughts of a growing in-tray back in the office) and for the rest of the team, who often must cover the delegate's normal work during the absence. For this reason there is a tendency to look for courses that cover as many relevant learning points as possible in the shortest time. It is important however to keep a balance and ensure that the delegate has enough opportunity to absorb what is being taught: a course that covers too much in a short time may be wasted if it goes so fast the delegate cannot take it in. Being away from the desk may seem a disadvantage; it is also a good thing in the sense that the delegate is able to concentrate on learning the new skill, away from distractions and other pressures. Often, some extra work will be needed on the delegate's return to the office, to relate the lessons of the course to the tasks of the job. The assimilation process can be helped greatly by support from the team leader, as we shall see in Chapter 5.

3.3.3 When to Use a Taught Course

When is a short course an appropriate training method? In a nutshell, when there is a suitable course available. There are many factors that affect availability of a "suitable course":

- Focus of the topic – is the topic to be learned focused or narrow enough to be covered in a few days, or is it really too big to cover comfortably in that time?
- Existence of the course – is the course offered by anyone? Is there an internal training team or external company that teaches a course with the delegate's learning objectives?
- Availability of places – does any training supplier have an empty place on a suitable course within the right timescale for the delegate's needs?
- Delegate availability – is the delegate available to be away from work for the length of the course? Is he able to be away from domestic commitments for the duration?

- Practicality – is the training venue accessible to the delegate? Can any necessary travel arrangements be made?
- Budget – is there enough money in the training budget to cover the cost of the course, and any travel and accommodation expenses?

Any or all of these factors may mitigate against using a short course as the training solution, in which case there are many more options to choose from, as we shall see later in this chapter.

3.3.4 Selection Criteria

Suppose for the moment that there are several suppliers who offer similar courses on the required topic, how do we go about choosing one? Many large companies have preferred supplier arrangements in place with one or more training suppliers, based on expected volumes of training places to be purchased. If there is a list of preferred suppliers in your organization then that is the start point for your search. If there is not, then start your search on the internet.

In my experience of selecting courses with delegates, I have found the following half-dozen criteria to be key elements:

- Close match of training objectives to learning objectives.
- Quality of training provision.
- Match of training style to learning style.
- Venue and location.
- Quality of administration.
- Trainer accreditation.
- Price.

Let us look at each of these points in more detail.

Close match of objectives – the closer the match between the teaching objectives of the course, ie the course content, and the delegate's learning objectives, the more relevant the course is likely to be. This should always be the prime consideration.

Quality of training provision – the higher the quality of training given by the supplier and instructor, the more the delegate is likely to gain from the course and the better value for money it is likely to provide. For suppliers you know already, quality can be measured by evaluation of previous course attendance (evaluation is discussed in Chapter 6) and from feedback from previous delegates. For a supplier you may be using for the first time, it is possible to ask them for reference clients and to follow these up to obtain recommendations, or warnings of any problems other clients have had.

Match of training style with learning style – if the delegate's learning style is diametrically opposed to the training style of a course, it would be better to find a supplier or training method with a training style closer to the delegate's learning style. For example, it's no use putting an activist on a lecture course and expecting him to do his own theorising – he will be frustrated and miss most of the learning points. The size of the class has a strong influence here – the larger the group, the harder it is to provide practical exercises and ensure that all students have understood the learning points. In practice, however, most courses and any good instructor caters for all learning styles, often by adapting the course presentation to include practical activities as well as presentation and summary of theories.

Venue and geographic location – given a choice, most people would choose a training venue that is easy to get to and not too far away from home. This has the added advantage of keeping travel costs down. The venue should also provide a learning environment, one that is neither too cold nor too hot, neither too noisy nor too quiet. If the course is residential or the delegate will be staying in a hotel, accommodation should be reasonably close to the training venue and should provide some means of recreation.

Quality of administration – it is easier to deal with a training supplier whose administration is smooth and efficient than to deal with one who frequently cancels or changes courses at the last minute, or who sends out joining instructions very late. However, this is definitely a minor consideration in choosing a training course or supplier; it tends to be important when choosing a preferred supplier.

Accreditation – if your organization has a policy of, for example, only using ISO-accredited suppliers then this will have to be taken into consideration. In practice, most reputable training suppliers have one or other of the training accreditations, for example ISO-9000 series or accreditation from the Institute of IT Training (IITT).

Price – last (and least important) is the price of the course. If two or more courses are evenly matched on the above criteria and on timescales and place availability, then take price into account. In the training world as in so many others, you get what you pay for. Very often I have found the less expensive courses to be so crowded with delegates or teaching topics that practical activities were squeezed out and the delegate had to do a lot of follow-up activity with colleagues at work. If you are on a very tight training budget and must use the least expensive course, then price may well be the deciding factor. But you should allow extra time for the delegate to consolidate his learning on his return to work. Some training topics become like commodity goods, in that there are so many providers giving roughly equivalent instruction that price becomes a valid deciding factor: at the time of writing, the software tools (word processor, spreadsheet) training market is like this.

Choosing a course and supplier is an iterative process of working out the delegate's needs, seeing and comparing what is available in the topic(s) and finding a good balance matching as many criteria as you can. There are no hard and fast rules and every case is different – which can make it frustrating. But perseverance pays off in finding the right course for the delegate.

Example

Martin needed to find a course on Visual Basic, a commonly-used computer development language. Several suppliers provided this type of training so Martin compared the course contents with what he needed to learn. He found there was a lot of similarity among courses, but one included an in-depth case study so he chose that one. This supplier was also one that was highly recommended by several of his colleagues.

Example

Fiona needed to attend several courses to cover different aspects of database systems. Her team leader suggested she choose the most relevant ones for her needs from several courses run by two suppliers. She found that there was a great deal of overlap between the two suppliers' courses but that they mixed the topics slightly differently – one had an application design flavour while the other looked at the same topics from the database support point of view. Both suppliers provided excellent training and both gave similar courses with the same frequency throughout the year. The prices of the courses were equivalent and both suppliers were centrally located in a nearby city. Fiona chose one course from one supplier and three from the other, by balancing the training topics with the timings of the courses and a consideration of when she would need to be applying the various topics in her job.

Example

Michael needed to learn some techniques for influencing people not on his team. He looked at several course descriptions which included influencing skills. One was from a supplier new to him and his colleagues. One was from a supplier he'd heard mixed reports on. One was from a supplier he knew was good but not convenient to get to. He chose a course from the new supplier after talking to two or three of their previous clients. The chosen course seemed closest to his requirements for influencing techniques where you don't have any authority over those you need to influence.

Example

Thomas only had one day to spare to learn about time management; he had already attended a time management course some years previously but found it hard to stick to his plans – so much changed every day! He found several companies that presented 1-day seminars on time management, but only one that offered the beyond-the-basics level he was looking for. This included dealing with interruptions and how to prioritize and re-prioritize. He found that the company was planning to come to his home town so he didn't have to waste a lot of time travelling. Although the seminar was run as a series of large lecture sessions, the speaker was able to capture the audience's attention and used graphic examples and visual imagery to help the audience retain the learning points.

Example

Henry, a member of the senior management team, felt he needed a strategic course to refresh his thinking and help him develop strategic vision. He found that several business management colleges provided courses on strategic topics; he discovered that he was not at all clear on what he really needed. By comparing the course descriptions and teaching style with his own shortcomings and learning style, he decided to attend one that gave 3 days of instruction and exercise followed up (after 2 months back at work putting it into practice) with a further 2 days discussing the application of the theory and refining the skills.

Example

Jane needed to learn how to use the word processor on her PC and needed to learn fast. As there was no internal training team and she needed a very practical course with plenty of hands-on learning-by-doing, she chose a course with a local training supplier which charged a low rate and had courses running every week. She attended a 1-day course later that same week.

3.4 Self-Study

Delegates do not always have the time or training budget to attend a taught course; those who work part-time are not always able to commit to the full days usually needed to complete a training course. On the other hand, some training needs are so focused and self-contained that they do not require a full training course. Often, the delegate needs an overview or introduction to a subject for background information or as a taster of a new topic that is not yet an immediate need. In all of these circumstances, self-study may be the solution. Figure 3.2 shows the main characteristics of self-study training.

3.4.1 Description

Self-study is also called distance learning. There are some subtle differences, for example self-study usually requires the student to find the materials and glean from them what he will, whereas in distance learning someone has constructed the learning material to guide the student through the topics in a logical fashion, with each lesson building on previous ones. For our purposes in this chapter, however, this is a fine distinction and I will include in the discussion any material the student uses on his own without an instructor present. (I will use the term distance learning in a later discussion of part-time higher education courses.)

The many types of self-study material available can be grouped into four media types: computer-based, books, videos and audio cassettes. There is also some overlap, for example some courses are presented as audio tape with workbook; some videos have instructional texts with them. But for the most part, the groupings stand and I will describe them each in turn.

3.4.2 Main Features of Computer-Based Training

Computer-based training takes several forms these days. At one time the only format widely available was text-only with no graphics and with little if any

```
Main Features

Several media
        • Computer-based training
        • Internet-based training
        • Books
        • Audio cassettes
        • Videos
Delegate works at own pace
Can be at work place or away from work place


                     When to Use

No suitable taught course is available
Time is short
Time is available but in short periods
Topic to be learned is very specific
Introduction required for background information
Overview material for delegate interest
Preparation for long-term future requirement
Funds do not allow taught course attendance
To introduce concepts prior to taught course
```

Fig. 3.2 Self-study at a glance.

interaction – the student read the instruction and that was that. Such material still has its uses and can still be found on mainframe systems, often used as a refresher to remind the individual of how to do something. Screen-based teaching was often supplemented by workbooks or other paper-based exercise tutorials. Some courses had built-in exercises for the student to try.

With the advent of PCs and multimedia capabilities, computer-based training material has become very rich. The best courses now use a stimulating mix of graphics, sound, text, animation and interaction. This exploits the power of the hardware and keeps the delegate's interest by varying the presentation method. The student navigates through the course as he needs to, whether by hierarchy of topic or by module. Course design now includes frequent summarizing and questions for the learner, partly to reinforce the learning and partly to maintain interest by working to the different learning styles. With some reading, some analysis, some try-it-and-see questions, there is something for everyone and all delegates should find an approach suitable to their preference.

Computer-based training seems a likely medium for technical topics like programming languages and PC tools. Technical topics can readily be broken up into chunks, for example the different types of statement used in a programming language, or the different tasks covered by an application system. Can computer-based courses also be useful for interpersonal skills like team leadership? The answer, astonishingly, is that they can. To some extent, interpersonal skills can be broken down into different tasks and the tasks described and taught – for example, team leadership includes delegation, motivation, planning, communication and so on. Each of these aspects can be demonstrated both in what it should look like and in terms of how not to do it. Computer-based material often includes video clips and humorous sketches to illustrate the learning points. The learner is often guided through a simulation where he is asked which of several alternative actions he might pick at each point in the scenario, and the program proceeds to play out that option, demonstrating the results of the action. Good courses will also suggest a better or more appropriate response and what that would lead to – and then explain why that option is preferred.

Some computer-based courses can "sense" the level of expertise or understanding of the delegate and pitch the difficulty of questions and detail of instruction accordingly. This helps all learners to improve their skill, whatever their current expertise, and ensures that everyone develops the skill eventually.

Courses are usually structured in modules, each covering some major topic within the subject. Modules are further divided into topics and lessons. Students should be able to select the modules or topics to be covered – especially useful for a subject the delegate already knows something about. Most material allows navigation forward or backward in a topic, allowing the student to repeat or review a lesson or topic; he should be able to stop the session at any time. Most courses will remember or "bookmark" the latest stopping point, ready to continue next time. Most courses include objectives at the start of each topic, then the instruction material with summaries or reviews at the end of the topic. Questions, examples and exercises are sometimes interspersed and sometimes inserted as a quiz after the summary. The material is usually stand-alone, rarely including a paper-based workbook. Some courses include a print facility to allow the student to make hard copies of, for example, summary pages.

Some computer-based training materials include progress tests or proficiency tests. These systems can also track the use of the courses by different students and their scores on tests. This can be a valuable aid to monitoring progress of several students through required courses. They suit some organizations and circumstances well, particularly when delegates need to prove proficiency levels and qualification in a skill before using that skill on the job.

Computer-based training packages can be delivered in many ways. They are now available on mainframe systems (but rarely with graphics, I find) and on PCs, usually with graphics and with options for sound, animation and video clips. Material can be delivered on CD-ROM or, less commonly, diskette. It can also be delivered via networks, where the material is held on a central file server and accessed from the PC. Training material can also be delivered via the internet or on an organization's intranet; this delivery mechanism is becoming known as e-learning. For internet and intranet configurations, which have performance issues in transferring large course files, the courses are often divided into small topics or lessons. These are stored as separate files and are faster to transfer than the entire course, giving minimal delay to the learner and minimal impact on network performance. Many organizations have set up learning centres which contain several multi-media PCs networked in a dedicated training room. Some organizations loan out courses and laptops to allow delegates to train out of the office – at home or while travelling for example.

3.4.3 When to Use Computer-Based Training

When is computer-based training a useful solution? It is very effective at running simulations in which the delegate needs to explore the consequences of different actions. Managing a project, for example, can become very complex as the results of one decision may have repercussions further down the line. By trying out different responses in a relevant simulation package, the learner can see the results of decisions fairly quickly and work out which options might give better results. Computer-based simulations are also useful in situations where safety is an issue, for example controlling a chemical process or nuclear reactor. Mistakes can be made that have no actual consequences but that the student can learn from.

Another useful application of computer-based training is a training programme involving large numbers of delegates. It can be used to introduce a new technology to an entire department for instance, with each person doing the training as he becomes available. This can work well even if individuals can only be freed up for a short period at a time. The delegates can book the training to suit their current workload and do not all have to do the training at the same time.

Computer-based training is a very effective solution if the delegates are geographically dispersed in several parts of the country or the world. It is a very useful way of training people who are remote from the main group, for example field service engineers, who can download training modules onto a laptop and keep updated without having to spend days at headquarters. Some global multi-national organizations use computer-based training to ensure that staff in all parts of their organization receive the same training consistently no matter where they are (often translated into their native language); this could be difficult and expensive to achieve by other methods.

Computer-based training can be cost-effective but there is an initial outlay. Things to be considered are the cost of the equipment and the cost of the software. You will need to decide how big an operation it is going to be: will it be one stand-alone multimedia PC? Will it be a network of several PCs in a learning centre? Or will you use laptops for people to borrow? It is tempting to try to put training at the workstation, as the PCs are likely already to be in place. If the equipment can support the training material, this can be a workable solution. However, some provision must be made to avoid interruptions to the training session so the individual can learn without distraction.

There are three options for obtaining computer-based training packages: purchase, lease or build. It is certainly possible to develop your own training material, although it can be costly and time consuming. Where the training is to be tailored specifically to a system being implemented or where your own organization's culture or message needs to be put across, developing a package can work well. There are a number of companies now that can provide this service. There are also several excellent authoring packages that help you develop your own material. For generic or common topics, however, there is much material already developed and on the market, covering technical topics as well as non-technical. These can be purchased or leased, individually or as libraries of almost any size. It is possible and reasonably common to have a set of courses as a training library that can be swapped about periodically, typically once or twice a year.

3.4.4 Main Features of Books

Self-study material includes more than just computer-based packages. Books are a good source of instruction and information and there are several types to choose from. Textbooks provide accurate detailed information usually set out in a learn-as-you-read format. Many textbooks include review or study questions to consolidate learning and to provoke further thought. If the learner's preferred learning style is reflective or theorist then learning from textbooks can be effective. The learning can be reinforced and expanded if there is someone to act as a tutor, to discuss various aspects of the topic or to help with experimentation. Reference manuals are another source of information, but rarely include any instruction. Sometimes the manuals are all you have to work with – in this case, the learner will have to do a lot of experimenting to try out the various features of the new topic, language or system.

Instructional workbooks can also be a useful training method. These are usually formatted with questions and space to write the answers in the book. The usual structure of a chapter will be an introduction to the topic, some factual material, then questions interspersed with further factual material or discussion; topics and understanding build up as the chapter unfolds. There are some excellent workbooks on specific non-technical skills like time management; on technical topics there are some very good books that combine a textbook format with the instructional nature of a workbook but without the space in the book to write the answers.

Books are a rich source of material; they are portable, often inexpensive, and can be used by more than one person (although not all at the same time). Learning from books needs some effort on the part of the learner, particularly if his learning style is less theorist and more activist. However, the book is still there for reference purposes, which a course instructor usually is not.

3.4.5 Main Features of Training Videos

A further form of self-study comes in videos. Many technical topics used to be covered by videos; many of these have now been converted to CD-ROM or some other computer-based medium. Videos are still an excellent way of delivering training on non-technical topics, especially in the realms of interpersonal skills. The most effective training videos use humour to get the point across. These use part of the video to instruct and give facts and background. Part of the video demonstrates how *not* to carry out the task, for example how not to run an interview. After reviewing the results of poor techniques, for example an aggressive interview style, more instruction reinforces the learning points. The video typically reruns the scenario but does it "properly" the second time. A summary reiterates the main points. These training videos are typically about half an hour in length and sometimes come with a booklet outlining the main points. Training videos can be used by individuals or by groups for instruction and discussion. The videos are surprisingly memorable and do help people learn and remember how to carry out various interpersonal tasks.

3.4.6 Main Features of Audio Cassettes

The last self-study method I discuss here is audio cassettes. Again these are mostly on interpersonal and lifestyle topics rather than technical topics. They are suitable for listening to while travelling for instance, or when sitting in a quiet environment, whether individually or in groups. Audio cassette courses are sometimes formatted in a similar way to videos. They can also take the format of a series of talks by experts interspersed with discussions between groups of people. Sometimes they are recordings of seminars on specific topics such as coaching. Some audio material stands on its own; other material is accompanied by a text or workbook with questions to develop the delegate's understanding of the subject.

3.4.7 Selection Criteria

There is, then, a wide variety of self-study materials and methods. Each is useful for some circumstances. How to choose between them? Again, it is a question of balancing the needs of the learner in terms of topic and availability to train against the quality of the materials and its cost and availability. The match between the delegate's learning objectives and learning style and the material's training objectives and presentation style should be the most important criterion in choosing the self-study method and solution. You will also need to take into consideration longer-term objectives of the team and/or department in deciding what sort of solution to go for and how much of an investment you need to make.

Example

Katherine, a systems tester, needed to understand the background of writing SQL statements in Cobol application programs. She found a suitable CD-ROM course in the training library and borrowed it to use at home. She did the course in half-hour chunks, finishing it in 10 days. The course gave her enough of an insight to be able to understand SQL statements in programs and to request clarification from the developers. She took some written notes as she did the course and used them to refer back to when she needed to.

Example

As training manager, Amy needed to understand the issues involved in team leadership. She was not convinced that such a topic could be learned from computer-based techniques but she could not justify attending a taught course within the timescale she needed. She tried a CD-ROM course on leading teams and was surprised at how much she did gain from it. She found the concepts easy enough to understand but not always easy to remember. The package she used had several scenarios or problems built around the same hypothetical company. She had to choose which of several actions she would take in any given situation. She also had to decide what the priorities would be for the different members of the team. Amy found that she learned a lot about human interactions from playing out the different scenarios and discovering what might happen as a result of her actions. She gained an appreciation of leadership issues as well as first-hand experience of using the materials in her library.

Example

A global multinational company needed to improve the project management skills of its consultants in all of its sites in America, Europe and Asia. It couldn't bring all the consultants to any one centre for class-based training as this was too expensive and highly impractical. Instead it developed a computer-based training package that combined instruction with practice. In two parts, the package included several modules of project management theory covering planning and monitoring, and outlining the different relationships to be developed during any project. The second part gave a simulated project for the student to run, from project inception through to completion and project close. In the simulations, students were able to retrieve the instructional material if they needed a refresher. The package allowed them to track their own progress through the simulation, experimenting without affecting real clients or projects. All the consultants in the company worked to the same standards and were able to put the theory into practice on their real assignments. The training and the learning were remarkably consistent despite the cultural differences and geographic spread of the delegates.

Example

Bill needed to learn a little about the programming language Java, enough to write simple programs for test purposes. He didn't feel that a 3-day taught course would be necessary as he was already familiar with other similar languages. He borrowed a book on Java and read through it, trying out each new concept on programs of his own. When he had finished the book, he tried working out what some existing Java programs did. He was soon able to amend existing routines and write new ones to create the test environment he needed.

Example

When Frank needed some training on time management, he assumed he would have to make the time to go on a 2-day course. He was surprised to find some useful workbooks in the training library. Working for about half an hour a day, he found he could learn the main concepts of planning and prioritizing his tasks and managing time and interruptions. Within a few weeks he had enough confidence to put it into practice in his working day and found he was able to manage his time much better.

Example

John needed to be able to make presentations that were influential as well as interesting and informative. He borrowed several videos on presentation skills to see which would be best. He found that he picked up some pointers from each of them. Despite the videos having different approaches and covering slightly different areas of presentation skills, he got what he needed from them. Because the videos used well-known professional actors, and showed both good and bad presentations, John found he remembered the learning points very well. His presentations improved and he even started to enjoy them.

3.5 On-the-Job Training

3.5.1 Description

Sometimes there are no ready-made training solutions available, no courses, no self-study material. What then? How does the individual learn the required new skill(s)? Training must take place on the job, as part of the normal work. The essence of on-the-job training is that the individual carries out the task(s) to be learned, with guidance from someone else. The learner is encouraged to think about the task and how to carry it out, then to go through the relevant steps, then to think back and understand what happened and what he learned from it. The main characteristics of on-the-job training are summarized in Fig. 3.3.

To be effective, on-the-job training must be carefully planned so that the training is integrated with job tasks and the learning points are recognized. There is often a more experienced person acting as coach and helping the delegate to gain the understanding and experience needed. The coach can be the team leader, or it can be a fellow team member – it doesn't really matter so long as the coach has time to help the delegate. Other people will be involved in the training, but the prime relationship will be between the learner and the coach.

3.5.2 Planning

In terms of planning, on-the-job training needs to be thought through. Figure 3.4 shows a simple form for use in planning on-the-job training; Fig. 3.5 gives a sample set of guidance notes and example training activities.

Main Features

Training takes place in the work area
Delegate carries out work tasks with guidance
Action plan with specific tasks
Progress against plan
Delegate thinks about learning points

When to Use

No relevant training materials exist
To reinforce learning from another training method

Fig. 3.3 On-the-job training at a glance.

SECTION 1 - Staff Details and Team Leader Approval
Name:
Team Leader: Sign:
Team:
Date Raised:

SECTION 2 - Training Objective
Skill:
Purpose of training exercise(s) (please tick most appropriate box):
☐ learn new skill   ☐ practise recently-acquired skill   ☐ expand current skill

---

SECTION 3 – Plan
exercise(s) or action(s)   target date(s)   completed date(s)

SECTION 4 – Progress
(Use this space to record any problems that arise and reasons for any alterations to the plan.)

SECTION 5 - Sign-off (when plan complete or terminated)
Team Leader: Sign:
Date:

At your next development review, consider whether the training worked: did you feel able to apply the new knowledge within acceptable timescales? Is further training needed?

Fig. 3.4 On-the-job training form.

When planning on-the-job training, try to keep it fairly specific so the delegate can focus the activities on the skill being learned or practised. The training objective is the skill to be developed together with the main purpose, whether to learn an entirely new skill, to practise something learned recently (for example, on a taught course), or to expand on a current skill. Some specific actions should be highlighted and noted on the plan. These activities can be taken from the suggested

Definition   On-the-job training is broadly defined as informal training carried out within your normal place of work and within your normal working day.

Activities which might be carried out are:

- viewing specific training video
- using specific PC courseware
- reading specific book or journal
- tasks given specifically to reinforce or practise a newly-acquired skill, maybe after a formal course
- regular development meetings with team leader or other coach/mentor
- secondments designed for development experience
- participation in working parties if done to expand experience

The following would NOT be considered on-the-job training:

- formal courses whether in-house or external
- PC courses or training videos done outside work time
- long term college-style or open university education
- normal work tasks using the new skill

Usage   Use this form to plan your on-the-job training and to record progress and issues.

Section 1   **Staff Details and Team Leader Approval**

Name	your name
Team Leader	your current team leader
Sign	signature of your team leader
Team	your current team or project
Date Raised	date the form is raised

Section 2   **Training Objective**

Skill	the particular skill you are trying to develop
Purpose	tick the purpose of the training

Section 3   **Plan**

Use this section to plan the activities to be carried out in developing this skill.

Exercise(s) or Action(s)	activities to be carried out as part of training; examples are given in the definition above
Target Date(s)	date by which you and your team leader agree the particular activity should be completed
Completed Date(s)	date of actual completion (or agreed abandonment) of the particular activity

Section 4   **Progress**

Use this section to record any problems that arise. If the plan needs to be altered at any time, use this section to record the reasons and the changes. If and when any activities are found to be unnecessary, put the date you cancel the activity in the Completed column in Section 3.

Fig. 3.5 On-the-job training form – process.

list in Fig. 3.5, or they might be different ones relevant to the skill and the delegate's current workload. Perhaps some new tasks can be assigned as learning exercises. As with other types of training planning, a target date should be agreed on to make the training timely and to keep it from drifting on indefinitely.

3.5.3 Progress

Progress on the planned activities needs to be noted, with learning points and learning obstacles indicated. These will aid the discussion and memory later in the year at the normal development review. Sometimes a planned activity becomes out of date before it can be carried out; actions that are no longer relevant should be cancelled and signed off on the form. When all the actions on the form have been completed (or cancelled) then the on-the-job training can be signed off. The learning points should be reviewed at the next opportunity, as part of the usual discussion of how the training went and what further training may be needed. A brief look at the effectiveness of the on-the-job training experience can also help with choosing training methods for this individual and for other team members in the future.

Example

Figure 3.6 shows an on-the-job training plan which is still in progress. Joe planned to reread some notes from a previous course and then to get some practice developing his new skill in JCL programming. In the event, he was called on to use the new skill in a real situation before he had had a chance to try it in a practice situation. Afterwards he went back to check out his understanding of the JCL he'd written "for real". He also looked closely at some other JCL routines and developed a more in-depth understanding of the subject. When he has had a chance to write some JCL for the live environment, he will feel able to sign off the training plan.

Example

Mike has just been promoted and now has to manage a cost centre in the IT department. He is not yet familiar with cost centre management. He has started working through the plan of action in Fig. 3.7, which will help him acquire the skill. He is currently wrestling with the draft budget and finance return and has had a lot of support from the Finance Manager.

Example

In Fig. 3.8 we see that Ann needs to expand her presentation skills. She has a plan of action but has not yet started to carry it out. She will be using her team leader as a coach, plus another person who has not been assigned yet, probably from the business user department. She will thus learn to prepare and give more influential presentations and at the same time get to know some of her key business contacts.

SECTION 1 – Staff Details and Team Leader Approval
Name: Joe Smith
Team Leader: Frank Lee   Sign: Frank Lee
Team: Support Team
Date Raised: 4 December 1997

SECTION 2 – Training Objective
Skill: JCL programming
Purpose of training exercise(s) (please tick most appropriate box):
☐ learn new skill   ✓ practise recently-acquired skill   ☐ expand current skill

SECTION 3 – Plan

Exercise(s) or action(s)	target date(s)	completed date(s)
Re-read course notes	Feb 98	can 3/98
Analyse an existing JCL routine	Mar 98	Mar 98
Amend and test an existing JCL routine	Apr 98	Jan 98
Write new routine for test environ.	As reqd	Feb 98
Write new routine for live environ.	As reqd	

At each stage, talk to Fred Brown to check I'm on the right
track

SECTION 4 – Progress
(Use this space to record any problems that arise and reasons for any alterations to the plan.)
Didn't have time to reread course notes properly. Needed to
amend existing routine and did it successfully. Later
looked at several other processes to see how they did
what they did.

SECTION 5 –Sign-off *(when plan complete or terminated)*
Team Leader: Sign:
Date:

At your next development review, consider whether the training worked: did you feel able to apply
the new knowledge within acceptable timescales? Is further training needed?

Fig. 3.6 On-the-job training form – example.

SECTION 1 – Staff Details and Team Leader Approval
Name: Mike Jones
Team Leader: Dave Green   Sign: Dave Green
Team: Testing and Support
Date Raised: Feb 97

SECTION 2 – Training Objective
Skill: Cost Centre Management procedures
Purpose of training exercise(s) (please tick most appropriate box):
✓ learn new skill   ☐ practise recently-acquired skill   ☐ expand current skill

---

SECTION 3 – Plan

Exercise(s) or action(s)	target date(s)	completed date(s)
Look at relevant procedures	Feb 28	Feb 20
Talk to Finance Manager	Feb 28	Feb 21
Draft first month's cost centre return	Mar 97	
Discuss draft with Finance Manager	Mar 97	
Amend finance return and budget	Mar 97	
Submit to Finance Manager	Mar 97	

SECTION 4 – Progress
(Use this space to record any problems that arise and reasons for any alterations to the plan.)

SECTION 5 –Sign-off *(when plan complete or terminated)*
Team Leader: Sign:
Date:

At your next development review, consider whether the training worked: did you feel able to apply the new knowledge within acceptable timescales? Is further training needed?

Fig. 3.7 On-the-job training form – example.

SECTION 1 – Staff Details and Team Leader Approval
Name: Ann Brown
Team Leader: Frank Lee   Sign:
Team: Support Team
Date Raised: 10 April 1998

SECTION 2 – Training Objective
Skill: presentations — more challenging ones
Purpose of training exercise(s) (please tick most appropriate box):
☐ learn new skill   ☐ practise recently-acquired skill   ✓ expand current skill

SECTION 3 – Plan
Exercise(s) or action(s)   target date(s)   completed date(s)
Get more involved in presentations that have to influence
· Join the change management team for project XYZ
· Decide who needs to be influenced to do what
· Work out how to influence each player
· Discuss with line manager/coach
· Meet each player individually and decide how to influence each
· Prepare talk — discuss with coach
· Hold talk
· Discuss after — did I influence everyone? Was it agreed?

SECTION 4 – Progress
(Use this space to record any problems that arise and reasons for any alterations to the plan.)

SECTION 5 –Sign-off *(when plan complete or terminated)*
Team Leader: Sign:
Date:

At your next development review, consider whether the training worked: did you feel able to apply
the new knowledge within acceptable timescales? Is further training needed?

Fig. 3.8 On-the-job training form – example.

SECTION 1 – Staff Details and Team Leader Approval
Name: Charlotte Green
Team Leader: Mike Jones   Sign: Mike Jones
Team: Testing and Support
Date Raised: 12 Dec 1998

SECTION 2 – Training Objective
Skill: presentations and business awareness
Purpose of training exercise(s) (please tick most appropriate box):
☐ learn new skill   ☐ practise recently-acquired skill   ✓ expand current skill

SECTION 3 – Plan

Exercise(s) or action(s)	target date(s)	completed date(s)
prepare and deliver talk to school party on IT in business, using this company as an example		
- Talk to some people in various business departments for overview of their functions, eg marketing	Feb	27 Feb
- prepare talk and discuss with colleagues	5 March	9 Mar
- rehearse talk to contacts in departments and colleagues	10 Mar	12 Mar
- deliver talk to school party	17 Mar	17 Mar

SECTION 4 – Progress
(Use this space to record any problems that arise and reasons for any alterations to the plan.)
Found out lots of new things about company and consolidated previously vague ideas about the business. Preparing the talk took a lot of time, had to work on it every evening! Rehearsal was very useful and showed I would overrun.
Talk delivered to school party, went well and was well-received.
Have been asked to give it again to a different school. Gained confidence.

SECTION 5 –Sign-off *(when plan complete or terminated)*
Team Leader: Mike Jones   Sign: Mike Jones
Date: 5 April 1998

At your next development review, consider whether the training worked: did you feel able to apply the new knowledge within acceptable timescales? Is further training needed?

Fig. 3.9 On-the-job training form – example.

Example

Charlotte also needed to expand her presentation skills, but in a different way; Fig. 3.9 shows her on-the-job training plan. Charlotte gave a talk to a group of school students about IT and how it supports business functions. To do this she needed to consolidate her own understanding of business functions, then she applied her IT experience to putting IT into the business context. She found the whole exercise very informative. She then filled in the gaps in her understanding of the business areas. She also discovered the need to take into account the needs and current knowledge of the audience. She discovered that preparing a talk is very time-consuming.

Although she thought she would not need much rehearsal time and felt silly doing it, in fact she was glad she had rehearsed as she was able to concentrate on the audience at the school without worrying about the flow of the talk. She did so well that she has been asked to give the talk again to a similar group from another school. The training plan has been signed off, as all actions are complete.

3.6 Summary

In this chapter we have looked in some detail at three major methods of training within short-term timescales:

- Short taught course – providing intensive training including instruction and practical exercises. Taught courses are excellent for learning a specific skill in a short time, but can be expensive and requires full attendance.

- Self-study materials – can be an effective way of learning a new skill but requires self-discipline to get the most benefit. Provides an excellent way of overcoming drawbacks of taught courses, in particular the cost and time requirements. Self-study is very flexible.

- On-the-job training – specific plan of exercises and activities to develop skills within the work context. On-the-job training is good where the learning objective is relatively self-contained and well-integrated into the normal workload and where there is a more experienced member of staff available to help with questions.

In the next chapter I deal with training methods on a longer timescale or with less specific training needs covering a range of topics within a subject.

4. *Choosing between Training Methods – Long-term Options*

■ ■

4.1 Introduction

In the previous chapter we looked at training methods that take place in a short concentrated period of time. In this chapter I consider training methods which take place over a longer period of time, and which often develop a set of related skills rather than a single skill. I begin with mentoring and discuss the many options available. I next look at the different kinds of accreditation schemes and consider their strengths. Finally, I look at higher education and how it helps individuals and organizations to develop staff and skill sets. As in Chapter 3, I will give a description of each training method, some indication of when it could be useful and some of the key points to bear in mind when deciding to use that training method.

4.2 Main Points of this Chapter

- Mentoring
- Accreditations
- Higher education

■ ■

4.3 Mentoring

4.3.1 Description

We have seen in the previous chapter that coaching can be a useful part of on-the-job training. We will see in the next chapter that coaching also forms part of ongoing learner support. Having someone with him to discuss new concepts can help the learner to develop his understanding.

Coaching can also be used for long-term development, particularly for developing the so-called "soft" skills such as leadership or political acumen. Long-term coaching is often referred to as mentoring. Whereas coaching tends to be used for specific job-related skill development, mentoring is a longer-term development process. A skills coach helps the individual to improve his proficiency at a particular set of tasks. A mentor helps the individual to better understand his role and aspirations, and to equip himself to fulfil his potential. At the heart of mentoring is the tutorial relationship between mentor and learner, in which the mentor guides the learner through a process of self-development. Mentoring schemes can be formal or informal, individual or organizational, focused or wide-ranging. Figure 4.1 shows the main characteristics of mentoring as a training method.

4.3.2 Main Features

Let us briefly consider the major aspects of mentoring relationships.

Long-term – any mentoring relationship is a long-term commitment, typically lasting 6–24 months. There has to be time to consider the purpose of the relationship in terms of what skills are to be developed, and for the relationship to grow to the point where the learner feels confident that the mentor will be able to help. The learner is often trying to see organizational issues unfold; these typically take several months to reach a conclusion. One major purpose of a mentoring relationship is to help the learner develop a new perspective and to be able to act within a new sphere of influence with confidence; it takes time to build up that confidence.

Definite purpose – the mentoring relationship will have a definite purpose, typically to develop a set of interpersonal skills or business awareness within the organizational context. So a mentoring agreement may be to help an individual wishing to develop his leadership skills, for example, or to get an understanding of how senior management operates, by say following one or two issues from proposal through to implementation. Both parties to the relationship need to know what they are expecting from the relationship and how they will know when

---

```
                          Main Features

          Tutorial relationship between learner and mentor
          Long-term commitment (6-24 months typical)
          Definite purpose, eg to develop interpersonal skills
          Regular but not too frequent meetings
          Outside the formal reporting line
          Relationship is nurturing
          Confirmed in a mentoring agreement

                           When to Use

          Long-term development desired
          To gain deeper understanding and different perspective
          To help realize potential or meet aspirations
```

Fig. 4.1 Mentoring at a glance.

they have achieved the objective. The relationship should not be allowed to become all-embracing or open-ended, lest it become a drain on both their energies.

Regular contact – the learner and his mentor agree to meet regularly but not too frequently. This will vary with time and circumstances. Typically they might meet fortnightly or monthly to begin with, as they develop a mutual understanding of the purpose and come to an agreement about how to proceed. Thereafter they might meet monthly, every two months or even quarterly to discuss progress since the last meeting and to identify action for the next one. A large part of the mentoring relationship is the opportunity to take a step back from daily routine and to see the work and the organization from a different perspective. The long-term view of events is considered at longish intervals, when there has been time to see both actions and consequences. It also allows "the dust to settle" before coming to conclusions about the effectiveness or otherwise of various options and approaches.

Outside the reporting line – the mentoring relationship is outside the formal reporting line in order to give that different perspective and to avoid the temptation to let routine matters get in the way. The learner's team leader is already involved in his development within the job; mentoring is used to develop skills that are wider than a single role. This is not to exclude the team leader altogether; on the contrary, the team leader is kept up to date with progress and may well wish to discuss with the learner what development is taking place. It may be that the learner gains valuable insight into the team's place within the organization that can help the team leader to grow the team as a whole. But as the purpose of a mentor is to provide an outside perspective, so the mentor is better equipped if he operates outside the line.

Nurturing – most importantly, the mentoring relationship is nurturing. The learner is trying to see the world of work from a new point of view, he is trying to gain confidence in a new sphere of influence. Thus the mentor encourages the learner to open up and express opinions without fear of being laughed at or shot down in flames. The mentoring discussions are sometimes theoretical but more often practical, considering how things happen in practice as opposed to how they ought to happen in theory. Discussions are of experience, how things went, how it felt, how people reacted, rather than about giving instruction all the time. Of course, some instruction may be needed and welcomed, but the relationship is more than just a course. Within the mentoring relationship, the learner is able to experiment, to consider what would happen if circumstances were different, ponder why a certain action prompted a particular reaction, to think through how it could be handled differently and what might be a realistic expectation of the various outcomes.

Mentoring agreement – a mentoring agreement is often noted down but can be as formal or informal as the learner wants to make it. Typically it might be a memo sent to the mentor and copied to the learner's team leader confirming that the new relationship exists and for what purpose. Any tentatively-booked meetings can also be included. The learner or team leader might like to file the memo with the usual review papers, to remind them to discuss progress along with other skill development at the next development review. Mentoring also forms part of some professional development schemes and for this the record keeping is somewhat more meticulous, according to the requirements of the scheme being used.

4.3.3 Choosing a Mentor

What makes a good mentor? What qualities do we look for? A good mentor is someone who is experienced in applying the set of skills the learner wishes to develop. Often, a mentor is someone who is looked to as a role model, although this does not mean they have to be an expert. More importantly, a good mentor is someone who is nurturing. A good mentor will help the individual to develop his skills and to gain a new perspective. The mentor needs to be able to pass on his skills to other people; training is available in mentoring and coaching skills for those who wish to become mentors.

The mentor needs to be able to establish a rapport with the individual being coached, and to maintain a tutorial relationship which is outside the usual work patterns. We expect a mentor to be enthusiastic about developing other people and seeing them grow.

The mentor can be in the same organization as the learner, and often is; equally, the mentor can be outside the organization. It can be very useful to have an outsider's perspective with a different set of practices and company norms. Indeed, an external view can aid the exploration of what the skill is all about and the many different ways to put it into practice. The mentor does not even have to be in the same industry as the learner, so long as there are enough similarities that the two can relate to each others' work settings. On the other hand, a mentor might be sought out because he or she plays a particular role or function that the learner wants to understand, for example chairing a committee. Thus the learner can shadow the mentor and discuss the various aspects of that role both visible and behind-the-scenes.

The learner will learn best what he discovers for himself; the mentor's task is to direct discussion through challenging questions. The mentor can suggest possible avenues of exploration but should certainly encourage the learner to be enquiring, to seek out other opinions, to experiment and try things out in different circumstances, to see what works and what does not. The mentor can also help the learner to put his findings in perspective, and can give examples from his own and his colleagues' past experiences to help enlighten the learner's path. Naturally a good mentor is willing and able to make himself available and to introduce the learner to relevant people and situations.

Of the learner, we expect open-mindedness and a strong desire to develop the skills in question. Keeping an open mind is essential and will lead to exciting discoveries of new approaches and different ways of doing things. The learner has everything to gain but may well feel out of his depth working in a different sphere of influence to his usual one. He will also be exploring new ways of thinking and new perspectives. These may be unfamiliar and uncomfortable at first, but with support and encouragement they will become easier. As he develops confidence and tact in dealing with people outside his usual set of colleagues, he also learns to relate effectively to people much more senior than himself, and to understand their perspective as well as his own.

4.3.4 Success Factors

There are some issues peculiar to mentoring as a training method, and these need to be addressed by each learner–mentor pair. First, there needs to be a recognition that mentoring is a legitimate form of skill development. Time needs to be allocated to both sides of the process, both to the learning and to the mentoring. The relationship should be seen for what it is – a form of training event – and reviewed periodically as part of the individual's usual performance and development review. As the skill is developed, so it needs to be incorporated into the job to help improve performance, lest the lessons are lost. The time that both parties spend on the mentoring and learning must be recognized as time well spent. Other people within the organization, notably the line managers of both the learner and the mentor, must respect the time devoted to the exercise.

Second, it is important to know when to stop. Ideally, the initial agreement includes some description of what is to be achieved and how you will know when it has been achieved. Life doesn't always go according to plan, however. Both the learner and the mentor should stay sensitive to the changes in the relationship as the learner's skills develop. Either one of them can call for a review if the relationship seems to be getting stale, if this happens before the learner has developed as he expected to. It may be that the learner's team leader is the first to spot that the skill has been developed. Equally, the mentor may sense that the learner is ready to be launched on his own and no longer needs to be mentored.

A third issue is that of confidentiality. Clearly, the learner is expected to respect any confidential or commercially-sensitive information he may come across during discussions, research or tasks. At the same time he will trust his mentor not to reveal details of mistakes or learning points to all and sundry. Both the learner and the mentor must explicitly agree to respect confidentiality where appropriate, in the same way that confidentially is maintained in normal business relations.

A fourth issue is that of record-keeping: how much to write down, where and for how long? The short answer here is "whatever seems appropriate". The learner might want to keep some notes of what he is learning as he goes along. He might want to keep track of tasks, how he approached them and what the outcome was – progress notes, in other words. Or he might just want to keep a note of whatever milestones there have been, what has been achieved. Some reference to the learning process should be made in the regular development review notes; beyond that any written records can adequately be kept by the learner for his own benefit. He can then keep his notes for as long as he finds them useful.

4.3.5 Mentoring Schemes

Some organizations and some professional societies run formal schemes for mentoring. Here, a central administration team co-ordinates the various mentoring relationships, helping to keep track of people and progress. Typically they maintain a list of those willing to act as mentors, along with notes about their speciality, how many individuals they are willing to support at any one time, as well as who they are currently supporting and when these relationships are expected to finish. An individual seeking a mentor then asks the administration team to find a suitable mentor and the team makes the first approaches and introductions. When they have helped the learner and mentor to choose each other, they explain the local arrangements, ensure a first meeting has been arranged, and then leave them to it.

A central administration team may or may not ask for progress notes periodically. This could serve several purposes – to remind the learner and mentor to keep meeting; to monitor the learning process; to track when the mentor may be free to take on another student; to highlight any issues of stagnation or other obstacles in the way of progress. In some more formal mentoring schemes it is possible that the mentor provides an assessment as well.

Some mentoring schemes are fairly general and open to all who wish to take part. Others are aimed at specific audiences, for example new entrants into IT or junior managers who aspire to senior management positions. An organization can set up a mentoring scheme for any group that seems to need extra help in developing particular skills, for example women returning to work after a career break for raising a family, or technical experts taking on their first line management role.

Thus a mentoring relationship can be completely self-contained and standalone, or it can be part of a wider training provision, or it can be part of a more formalized process. Many large companies run internal mentoring schemes and several professional societies operate external schemes to aid skill development within their industry.

Example

One IT department had several new entrants to IT, primarily people who had moved from the business side of the company to the IT side. They were each assigned a "buddy" in their respective teams and had training programs developed for them. They also had mentors assigned from among middle managers within the IT department. The trainees' mentors helped them understand the technical background and how their previous business experience related to the IT projects they now worked on. The project allocation team administered the mentoring relationships, keeping the relevant records of assignments and progress. All the new entrants found that their mentors helped them to understand the technical world and to find their own place within it.

Example

Paul, a young manager who had previously joined the IT department from a commercial department, felt there was something missing in his understanding of how the IT department operated. He found a mentor amongst the senior managers and with his help explored the various functions of IT management. This mentoring relationship was very informal but Paul gained a lot from it, eventually becoming a senior manager himself and acting as mentor for other future managers.

Example

Henrietta found that as a junior manager she was not progressing very fast and often could not see what influences were at work amongst her colleagues and her superiors. She approached one of the senior management team and asked her to explain things. This turned into a mentoring arrangement that lasted about a year. By that time she had come to understand the different perspectives of junior and senior managers and to be able to influence people within those perspectives.

4.4 Accreditations

4.4.1 Description

Accreditations as a training method can be grouped into three major types: National Vocational Qualifications (NVQs), proprietary certifications such as Microsoft Certified Systems Engineer (MCSE), and professional society qualifications such as Information Systems Examination Board (ISEB) qualifications or professional society membership. They are particularly suited to practical topics, especially where much of the learning happens within the normal job context. These training methods include some instruction but the main emphasis is on demonstrating competence at various job-related tasks, proof being provided by a portfolio of evidence, examinations, or both. The timescales involved are generally around 3–9 months, making accreditations a long-term training method. The main characteristics of accreditations are shown in Fig. 4.2.

```
                            Main Features

        Three major types
              • National Vocational Qualifications (NVQs)
              • Proprietary certifications
              • Professional society qualifications
        Formal scheme of administration
        Formal assessment of knowledge and competence
        Syllabus based on formal standards
        Skill-based rather than purely knowledge-based
        Wide recognition of qualification


                            When to Use

        When other training methods do not exist
        To gain formal recognition of existing skill
        When other training methods are not appropriate
        To develop skills and gain qualification at the same time
        To gain thorough understanding of proprietary products
        To gain membership of professional society
```

Fig. 4.2 Accreditations at a glance.

4.4.2 Main Features

Although there are three main types of accreditations, they share the same features.

Formal scheme – most accreditation programs have a formal scheme which structures the administration. Candidates register their interest and commitment to the program and are assigned an assessor or an assessment team. Whatever form the assessments take, they are booked and attended as discrete events, with a time and place. The administration scheme helps to keep track of these assessments and their outcomes. The awarding body also ensures that the syllabus and assessment methods are kept up to date and that any instructional material is current and relevant, and is made available to delegates at the appropriate time. When the candidate has passed the assessment(s), the relevant certificate is issued in accordance with the scheme's rules.

Formal assessment – all accreditations involve formal assessment of some kind. For proprietary certification and professional qualifications the assessment is likely to be by examination. An examination or set of exams is clearly a formal assessment; some are written papers and some are practical sessions based in a computer centre. Some examinations are presented in computer-based format, without diminishing the rigour of the assessment. Candidates' answers are marked against correct or acceptable solutions and the resulting score is compared to the required pass mark established by the awarding body.

In the case of NVQs, the assessment is just as rigorous but is usually based on a portfolio of evidence of competence. The portfolio is built up by the candidate and includes documentary evidence of work tasks performed satisfactorily. It might include any of the following items:

- Reports completed as part of normal work.
- Feedback or comments from colleagues and customers.
- Written notes of processes followed and the outcomes.
- Notes of progress from the team leader.
- Notes of learning points made by the candidate.

The assessor reads through all this material, marking it against a benchmark standard, and then discusses it with the candidate. This discussion allows the assessor to probe the candidate's understanding of the topic and the context, allowing them to explore the extent of learning and competence in the relevant skills.

Syllabus – both types of formal assessment are based on a comprehensive syllabus of tasks and activities. The syllabus will have been designed to encompass all the common aspects of a topic, installing a piece of software for example, as well as many of the less obvious ones, for instance designing the testing of that software in situ. The topics are not left in isolation, but are generally linked to each other to reflect the context in which the tasks will be carried out. Thus handling a call to the help desk is seen as including not just the call itself but also a description of the problem, the solution, and the follow-up to check that the solution actually solved the user's problem.

Recognized standards – the syllabus itself is based on a recognized set of standards. IT NVQs are based on the National Training Standards agreed by the

Information Technology National Training Organization (ITNTO). The training standards reflect the expertise and views of a wide range of experts in the field, including companies which are IT users, IT manufacturers, or IT service suppliers, as well as educational establishments and research organizations.

Proprietary certificates, on the other hand, are driven by standards laid down by the relevant manufacturer or supplier, for example Microsoft. These suppliers have built their products to be operable within a wide variety of hardware and software configurations. Suppliers naturally prefer that their products are installed and maintained in an appropriate fashion; certification is one way of ensuring that those who look after the products are qualified to do so and have proven that they meet the same high standards as the suppliers' own personnel.

Professional qualifications are based on standards of competence agreed by or within the professional society making the award. These standards are likely to be embodied in a code of practice for the society's members. Professional standards may also include important items from the National Training Standards, which is not surprising since the latter have often been developed from many of the former.

Practical nature – accreditations, as distinct from university degrees and other education diplomas, are essentially practical. They demonstrate assessed competence in a skill or set of skills. They demonstrate that the candidate has the relevant background knowledge, and understands the principles involved, as do academic qualifications. Accreditations go further, however, and also demonstrate that the candidate can and does apply that knowledge to solve real problems and to complete real tasks. Thus the candidate's competence and skill level are tested; the successful candidate has demonstrated that he can do the job.

Wide recognition – there is a wide recognition of the qualifications offered through accreditation. They are seen to be relevant to the IT industry and to keep up with new developments. They are also credible and have proven themselves to be a valid predictor of performance in the relevant tasks and activities. Thus if an individual has gained such a qualification, employers (current and prospective) can be sure that he can actually perform these tasks. Having said that, there is still no real requirement within the IT industry that practitioners must be accredited in the same way as, say, doctors must be qualified before they can enter general practice. Even proprietary accreditations, while increasingly common, are not actually required for user organizations. However, the process of gaining an accreditation is still a valid and useful training method. The advantage for the employer is the guarantee that the learner has developed the skill; the advantage for the individual is that he has gained a marketable skill.

4.4.3 Different Purposes

We have looked at the salient points about accreditations. What are the main differences between the three major types? The differences fall into two major categories: purpose and assessment methods.

The different types of accreditations have different drivers and different purposes. The main purpose of the NVQ scheme is to provide a benchmark to assess and to describe a person's competence in a skill. NVQs were initiated as part of the government's provision of education and training for young people preparing for employment and for continuing skill development throughout a person's working life. They are administered in conjunction with the national network of local Training and Enterprise Councils (TECS; SCOTVECs in Scotland). NVQs for IT address training requirements at all levels of experience and seniority, in five levels ranging from an IT user to a senior development manager setting strategy. The highest level NVQs are equivalent to university degrees at undergraduate and graduate levels. The driver for creating the NVQ scheme, then, came from concerns about the educational provision in the UK.

The driver for proprietary certifications, on the other hand, came from the major suppliers of software and operating systems within the industry. For these companies, the main concern was and is to ensure best use of their products by user organizations. Through their accreditation schemes, these suppliers help their customers to obtain real business benefit from their software purchases, both initially and as features are added in upgraded software releases. The certification schemes ensure that relevant training is available when it is needed. Thus the main driver for proprietary accreditations is largely commercial.

Qualifications awarded by professional societies are driven more by a desire to ensure that professional standards are adopted throughout the software industry. These qualifications provide a training scheme that is essentially practical in nature and focused on the requirements of, say, project management, as distinct from the wider coverage of a university degree in computer studies. For many of the professional qualifications, the training schemes also represent a major route to gaining full membership of the awarding body.

4.4.4 Different Assessment Methods

The three major types of accreditation scheme use different training and assessment methods. We have already seen that the NVQ scheme is generally work-based and assessed on a portfolio of evidence. Training in individual topics may take a variety of forms, including taught courses, computer-based material, self-study and on-the-job training. Very often an NVQ scheme is used to tie it all together, as it were, and will include more on-the-job training than taught course attendance. Doing an NVQ, the individual is encouraged to look at various aspects of the tasks and to consider them from different perspectives, for example not just looking at his own part of handling a help desk call but also considering the viewpoint of the caller. The individual then consolidates his learning points as part of the NVQ evidence portfolio. This process reinforces the learning and helps to highlight ways of improving the service he provides.

Training for proprietary certifications usually takes the form of a series of taught courses plus some experience applying and consolidating the learning. The courses are given by a training supplier which is certified or accredited to deliver the training on behalf of the software supplier – a Lotus Authorised Education Centre, for example. Each of the major proprietary accreditations has established an international network of such authorised training centres and training companies. The post-training experience is typically in the normal job context. The examinations are taken at an authorised testing centre, which might be run by the accrediting company or might be at an independent authorised examining centre. In any case, the whole process is run according to the requirements of the particular accreditation scheme.

Training for professional qualifications is usually provided on taught courses. Some professional societies run their own programmes of courses; others use approved training suppliers. As we have seen earlier, assessment is often by examination. Many societies have non-examination routes to membership and qualification, to recognize an individual's knowledge and experience gained over several years of working in IT. One example of this is the British Computer Society's points-based membership system, in which qualification entry levels are derived from a combination of previous experience, academic qualifications and relevant training undertaken (British Computer Society, 1999d).

4.4.5 When to Use Accreditations

Accreditation as a training method is appropriate in some circumstances where other training methods do not exist. If a learner wants to develop skills and at the same time wants to gain a qualification, then accreditation can be a useful way of combining both objectives. If, on the other hand, an individual wants to expand on a skill he already has and to fill in the gaps, then going through an accreditation scheme can prove flexible enough to recognize prior experience and to highlight and address existing training needs. Sometimes an individual wants to gain formal recognition of a skill already gained, and most types of accreditation scheme can support this objective.

Sometimes an individual needs to further develop skills and experience but no formal training exists at the advanced level required. In this case an accreditation scheme can help provide the framework for consolidating and expanding the skill set. NVQs are particularly useful in this instance, as they combine many different forms of training and encourage the recognition and reinforcement of learning gained on the job. The assessor can also help to highlight further developments that can be made. The assessor's different perspective can help the learner to consolidate new angles he had not seen before.

Accreditation schemes are very useful for those individuals who cannot or do not wish to embark on the longer-term education afforded by an educational qualification. It may be that a part-time degree course will take too long, or may call for a commitment the individual is not able to give. Or it may be that the individual has a highly pragmatic learning style and thus would find an academic solution too dry and frustrating.

Accreditations, being more focused than most degree or diploma courses, may better fit the individual's learning objectives in terms of being related to the job. For example, the ISEB qualifications administered by the BCS specify training and assessment in a variety of information systems areas such as Business System Development (British Computer Society, 1999c). Accreditations are just as rigorous as academic qualifications, but usually have a narrower focus that is treated in some depth on a practical basis. Some accreditations, particularly the proprietary certifications, may be the obvious solution when faced with the need to train in a particular supplier's products, and to gain a thorough understanding of those products and how to manage them.

4.4.6 Selection Criteria

Having decided that the learner's objectives warrant the use of an accreditation scheme, how do you choose which one to use? The main purpose of the training will indicate the type of scheme to go for. Thus for an individual needing to develop a skill in a highly practical way, probably based on work done on the job, an NVQ is the obvious choice. Where an individual needs to be able to work effectively with a specific software product, the relevant proprietary certification is the one to choose. Where an individual needs to learn and apply best practice in a particular branch of the IT industry, maybe with a view to joining a professional society, a qualification provided by that society would be the best option.

Accreditations, then, are many and varied. They provide a focused, practical training method for developing or enlarging a set of skills needed for one particular function within the IT industry. They are rigorous enough to demonstrate real competence, yet flexible enough to allow several different training options to be used as required.

Example

Several members of an IT helpdesk team needed to enhance their skills in handling calls and providing first-line support to users. All the available training courses covered the basics of the skills they needed, but no advanced training could be found. They decided to do an NVQ in Customer Service, using a training and development company approved by the City and Guilds Institute. Working over a 6-month period, they worked within the helpdesk environment to identify and address areas of improvement both individually and as a group. Basing their training needs analysis on the standards required by the NVQ, they used team discussions and customer feedback to improve the service they provided. Working for and gaining the NVQ gave them a lot of confidence in their work, as well as a better understanding of their working relationships with both the customers calling the helpdesk and with the second line support teams they often call upon.

Example

Tom was joining the Network Support team and had to be quickly trained in all aspects of setting up the full range of local area network software. Most of the existing team members had taken the Microsoft Certified Network Engineer (MCNE) training and exams and Tom chose to do the same. He registered for the certification and attended several courses as required to gain the knowledge, putting the new skills into practice on the job. After about 10 months he took the exams, passing them first time. He reported that the exams were hard but fair and that he was glad to have the opportunity to prove his competence.

Example

Alan was interested in learning more about project management. His job as a project leader had shown him that managing projects is fine when all goes well, but he suspected that there was more to it than that. He felt there were ways of ensuring that a project would go well, that planning and monitoring were complex tasks in their own right. He investigated some courses on project management and contacted the Association for Project Management (APM). He chose to take the exams to gain membership of the society. To prepare for the exams, Alan attended some courses, did some computer-based simulation practice and prepared a portfolio of evidence built up from what he learned in training and how he'd applied it to his work leading projects. He did gain membership of the society. He found the process rewarding and enlightening, giving him a broader understanding of project management than he'd had previously.

4.5 Higher Education

4.5.1 Description

Degrees and diplomas gained from higher education are generally more wide-ranging than qualifications gained from accreditations. Academic courses often give an appreciation of latest research as well as a deeper insight into current practices. Whereas training courses and accreditations are predominantly practical and skill-based, education is more theoretical and knowledge-based.

There are many higher education courses open to part-time students who are in full- or part-time employment. It is perfectly possible for an employee to take a full-time education course, but this is less common for the very practical reason that it usually entails taking time off unpaid. Therefore I will concentrate on the various modes of part-time study.

There are essentially three types of part-time degree course, relating to the different patterns of attendance required:

- Campus-based courses requiring some weekly attendance at the college or university. The student often attends for one day a week on a day-release basis and this mode is often referred to as a day-release course.

- Distance learning, in which the student receives the course material in the post, in the form of written or recorded discussion, readings and questions. The student works through these at his own pace.

- Open University or open learning, in which lectures are recorded and broadcast via television, augmented by written materials sent in the post or via the internet. The student works through the materials on his own at his own pace.

Figure 4.3 summarizes the main characteristics of higher education courses.

Main Features

Part-time study fits in with full- or part-time working
Long-term (2–7 years typical)
Wide-ranging topics within a subject area
Theoretical and knowledge-based, academic in nature
Teaching includes instruction and individual work
Time commitment 15-20 hours per week
Leads to degree, diploma or certificate
Formal assessment of knowledge and understanding
Based around academic year

When to Use

Delegate has strong desire for academic qualification
To continue education during career
Delegate is able to make the necessary commitment
To provide theoretical foundation for practical skills
To update skills across a whole subject area

Fig. 4.3 Higher education at a glance.

4.5.2 Main Features

Whatever mode of attendance is chosen, there are some points of similarity amongst higher education courses; these points are also true of full-time courses.

Long term – higher education courses provide a long-term training method. A typical part-time course will take between 2 and 5 years, depending on the level of the course. Thus a Post Graduate Diploma, for example, may take 2 years while an undergraduate degree with a foundation year might take 5 years. It is possible to spread the workload more thinly, taking fewer subjects each year, and extend the period of study to 7 or 8 years or more. The Open University, for example, offers just this flexibility and it has proved very popular.

Wide-ranging – a degree or diploma course usually has some major subject, for example Computer Studies or Software Engineering. The course syllabus will cover many topics within the subject. Most courses aim to give a broad understanding of the subject and so cover some three or four topics each term or year. There will be some core topics included for common parts of the discipline, for example systems analysis and design within Computer Studies. There will also be some topics which relate to research currently being carried out or topics of special interest to the teaching staff at the institution, for example distributed data architecture within Computer Studies, or graphical animation within Software Engineering.

Academic nature – the material presented on a degree course is academic in nature, by and large. Whereas other training methods aim to develop a student's skill at a particular form of task, e.g. Cobol programming or network installation, education courses aim to develop the student's knowledge and understanding of the principles and issues involved in the subject. The part-time student is usually carrying out the tasks in his workplace, applying his skill; the academic course provides the background and theoretical basis for the practice. The student doesn't so much learn how do it better, so much as why it needs to be done and where it fits relative to other tasks. The long-term course has time to develop the rationale behind a set of techniques, to examine the pros and cons of different techniques, and to give an understanding of the issues involved in choosing and applying a technique to a given problem.

Teaching methods – the teaching methods used on education courses include instruction and independent follow-up work. We will see later that there are distinct variations in the way the instruction is delivered. Yet all the delivery mechanisms include a form of factual presentation and some trigger for comparative thought and critical analysis of the topics and ideas. The material is generally built up from first principles, introducing to the student both the concepts within the topic and a framework for discussing and explaining those ideas. The independent follow-up work then encourages the student to explore the concepts further, allowing him to develop his own understanding of what the principles mean and how the theories both explain and predict observable results from experimentation. At some times in the development of the subject, the student explores ideas and concepts and may be required to write essays about, say, relative merits of software design processes; at other points he experiments with applications and their results and may be required to do "hands-on" hardware or software application work about, say, factors affecting performance of operating systems. All types of academic course offer students an individual tutor or supervisor who can be contacted about problems with course content or with other problems such as workload management or study skills. The tutor thus provides valuable backup to whatever teaching methods are in use.

Time commitment – a degree or diploma course represents a significant time commitment on the part of the student. Whatever the mode of attendance, a part-time course is likely to require 15–20 hours per week (where a full-time course would require at least double that time). For a part-time student who is also doing a full week's work, and presumably has some sort of domestic responsibility as well, this can present a real difficulty. The team leader can help tremendously by keeping an interest in the course and how the current topics relate to the work being done on the job. We can also help by being as reasonable as we can about extra effort needed at work – there will be times when the demands of the job peak at the same time as the course workload, and knowing his team leader will be flexible most of the time helps the student to balance the demands.

End result – education courses demand a large commitment; successful completion represents a great achievement. The tangible result is a degree, diploma or certificate; the intangible result is a tremendous feeling of satisfaction in meeting the challenge. An academic qualification is recognized universally as evidence of conceptual understanding and an ability to apply principles in practice.

Formal assessment – academic courses are assessed using a variety of formal methods; which methods are used depends as much on the subject matter as it does on the mode of attendance. Formal end-of-year examinations are common; students must answer a range of questions under controlled supervision. Exam questions are generally designed to allow the student to demonstrate his understanding of the topic, rather than to catch him out and force mistakes. We can help as team leaders by getting him to explain or outline what he knows about the topic, to help focus his thinking on the central concepts and how they might be applied. Another common assessment method is the project or case study. This is an extended piece of work covering several weeks or months. It often brings together all of the topics within a year or even all the parts of a course. Some projects are done individually while others are group efforts. Many courses use extended essays as part of the assessment, although this is less common with purely technical subjects where arguments alone cannot demonstrate understanding of concepts and implications. More common in these circumstances is the use of assessed coursework (as opposed to unmarked assignments used to provide practical insight). In assessed coursework the student demonstrates an ability to apply the theory to some practical problem and come up with a working solution, for example developing a complex database system and running some set of queries against it to produce reports of some kind.

Academic year – academic courses are based around the academic year, which seems obvious but is often overlooked within the year-round world of work. Some institutions organize their teaching year into three terms of about 10 weeks each, others into two semesters of about 14 weeks. In a term-based year, it is usual to teach all the topics in modules running concurrently throughout the three terms, with exams and project presentations in the third term. In a semester system, on the other hand, one commonly finds the topics in modules that are completed within one semester, with exams and project presentations at the semester end; the student generally does half the modules in each semester. The academic year is often shorter than the calendar year; this is an important distinction for part-time students. During the academic year, the part-time student is under intense pressure on his course and so needs to avoid over-commitment at work. During the academic breaks, there is more time to do that bit extra at work to catch up on anything that was postponed. With forward planning, the work load and the study load can be successfully balanced across the entire year so that everything gets done satisfactorily.

4.5.3 Different Modes of Attendance

We have seen the points of similarity between the different types of education course. What are the variations? There are three major points of difference: mode of attendance, use of teaching methods, and course structure.

I referred to the different modes of attendance at the start of the discussion of education courses. Here I consider the three types in more depth.

Campus-based courses, as we have seen, require attendance at lectures and other teaching events. Attendance is usually required weekly, typically for a period of 6–8 hours. Different courses will have different teaching patterns, some requiring one day a week, others one afternoon plus the evening, still others being held over two evenings. The student is expected to put in another ten hours a week in his own study time, to reread course notes, read any reference material and do assignments and coursework.

Some employers support day-release for their students, others ask the students to work extra hours on their days in the office to make up the time away. As a general guideline, I would recommend most part-time students to attend colleges or universities within about an hour's travel time from their home. Much further than this generally leaves the student too tired to keep up with the work – but of course this is only a guideline. The highest priority should always be given to the match of the course syllabus with the student's learning needs.

Distance learning courses require little or no campus attendance and can thus draw their students from any geographic location. Course materials are sent to the student at regular intervals. Distance learning materials are designed and written to be used by the student on his own with little extra input from the teaching staff. Much of the material is in text format; on practical courses there is also relevant software to use on a PC. For this type of course, the student must spend the equivalent of class time reading through the course material and any supporting reference material, as well as his own time working on assignments and course work. The time commitment is still about 15–20 hours a week, but of course the student can schedule this in whatever hours he chooses to suit his existing commitments, for example late evening when the house is quiet, or on the train while commuting to work.

Many distance learning courses also offer optional residential sessions, typically one weekend per module or 1 week per year. The residential session gives an opportunity for students to exchange notes on progress and issues, and to gain mutual support. Distance learning can be a very isolated mode of study and this isolation is alleviated to a great extent by the periodic contact with fellow students. Residential sessions also provide a valuable opportunity to meet the teaching staff and air any problems there may be. The staff are able to highlight the important points in any part of the course and to provide an insight into recent developments in the field.

Open learning courses, in particular those run by the Open University, make extensive use of public broadcast channels and the internet (Open University, 2000). Lectures and practical demonstrations are recorded for the course and broadcast on television (or sometimes on radio), often in the middle of the night or early morning. Many students record the broadcasts for later viewing if the broadcast times are inconvenient. The broadcasts are supplemented by written textbooks and course notes similar to those prepared for distance learning courses, as well as any computer software that is needed; indeed, on some courses the broadcasts are really a supplement for the written materials. Again the student is expected to put in about 15–20 hours a week viewing and reading the material and working on assignments.

Open University courses also include optional residential summer schools of about one week, which give the staff and students a chance to meet and exchange progress and discuss issues. The written material presented during the year is augmented and reinforced by teaching sessions, and the students develop their ideas in discussions and practical sessions.

Open learning is also being conducted on the internet, as universities begin to exploit new communication channels for education purposes. (The internet is not a new channel for universities, of course, but its wide availability to the general public is a recent phenomenon.) Open learning delivered via the internet is often referred to as e-learning. Recent developments include downloadable recordings of lectures and demonstrations, available to students registered on a course. Course materials can also be distributed in this way. Some courses provide on-line tutorial help, sometimes in real time with a lecturer in attendance. Some of the tutorial support is in off-line mode, with the response following some hours or days after the enquiry. The widespread access to the internet is sure to trigger more innovative approaches to education delivery.

4.5.4 Different Teaching Methods

Another variation between part-time courses is in the use of teaching methods. On attendance-based courses the instruction takes the form of lectures, classes, practical sessions and tutorials. Lectures are used to deliver and explain conceptual information; being essentially one-way communication, a lot of material can be presented to a large number of students at once, say 50 or 100. Classes are held with smaller groups, say 5–20, and provide a more interactive exploration of theories, their consequences and their practical applications. Where they are appropriate, practical computer lab sessions provide the students with a chance to try it out for themselves, to put the theories to the test and to experiment with the applications, drawing their own conclusions on some of the related issues. Tutorials are generally held in very small groups of 1–3 students, giving them the opportunity to put all the topics into perspective and develop an understanding of the subject as a whole. Tutorials generally include discussion of all the topics or modules a student is following, whereas lectures, classes and labs are usually devoted to one topic or module within the course.

Distance learning teaching methods also include instruction and tutorials, although in a different format. Here, the instruction is often in the form of directed reading, in which the lecturers have interleaved explanatory and discussion notes with reading material taken from the literature. These might include current books, journal articles and conference papers covering different aspects and concepts within the topic. Working through this material can be very like having a panel of experts all to yourself! Sometimes there is software available for the student to use on a PC to carry out practical work and experiment with applying the instruction and theory; students work on computer-based applications and send samples to their tutors.

Most distance learning courses offer optional residential sessions, as described earlier. Individual tutorials are generally offered at these sessions, as well as lecture-style explanation of the main points in the topic. Students are of course welcome to contact their tutors at any time; the residential session gives a chance to talk face-to-face.

Open learning teaching methods provide instruction and tutorials in yet a third combination. Some lectures are recorded for broadcast, and deliver factual material explaining and expounding a topic. Recordings are augmented by written materials, text books and sometimes computer software in a similar fashion to distance learning teaching methods. Many open learning courses also offer residential sessions for students and staff to exchange progress and discuss issues. Open learning teaching methods thus combine methods used in campus-based and distance learning courses.

One form of open learning which is gaining ground in recent years is the on-line or virtual university. This combines internet-delivered self-study material with tutorial support and is often accredited by a university. The student registers for a course of study and selects his options from the syllabus presented online. Material is accessed via the internet (usually downloaded for later perusal); assignments and reading lists are also issued in this way. Tutorial support can be provided on-line, typically via email, or off-line using email, telephone, or other communication media.

4.5.5 Different Course Structures

The third point of variation between the different types of higher education courses is in the area of course structure. By and large, campus-based courses consist of several subjects running concurrently for each academic year. Thus a part-time Computer Studies course might include systems analysis and design, data structures, network principles and object-oriented programming during the first year, with four further subjects in the second year. There is often a project in the second or third year, running for the duration of the academic year. Preparation for the project often includes instruction and practice on project management. The project itself is frequently a self-contained piece of work from the workplace, for example, designing and implementing a prototype staff administration system.

Distance learning courses, on the other hand, are frequently structured in three or four modules running one after the other. Such courses are rarely tied to the academic year, but continue throughout the summer when university teaching generally takes a break. The student concentrates on one subject at a time, completing the assessment for one module before starting the next. There is often a wide-ranging piece of work to do as a final task, for example a project or dissertation, which typically pulls together all the subjects covered in the modules; this follows the last module.

Open learning courses are more flexible than either of the other two types. The student is able to follow several modules together within an academic year, or can choose to do only one each year, depending on his own workload and available study time. Again there is often a project that pulls much of the course teaching together.

4.5.6 When to Use Higher Education

When is a degree course an appropriate training method? There are some circumstances in which a part-time degree course is an ideal solution. Where an individual wants to study for a degree but cannot take time out of his career to study full-time, a part-time degree is the obvious answer. Not everyone goes straight from school or college to university, and part-time degree courses give these people a chance to continue their education later on once their career has started. Of course, the student must be able to spend the necessary time to do the studying; sometimes this is more a factor in deciding what mode of part-time study will be followed than in deciding whether or not to go for a degree or diploma.

A degree course is a clear choice if the individual wants to learn about a wide range of subjects within the learning objective. If the learning objective is narrow and focused then some other method of training will probably be better. If the learning objective includes a wide range of topics then a part-time degree or diploma course will likely be suitable.

Another reason for choosing a degree course is that the individual may wish to update his skills in the subject as a whole; here, the wide range of topics – and the inclusion of leading edge approaches still under research – support the learning objectives very well indeed. This is also true of an individual who is changing from one career to another and needs to learn a lot about the new subject, both theory and application, in a way complementary to the job role and tasks. Part-time study is a good training method for anyone who wishes to understand and explore the theory behind his subject and the background to the practice of his craft.

4.5.7 Selection Criteria

Choosing a course of part-time higher education study is again a question of balancing several considerations:

- subject area and match of learning objectives to syllabus;
- mode of attendance and how it relates to learning style;
- locale if it is necessary to attend classes regularly;
- study pattern and how it fits in with work and domestic life.

In this decision process, the different criteria cannot be considered in isolation but must be balanced against each other.

The match of the individual's learning objectives to the teaching objectives as embodied in the course syllabus is the most important factor in this decision. But the combination of mode of attendance, distance to be travelled regularly, and how the study commitments will fit into existing work and home commitments also needs to be taken into account. It is worth looking at several courses to see which syllabus gives the best coverage while still being practical in terms of the other factors. You will need to look fairly closely at the content of each course and consider which one gives the best fit to what the individual needs.

For example, Computer Studies might include commercial system design and management topics, while Computer Science might include hardware and operating system topics. Similarly, one institution's Computer Studies syllabus might look the same as another's Computer Science syllabus: the same course title does not imply the same course content.

The prospective student must look at his own learning style and consider how it fits with the different modes of attendance. If, for example, he prefers to learn with other people then he might find a distance learning course very isolating and hard to sustain – although course leaders are well aware of this problem and encourage students to get together with other students in their local area.

The student must also look realistically at his work and domestic commitments. Are these likely to stay the same as at present, or increase or decrease? Then consider how each different type of course might fit with these commitments. If, for example, the student can be available on a day-release basis, then a campus-based course may be just the thing. If on the other hand he cannot be available on the same day every week, then a distance or open learning course would be indicated.

If a course demands a work-based project then this should be factored into the decision. Such projects need to be self-contained, completed by the student alone and fit into the required timetable. Some courses require projects to be conducted on one day a week for an academic year, often in conjunction with project management instruction; other courses require concentrated effort for a month or two after all other teaching has finished. Although it is not impossible to find suitable projects outside the work environment, it is much easier for the student to use a real piece of work for a course project – doing so reduces the extra workload and also relates the teaching back to the work place, reinforcing the learning points.

Choosing a course is thus a balancing act and should be discussed between the individual and his team leader and also with his partner or anyone else whose life will be significantly impacted by the extra demands of an extended course of study.

Example

Paul wanted to do a degree course in computer studies and management. He didn't really have any specific topics he wanted to cover, but he knew he would not be able to commit to attendance at classes much beyond the first year. His learning style was reflective-theorist, and he had strong self-discipline, so he knew that he would be able to sustain his studies in relative isolation. He chose to pursue an Open University degree. This gave him the flexibility to do two modules in the first year when he had more availability and only one in subsequent years when his availability would drop. Although this meant it would take longer to finish the degree, he was happy to continue for as long as it took. He found that the things he learned in the modules were of immediate use in his work, bringing new approaches to his attention and challenging him to re-think some of his work practices. He was also able to share some of his understanding of new approaches with his colleagues, who appreciated the fresh insights.

Example

Sally, Frank and Jim attended the local university's part-time degree course in Computer Studies. This was a campus-based course where students attended one day a week during the academic year. The course led to a BTEC Higher National Certificate (HNC) after 2 years, Higher National Diploma (HND) after 3 years, Bachelors degree after 4 years, and Bachelors (Honours) degree after 5 years. Sally started in year four as she had an HND already, and completed her honours degree in 2 years. Frank had started a degree course straight after leaving school but had not finished it; he started in the second year to gain his HND before going on to the degree itself. Jim started with the first year and finished the first 3 years with an HND, then took a break for a year and returned to finish the final 2 years of the degree course. They all found it very worthwhile but hard to keep at the studying. They all had various life changes within their years of study, for example Frank got married and Jim changed to a different type of system development work. Despite the difficulties, all three spoke highly of the course and recommended it to their colleagues.

4.5.8 Corporate University

Another form of open learning is the corporate university. Corporate universities are typically organized as a partnership between an individual company and a training supplier or university specializing in this type of training delivery. Many of the newer universities are forging this type of link to industrial and commercial organizations. Conversely, many large organizations run their company universities entirely within the organization.

However it is organized, the corporate university combines several different teaching methods, especially self-study, taught courses, mentoring and tutorial support. They provide a global company-wide education service, supporting people who are new to the company as well as those who are developing or even changing their careers within the organization. In most cases, the topics covered include the specific skills needed by the organization, for example industry-specific or company-specific topics, as well as more general skills such as team leadership or professional development topics.

Some corporate universities award internal certificates, recognizing and accrediting progress and skill development in a format understood throughout the organization. The individual not only increases his skill set but he does so in a way that facilitates his career development within his organization. Some corporate universities are moving toward linking their qualifications with nationally recognized qualifications such as NVQs. This gives the individual a more widely-recognized accreditation while developing his skills in line with his organization's skill requirements.

Because of the focus on skills for the company, corporate universities do not really provide higher education courses at all, but a novel way of organizing training delivery and recognizing skill development. Nevertheless, I suspect that we will see more large companies using in-house universities to develop their people in future.

4.6 Summary

In this chapter we have looked in some depth at three types of long-term training:

- Coaching or mentoring, in which an individual is helped to learn about his role by discussing it with an independent mentor, observing role models, trying things out for himself, and reflecting on a wider perspective.

- Accreditations, in which instruction and experience are closely integrated, so the student both learns about the work and demonstrates competence in the required tasks.

- Higher education courses, in which part-time study over a number of years leads to academic qualifications and provides an understanding of the theory behind an area of work and the background to the practical tasks within that work.

These long-term training methods complement the short-term training methods we looked at in Chapter 3, namely taught courses, self-study and on-the-job training. In the next chapter I consider ways in which the team leader can support the learner, whatever type of training method is in use.

5. *Learner Support*

5.1 Introduction

So far in this book we have identified a training need and decided how to meet that need. Now it is time to recognize the learner as a person and not as a bucket into which we pour knowledge. People are social beings; anyone learning a new skill will develop their expertise more quickly if they are supported by someone else. This can be someone who has the skill already, or someone who is learning at the same time – or just someone who is interested and can help the learner talk through what is being learned. I have often found that just by recapping a recent training course to me, my colleagues have recalled and reinforced the things they learnt. Explaining something to another person helps us to both understand it better and to see it from a different perspective.

In this chapter I look first at the support we give our people before their training, to prepare them for it. I then look at the support we give after the training, to reinforce the learning that took place. Next I consider the continuation of the learning process, often done by coaching the learner to ensure ongoing development. Finally, I look briefly at action groups that provide mutual support for a group of people learning at the same time.

5.2 Main Points of this Chapter

- Pre-training support
- Post-training support
- Coaching the learner
- Action groups – mutual support for a group of learners

5.3 Pre-Training Support

In some ways, pre-training support began with the identification of the training need and the ensuing discussions between the delegate and the team leader. This was the start point for the learner to consider the skill gap and, in particular, what

65

the new skill will look like and feel like. Pre-training support then takes the form of recalling that discussion and bringing the learning objectives back into focus. Whatever training method is chosen, a pre-training briefing can be used to clarify these objectives a short time before the planned training activity.

5.3.1 Pre-Training Briefing

This briefing session, which might last anything from 10 to 30 minutes, can be structured around a pre-training briefing form or checklist; Figure 5.1 shows an example which is used to describe the process.

Training selection – some of the information requested is for analytical purposes to support the training decision-making process, for example how the training was selected. This will also remind the learner and the team leader what the main purpose of the training is to be. If the training was selected during an annual review for example, it might indicate a long-term development need rather than an immediate requirement. A brief reminder of the reason for nomination will confirm whether this is a short-term or long-term need and where this training fits into the individual's long term plans.

Timeliness – by considering the timeliness of the training, you should be able to highlight any potential problems. If a particular course is the best one for the delegate but the only available place is too early or too late, it alerts you to expect difficulties with an unfamiliar topic or an over-familiar topic – and hence a bored delegate. Forewarned is forearmed; the team leader can help by giving a bit of background in the topic and by being tolerant of any later frustration on the learner's part. The learner can help by being understanding of a potentially frustrating course if the timing is not ideal.

Objectives – looking at the training objectives and the individual's learning objectives was part of the training selection process and one would hope that the training activity was chosen to closely match the learner's training needs. But this briefing session is a good opportunity to see if anything has changed since the training was selected. Are the previously-identified objectives still valid? Have any further objectives arisen, maybe through recent familiarisation with the topic or work area? What other benefits will the training bring, what other objectives? Perhaps the individual will have the opportunity to make contact with people in other companies, perhaps he wants to do some recreation before or after a course.

Pre-training work and post-training opportunity – some training activities have familiarisation work to be done before attendance, and the briefing session is a chance to check that this has been done and understood. The team leader can help to iron out any problems or explain the background. The learner should try to think what he expects from the training activity. Will there be an opportunity to use the new skill soon after the training? What new skill or topics does he expect to find out about? What does he expect to be able to do after the training? What does he expect to use straight away and which job tasks will it help with? How soon does he expect to be able to use the new skill? If there is no opportunity to use the new skill within a few weeks, the skill will fade and will have to be remembered or refreshed before it can be applied. Can any measures be identified so you will be able to tell if the training was adequate and effective? At this stage, such

---

Name: Briefing Manager:
Course/Material: Training Date(s):
Supplier:

1. How did you select this training:
   ☐ Performance Review   ☐ Self
   ☐ Team Leader   ☐ Training Manager
   ☐ Other please state

2. Reason for nomination:
   ☐ Immediate Job Requirement   ☐ Change of Job
   ☐ Long Term Aspirations   ☐ Team Development
   ☐ Other please state

3. Is the timeliness of this training:
   ☐ Too early   ☐ About right   ☐ Too late

4. Are all training objectives relevant: YES / NO
   if NO what percentage of training objectives are relevant?
   ☐ 20%   ☐ 40%   ☐ 60%   ☐ 80%

5. Do you have any personal objectives over and above the training objectives?
   YES / NO (If YES please write them down overleaf)

6. How much of the training content are you familiar with:
   ☐ None   ☐ Some   ☐ Most   ☐ All

7. Are there any pre-training work or pre-requisite requirements? YES / NO
   if YES, have they been completed / fulfilled?   YES / NO

8. How soon will you have the opportunity to make use of your new skills and knowledge?
   ☐ Immediately   ☐ Within One Month
   ☐ Within Six Months   ☐ Within One Year

Book an appointment for Debriefing with Briefing Manager at earliest available date.
Please supply that date:

Delegate Signature:
Briefing Manager Signature:
Date:

Fig. 5.1 Briefing form

measures are likely to be fairly loose, for example "can work on his own to code programs without needing to ask too many questions" or "can put together informative presentations that spark useful discussion rather than lots of background questions".

The pre-training briefing session, then, gives the learner and the briefing manager a chance to revisit the reasons for the training activity and check those reasons are still valid. The briefing manager is usually the team leader – but could easily be someone else, a more experienced team member, say, or a skills mentor or the training manager. As we shall see in a later chapter, organizational structures can have a bearing on who is involved in training discussion and in developing the skills within a department.

Example

Ann is about to join a team using rapid application development (RAD) techniques to implement a new system. She is an experienced analyst programmer but has not come across RAD as yet. Her first priority on joining the new team is to learn about this development method. The training has been suggested by her new team leader, who briefs her about the course using the briefing form in Fig. 5.2. Fortunately there was a training place available on a suitable date so the timing is good. Some of the training objectives for this particular course will not be relevant to Ann as they relate to other roles. When Frank and Ann discuss the training objectives and her learning needs, they conclude that about 80 per cent of the course will be relevant. This alerts Ann to expect not to be able to use all of the course content. Being new to RAD, Ann's own objectives include meeting other people and seeing how they use the techniques in their companies. Frank gives Ann an overview of how RAD is used in their own company, as she is not familiar with the topic at all. There is no pre-course work and Ann will be able to use her new skills immediately, although both recognize that she will need practice on returning to the office. They book an early debriefing date right after the course has finished.

Example

Paul has been working as a technical specialist for some time and is recognized as one of the experts in the department. However at a recent review he expressed a wish to become more of an internal consultant than just a technician. His training need is to learn to be more influential, particularly as he has no direct authority over those he will be advising. Paul discussed his training needs with Amy, the training manager, and together they selected a suitable set of courses. Amy is also doing the briefing session for the first of these courses, on advanced communication skills. The briefing notes are shown in Fig. 5.3. Paul's reasons for doing the course are his long-term aspirations, which he has discussed in some depth with his team leader at his annual review and with Amy in their earlier discussions. Paul will shortly begin a project with very tight timescales and he decided to get started on his long-term development before the project gets underway. The follow-on course in influencing skills will not take place for another 12 months. In that sense, this training in communication skills is a little early for him but both he and Amy recognize this. Paul will put some effort into reminding himself of the course content when he needs to begin to use it. All of the course objectives are relevant, as they deal with various aspects of getting the message across to people. Paul's personal objectives go beyond the course objectives, as he wants to develop new communication techniques for himself, in readiness for the influencing skills course next year. He also wants to start practising! Most of the course content will be

Name: Ann Brown   Briefing Manager: Frank Lee
Course/Material: Rapid Application Devt   Training Date(s):   17–21 May 1998
Supplier: XYZ Training

1. How did you select this training:
   - ☐ Performance Review   ☐ Self
   - ☑ Team Leader   ☐ Training Manager
   - ☐ Other please state

2. Reason for nomination:
   - ☑ Immediate Job Requirement   ☑ Change of Job
   - ☐ Long Term Aspirations   ☐ Team Development
   - ☐ Other please state

3. Is the timeliness of this training:
   - ☐ Too early   ☑ About right   ☐ Too late

4. Are all training objectives relevant: NO
   if NO what percentage of training objectives are relevant?
   - ☐ 20%   ☐ 40%   ☐ 60%   ☑ 80%

5. Do you have any personal objectives over and above the training objectives?
   YES see how RAD is used elsewhere from other delegates

6. How much of the training content are you familiar with:
   - ☑ None   ☐ Some   ☐ Most   ☐ All

7. Are there any pre-training work or pre-requisite requirements? NO
   if YES, have they been completed / fulfilled?   YES / NO

8. How soon will you have the opportunity to make use of your new skills and knowledge?
   - ☑ Immediately   ☐ Within One Month
   - ☐ Within Six Months   ☐ Within One Year

Book an appointment for Debriefing with Briefing Manager at earliest available date.
Please supply that date: 28 May

Delegate Signature: Ann Brown
Briefing Manager Signature: Frank Lee
Date: 10 May 1998

Fig. 5.2 Briefing form – example.

relevant, although Paul has some experience of giving presentations so he and Amy feel that part of the course may be old hat to some extent; Paul will try not to get impatient in that session. There is no pre-course work to be done. Paul expects to be able to use any new techniques he picks up on the course within about 6 months; the new project is not likely to require him to persuade other people to do things. Paul and Amy tentatively book a debriefing date to fit in with the new project's time plans and both their holidays.

```
Name:              Paul Wilson              Briefing Manager: Amy Pink
Course/Material:   Advanced Communication   Training Date(s):  18-20 June 1998
Supplier:          internal training team
```

1. How did you select this training:
   - ☑ Performance Review   ☐ Self
   - ☐ Team Leader   ☑ Training Manager
   - ☐ Other please state

2. Reason for nomination:
   - ☐ Immediate Job Requirement   ☐ Change of Job
   - ☑ Long Term Aspirations   ☐ Team Development
   - ☐ Other please state

3. Is the timeliness of this training:
   - ☑ Too early   ☐ About right   ☐ Too late

4. Are all training objectives relevant: YES
   if NO what percentage of training objectives are relevant?
   - ☐ 20%   ☐ 40%   ☐ 60%   ☐ 80%

5. Do you have any personal objectives over and above the training objectives?
   ```
   YES develop communication techniques ready for influencing
       skills course next year
   ```

6. How much of the training content are you familiar with:
   - ☐ None   ☑ Some   ☐ Most   ☐ All

7. Are there any pre-training work or pre-requisite requirements? NO
   if YES, have they been completed / fulfilled? YES / NO

8. How soon will you have the opportunity to make use of your new skills and knowledge?
   - ☐ Immediately   ☐ Within One Month
   - ☑ Within Six Months   ☐ Within One Year

Book an appointment for Debriefing with Briefing Manager at earliest available date.
Please supply that date: 30 July

```
Delegate Signature:          Paul Wilson
Briefing Manager Signature:  Amy Pink
Date:                        9 May 1998
```

Fig. 5.3 Briefing form – example.

Example

May needs to learn how to use the REXX programming language in order to carry out her work. She is an experienced programmer so an external training course is not likely to be relevant. She needs to use the tool fairly soon so there isn't time to wait for a place on an external course. She looks in the department's training library and finds a computer-based course to run on the PC. May and her team leader discuss the training need. They conclude that the self-study solution is the best for her in this instance – the timing is right as she does not need to interrupt her other work too much. By setting aside two hours a day, she intends to finish the course in one week. The course materials appear to cover all of her learning objectives, which are to gain a basic understanding of REXX principles and language constructs and to be able to test and amend REXX routines. Their course briefing form is shown in Fig. 5.4.

5.4 Post-Training Support

Following the training activity, be it a course or some other form of training, the learning points will be reinforced by a short discussion of how the training went – a "lessons learnt" review, if you like.

The main purpose of a debriefing session is to check that the training was worthwhile, but there are several other offshoots of this dialogue. Sometimes a course was so instructive that a whole team may benefit from training in the topic, and the debriefing manager can highlight this from the meeting. During the debriefing session it may become clear that further instruction may be needed, or further experience with the new skill. The individual may be able to highlight areas of his job that have become easier or that need more practice. Sometimes the discussion can help to build and strengthen the relationship between the individual and the team leader. The debriefing session provides an opportunity for the individual and the team leader to sit back and take a look at the new skill from a different perspective. It gives them a chance to consider the job role and how the new skill works with other skills and how it feeds the work that must be done.

5.4.1 Post-Training Debriefing

Turning to Fig. 5.5 we see an example debriefing form, which will be used to describe the discussion.

Attendance – it is important to note whether the entire training event was completed, or whether for example days were missed through illness.

Relevance – the delegate did the training for reasons discussed earlier, in the briefing session; the training content may or may not have been relevant to those reasons. If someone was looking for an overview, for example, but the course or package turned out to be very detailed, then the content would not have been appropriate for the delegate. Cases where there is a serious mismatch between the stated aims of a course and the actual course content should be taken up with the training supplier, as the catalogue and prospectus may need to be updated.

Name: May Smith   Briefing Manager: John Brown
Course/Material: REXX Fundamentals   Training Date(s):   18–24 June 1998
Supplier: PDQ Materials Ltd

1. How did you select this training:
   ☐ Performance Review   ☑ Self
   ☑ Team Leader   ☐ Training Manager
   ☑ Other please state Training Library

2. Reason for nomination:
   ☑ Immediate Job Requirement   ☐ Change of Job
   ☐ Long Term Aspirations   ☐ Team Development
   ☐ Other please state

3. Is the timeliness of this training:
   ☐ Too early   ☑ About right   ☐ Too late

4. Are all training objectives relevant: YES
   if NO what percentage of training objectives are relevant?
   ☐ 20%   ☐ 40%   ☐ 60%   ☐ 80%

5. Do you have any personal objectives over and above the training objectives?
   NO (If YES please write them down overleaf)

6. How much of the training content are you familiar with:
   ☑ None   ☐ Some   ☐ Most   ☐ All

7. Are there any pre-training work or pre-requisite requirements? NO
   if YES, have they been completed / fulfilled? YES / NO

8. How soon will you have the opportunity to make use of your new skills and knowledge?
   ☑ Immediately   ☐ Within One Month
   ☐ Within Six Months   ☐ Within One Year
   follow-up with example programs for my current task

Book an appointment for Debriefing with Briefing Manager at earliest available date.
Please supply that date: 24 July 1998

Delegate Signature: May Smith
Briefing Manager Signature: John Brown
Date: 15 June 1998

Fig. 5.4 Briefing form – example.

Timeliness – now that the delegate has returned from the training, what can be said about the timeliness of it – has it turned out to be about right, or too early or late?

Objectives – were all the learning objectives met? Most course instructors work very hard to ensure that the course objectives are understood and covered, and to integrate the individual delegates' objectives as well. The supplier will need to know if they have not achieved this. By considering whether his objectives were met, the delegate has a chance to reflect on the learning experience both during and since

Name: Debriefing Manager:
Course: Course Date:
Supplier:

1. Did you attend the training? YES / NO

2. Was the training content relevant for the reason you were nominated: YES / NO
   (refer to Briefing Form question 2)

3. Having attended the training did you feel that the timeliness was:
   ❑ Too early   ❑ About right   ❑ Too late

4. Were all training objectives met:
   ❑ Fully   ❑ Mostly   ❑ Some   ❑ None

5. If any personal objectives were stated were they met:
   ❑ Fully   ❑ Mostly   ❑ Some   ❑ None

6. How much of the training content was familiar to you:
   ❑ None   ❑ Some   ❑ Most   ❑ All

7. Was the pre-training work or pre-requisite requirements relevant?
   ❑ Fully   ❑ Mostly   ❑ Some   ❑ None

8. Having attended the training do you feel that you will be able to make use of your
   new skills and knowledge?
   ❑ Immediately   ❑ Within One Month
   ❑ Within Six Months   ❑ Within One Year

9. How much has your ability to do your job improved after this training:
   ❑ 0% (no improvement)   ❑ 20%
   ❑ 40%   ❑ 60%
   ❑ 80%   ❑ 100% (could not perform this task before)

10. What main points did you learn from the training?
    How can you share them with other team members?

11. How do you feel the training could be improved?

Delegate Signature:
Debriefing Manager Signature:
Date:

Fig. 5.5 Debriefing form.

the training. This can and often does both reinforce the learning points and bring others to the fore.

Familiarity – some of the training content may have already been familiar to the individual, which could have provided a foundation on which to build the new skill. Some prior familiarity may be a good thing and ease the learning; a large amount of prior knowledge may undermine the usefulness of training and make it seem irrelevant or too easy.

Pre-training work – where there had been pre-training work or specified pre-requisites before attendance on a course, the team leader needs to know whether the prerequisites were relevant and actually useful, particularly if other delegates are to use the same training event.

Post-training opportunity – an important aspect of the timeliness of training is the timeliness of the support and use of the new skill – will this be immediate or more long-term? If this is likely to present a problem then that fact should be highlighted as it may affect job performance. There may also be a need for a refresher when the new skill *is* to be used if that will be a long way ahead.

Performance improvement – in the relatively short time since the training, does the delegate or team leader feel that improvement has been seen in use of the skill? This is a question that can usefully be discussed again at the next perform-ance review.

Lessons learnt – it is helpful to the delegate to write down the main points gained from the training. This serves both as a reminder and as a consolidation of the learning. These lessons can also be passed on to other team members. Perhaps the delegate could do a short presentation at a team meeting, for example, as a "Lessons for Us" session. Perhaps the lessons learnt could be written up and distributed, say as a set of Quick Tips. Highlighting and discussing the learning points can help the whole team to learn.

Improvements – Sometimes a delegate will have ideas on how the training could be improved. These suggestions provide valuable feedback both to the team leader (who can use the information in choosing future training) and to the training provider (who should consider seriously any such suggestions).

5.4.2 Reinforcing the Learning

The post-training debriefing session is a valuable part of the learning experience, giving a chance to think back on what was done and how it helped in the skill development process. It does not have to be immediately after a training activity, but should not be left too long – best to do it while the material is still fresh in the memory. It can help to reinforce the new skill and how it fits into the dele-gate's job role. I have found it particularly helpful for those people to whom it feels uncomfortable (those who are not naturally reflective in their learning style) as it encourages them to complete the learning cycle and ponder what they learned while beginning to put it into practice.

So we see that the post-training debriefing session can be an integral part of the learning process. The delegate is given a chance to go back over the training, discussing the "how did it go" questions. He can consider whether it was a learning opportunity and if not what were the blocks to learning? Are they also present in the day-to-day work environment? Do they get in the way of performance? The delegate also reviews the contents of the training and what was learned. Just consid-ering these can reinforce the learning for the delegate. An important part of classroom training is the set of new contacts the delegate can make. Will any of them be useful in the role? Are they purely social? Will he ever see them again or did they just help the learning process to happen?

In a debriefing session and other follow-up chats, the delegate is able to look at how the lessons learnt can be applied, which part of the job they relate to. It may be useful to share the learning points with the rest of the team. The training may have already highlighted some further development or practice which may be needed before the individual is highly proficient. Sometimes it is possible at this early stage to identify suitable measures of improvement or proficiency, for example greatly increased confidence in meetings, which can be observed both by the delegate and by others around him.

Example

In Fig. 5.6 we see the notes from the debriefing session held by Ann and her team leader. She went on the Rapid Application Development course and found the content of the course was relevant to her reasons for attending, as she is using this new technique in her new role. Although they had thought the course would be too early for Ann, in fact it proved fairly timely as she had started to understand the context of system development in the first few days in the job. The course objectives were mostly met, as were most of her personal objectives. She now has several contacts in other companies and will try to keep in touch with them from time to time. Being honest, Ann realized that she was familiar with none of the course content, only with some of the background context for rapid development. There had been no pre-course work. Ann expects to use the material learned immediately and her team leader agreed with this, as he was about to give her a set of initial tasks. As she had had no prior knowledge of the subject, Ann's improvement within the job was 100 per cent. Ann listed some of the main learning points but felt the rest of the team already understood them. She had no clear ideas of improvements to be made to the course – she thought it was well-run and covered most of what she needed. In a few months' time she might have a different view but at the moment she felt well-prepared to get down to trying out the new techniques.

Example

Figure 5.7 contains the notes from Paul's debriefing session with the Training Manager. His debriefing session was six weeks after the training, by which time he was beginning to see the benefits. He did attend the course, which addressed some of his long-term aspirations. This was a course in advanced communication skills to prepare him for further training in influencing people, particularly senior management. Although he had earlier felt the course would be too soon, in practice Paul found the course to be very timely. Only some of the course objectives were met for Paul, but as he recognized that his personal objectives didn't match very well with the course's training objectives, this was not surprising. Some of the material was already familiar to him while some of it gave him new angles on topics he had looked at before. There had been no pre-course work and

Name: Ann Brown   Debriefing Manager: Frank Lee
Course: Rapid Application Devt   Training Date(s):   17–21 May 1998
Supplier: XYZ Training

1. Did you attend the training? YES

2. Was the training content relevant for the reason you were nominated: YES
   (refer to Briefing Form question 2)

3. Having attended the training did you feel that the timeliness was:
   ☐ Too early   ☑ About right   ☐ Too late

4. Were all training objectives met:
   ☐ Fully   ☑ Mostly   ☐ Some   ☐ None

5. If any personal objectives were stated were they met:
   ☐ Fully   ☑ Mostly   ☐ Some   ☐ None

6. How much of the training content was familiar to you:
   ☑ None   ☐ Some   ☐ Most   ☐ All

7. Was the pre-training work or pre-requisite requirements relevant? N/A
   ☐ Fully   ☐ Mostly   ☐ Some   ☐ None

8. Having attended the training do you feel that you will be able to make use of your
   new skills and knowledge?
   ☑ Immediately   ☐ Within One Month
   ☐ Within Six Months   ☐ Within One Year

9. How much has your ability to do your job improved after this training:
   ☐ 0% (no improvement)   ☐ 20%
   ☐ 40%   ☐ 60%
   ☐ 80%   ☑ 100% (could not perform this task before)

10. What main points did you learn from the training? See attached
    How can you share them with other team members? Send them the attached
    document, but they won't need it

11. How do you feel the training could be improved? No clear ideas

Delegate Signature: Ann Brown
Debriefing Manager Signature: Frank Lee
Date: 28 May 1998

Fig. 5.6 Debriefing form – example.

Name: Paul Wilson   Debriefing Manager: Amy Pink
Course: Advanced Comm Skills   Training Date(s):   18–20 June 1998
Supplier: Internal Training Team

1. Did you attend the training? YES

2. Was the training content relevant for the reason you were nominated: YES
   (refer to Briefing Form question 2)

3. Having attended the training did you feel that the timeliness was:
   ☐ Too early   ☑ About right   ☐ Too late

4. Were all training objectives met:
   ☐ Fully   ☑ Mostly   ☐ Some   ☐ None

5. If any personal objectives were stated were they met:
   ☐ Fully   ☐ Mostly   ☑ Some   ☐ None

6. How much of the training content was familiar to you:
   ☐ None   ☑ Some   ☐ Most   ☐ All

7. Was the pre-training work or pre-requisite requirements relevant?
   ☐ Fully   ☐ Mostly   ☐ Some   ☐ None

8. Having attended the training do you feel that you will be able to make use of your
   new skills and knowledge?
   ☑ Immediately   ☐ Within One Month
   ☐ Within Six Months   ☐ Within One Year

9. How much has your ability to do your job improved after this training:
   ☐ 0% (no improvement)   ☐ 20%
   ☐ 40%   ☑ 60%
   ☐ 80%   ☐ 100% (could not perform this task before)

10. What main points did you learn from the training? Think about who you're talking
    to, try to understand their pressures and priorities, and try to
    predict their reactions
    How can you share them with other team members? Demonstrate in a talk

11. How do you feel the training could be improved? Follow up a month later to
    remind us of points and see if we're putting into practice; also
    more stretching exercises

Delegate Signature: Paul Wilson
Debriefing Manager Signature: Amy Pink
Date: 30 July 1998

Fig. 5.7 Debriefing form – example.

Paul had found the course content and new techniques immediately useful. He feels his performance is already improved by about 60 per cent. Amy noticed a new confidence about Paul as he talked in their meeting. Paul's main learning points were in the area of understanding people's motivations. He would give a talk to the team at the next team meeting to demonstrate what he had learned. Paul felt that the course could be improved in two ways: firstly to have more stretching exercises during the course, to challenge the delegates rather more (they were allowed to stay within their "comfort zones" rather too much, which dampened the learning points) and secondly to have a follow-up a month later to remind delegates of their learning points and to see if they are improving. Paul had to do this with a colleague.

Example

May and her team leader discussed the usefulness of the self-study material. She found that the material was very good but that she needed to spend some time consolidating each topic for herself before moving on to the next topic. As the material was self-paced, May was able to integrate the training with her other tasks. This helped to provide a break and some relief from the concentrated effort of learning a new programming language. The training was relevant and her objectives were met in full. May has since begun testing a REXX script for another team member and found she could do so very readily. She reported that debugging an existing script was a learning exercise in its own right. Computer-based learning proved to be a good option in this situation. Her debriefing form can be seen in Fig. 5.8.

5.5 Coaching the Learner

The bulk of this chapter has been about pre- and post-training briefings, in which the training event is discussed and put into the context of the job roles and responsibilities. But learning doesn't stop there; nor does learner support. Coaching is an important follow-up ongoing exercise, perhaps the most important part of the skill development process. It can be formal or informal, occasional or frequent.

5.5.1 Who Can Coach

There are a couple of key points to consider. Firstly, who should do the coaching? It is a natural leadership function and so can be carried out by the team leader. In this case, coaching and encouragement often take place as part of a regular progress review meeting, especially if this is on a one-to-one basis. In many situations it may be the learner's colleagues who do most of the coaching day-to-day. This may be particularly relevant where a new member of the team needs to become familiar with the way things are done in that team. If, on the other hand, the new team member is a trainee and has a long learning curve to go through, then one of the team may be assigned as a "buddy" and so would do most of the

Name: May Smith   Debriefing Manager: John Brown
Course: REXX Fundamentals   Training Date(s):   18–25 June 1998
Supplier: PDQ Materials Ltd

1. Did you attend the training? YES

2. Was the training content relevant for the reason you were nominated: YES
   (refer to Briefing Form question 2)

3. Having attended the training did you feel that the timeliness was:
   ☐ Too early   ☑ About right   ☐ Too late

4. Were all training objectives met:
   ☑ Fully   ☐ Mostly   ☐ Some   ☐ None

5. If any personal objectives were stated were they met:
   ☑ Fully   ☐ Mostly   ☐ Some   ☐ None

6. How much of the training content was familiar to you:
   ☑ None   ☐ Some   ☐ Most   ☐ All

7. Was the pre-training work or pre-requisite requirements relevant?
   ☐ Fully   ☐ Mostly   ☐ Some   ☑ None

8. Having attended the training do you feel that you will be able to make use of your
   new skills and knowledge?
   ☑ Immediately   ☐ Within One Month
   ☐ Within Six Months   ☐ Within One Year

9. How much has your ability to do your job improved after this training:
   ☐ 0% (no improvement)   ☐ 20%
   ☐ 40%   ☐ 60%
   ☐ 80%   ☑ 100% (could not perform this task before)

10. What main points did you learn from the training? Writing REXX scripts
    How can you share them with other team members? They don't need it

11. How do you feel the training could be improved? N/a

Follow-up: May has tested and amended an existing REXX script, the
week after concluding the training. She has the foundation on which
to build in writing REXX scripts for various tasks within the
current work.

Delegate Signature: May Smith
Debriefing Manager Signature: John Brown
Date: 30 June 1998

Fig. 5.8 Debriefing form – example.

coaching, both to show him how the team operates and to reinforce the lessons about what the job entails and how to carry out the work.

In many organizations, there are mentoring schemes in operation, as we saw in Chapter 4; this formalizes the coaching arrangement to some extent. In this case, someone who is outside the learner's direct reporting line is chosen as a mentor and this person coaches the learner on agreed aspects of doing the job. The mentoring relationship typically lasts between 6 and 24 months, until the learner has developed confidence in the skill he was seeking from the mentor. Mentoring is often used to develop non-specific all-roundedness, helping the individual to put it all together, so to speak.

So a range of people can be coaches. The main skills required are a willingness to listen and to nurture, to encourage the learner to develop and ask questions and to answer his own questions as far as possible. The main role of a coach should be to help the learner to learn, rather than to tell him all the answers – people generally learn best what they find out for themselves and explain to others.

5.5.2 What to Discuss

The second key point concerns the "what" of coaching – what to talk about? This will usually start off with a more detailed discussion of say the contents of a recent course, covering such questions as What did you learn and How much will you apply it to your day-to-day work. This leads naturally to discussion of aspects of the job and how they should be done, and how the learning or new skill will help. Depending on the individual's level of expertise, this could be fairly detailed or just an overview. The coach should also check the outcome of the work to ensure that the lessons are applied correctly – some tact may be needed here.

5.5.3 When to Coach

My third key point about coaching concerns the "when" – timing can be as frequent or seldom as necessary. In some situations, regular weekly meetings can be appropriate. In other cases, occasional chats are appropriate. For other people, each new task is a coaching opportunity to learn more about the job and its requirements. The cue should be taken from the individual and their performance within the role or team. At first, when the topic is still very new and the individual hesitant, coaching needs to be fairly frequent. This has the added benefit of encouraging the individual to be (or become) an active team member while developing the new skill. Later, the coaching can tail off as the individual gains confidence with the new skill.

Example

Following her RAD course, Ann was coached by her team leader. At first this took the form of talking through how RAD could be applied to the various aspects of Ann's work as an analyst. The coaching soon changed to one of the team showing her how to put into practice the theory she had learnt on the course. Ann felt well-integrated into the team and settled happily in her new role.

Example

Paul was surprised to find that his Advanced Communication Skills course would be useful so immediately. He found himself turning to one of his friends on a different team for informal coaching, to get their viewpoint and angle on various communication styles. He and his coach often compared notes on key people in the department and Paul found he learned a lot from the discussions and from a fresh pair of eyes.

Example

One of May's fellow team members gave her coaching and acted as a "buddy" in giving her increasingly challenging tasks and showing her what she needed to know to get started. She found this approach very helpful as she knew she could work at her own pace and learn for herself but that there was always someone she could turn to for guidance. Although her colleagues had to spend some time showing her how to do each task, it was time well spent as May was able to contribute productively to the team's work at an early stage. Although the team's role in technical support for the system developers was very demanding, she was soon able to provide effective support alongside the existing support team.

5.5.4 Supporting Long-term Study

Coaching is one of the main ways in which a team leader can support a member of staff who is doing a long-term course of learning such as a part-time degree course. Briefing and de-briefing forms are not really relevant, but the team leader can discuss with the individual what modules are currently being undertaken. Some of the projects on the job can be used or adapted to suit the needs of project or course work as a student; the team leader can encourage the student to find the points of similarity and decide what can be used and what cannot. The academic background knowledge may give the student a wider view of the work he is carrying out on the job. The studies may provide a theoretical underpinning to the practical applications. Those who return to academic study are expanding their skills not for today but for tomorrow, looking at what is currently in research or development but not necessarily as industrial-strength tools as yet. The student may be able to present or explain topics of interest to his colleagues, either as a group or as individuals. The team leader can encourage each of the team to widen their understanding and to share their new insights with the rest. He can also provide encouragement and time for them to put their new insights into practice.

5.6 Action Groups

Another form of learner support takes the form of action groups, in which a number of people all developing similar new skills get together for mutual support and encouragement. Action groups can be formal or informal, run as an integral part of the training course or as a follow-up support group. In my experience, three types of action group work well: those focusing on the same topic, those based on the same team or job role, and those centred upon the same entry date.

5.6.1 Topic-Focused

Action groups centring on the same topic typically arise from a training course, particularly where the new skill cannot be acquired just from considerations of the theoretical background, but must be applied to real situations before the learner can become a qualified practitioner. In some cases, especially on management topics, the course structure will include a follow-up day some weeks after the taught course. Here, the action group is the entire class and the purpose of the follow-up day is to consider how the new skill was applied to the job, what the difficulties were, how they could be overcome – in short, how the theory informs and shapes the practice.

Other post-course action groups are less formalized and may consist of a small number of delegates agreeing to get together to compare notes. Sometimes just a series of telephone or email conversations can help delegates to recall and reinforce their learning both for themselves and for each other. This network of contacts is often seen as a major reason to attend formal courses outside the organization and the benefit can be great if only to aid the learner in developing the new skill within a wide context. To have pre-briefed outsiders to use as sounding boards can be very valuable indeed, provided always that confidentiality is maintained.

5.6.2 Role-Focused

When a job role changes or is clarified, necessitating training for a whole group of jobholders, they will form their own natural action group. This can usefully be harnessed by holding regular (but not too frequent) reviews of progress with team goals or the new job roles, considering such things as lessons learnt, relative priority of different aspects of the job, any need to reprioritize specific goals.

The action group can also provide an opportunity to step back and look at the job in context, to get a different perspective from the usual day-to-day view. By inviting key people from other teams, it can provide valuable feedback on interactions with different parts of the job environment and can thus help the team to work better with other areas. This type of action group can also provide a focal point for discussing further training on specific skills that the team and role may require. Even just highlighting the need to use a skill that everyone has can help the team to perform better as a whole.

5.6.3 Entry-Focused

A third type of action group consists of people who have all joined a team or company at about the same time, typically a group of graduate entrants all starting in the same month. Whether or not they follow the same detailed training plan, they will integrate into the company much more easily if they are encouraged to get together to exchange notes on a regular basis while they are still trainees. Some companies run formal schemes of social gatherings once a quarter, others have feedback meetings in which each graduate describes their recent work and shares what they found out (this has the added advantage of giving the trainees experience of semi-formal presentations). Other organizations have informal gatherings on an ad hoc basis. All are equally valid, so long as the action group provides mutual support for the individuals within it. Often this type of action group fades away as its members become fully integrated into their new teams and as they move out of the trainee role to become junior practitioners.

Example

A group of people from different teams attended a business analysis course, to learn how to gain a better understanding of the business area for which they were designing systems. Some of the delegates came from the business area and others came from the systems analysis team. They found that business analysis is a halfway house between carrying out the business functions and designing the computer systems that are used in the business. Following the course, they formed an action group to review the lessons they had learned from the course and to apply those lessons to the roles they carried out. As they all work on business analysis but in different teams, the delegates found the action group very helpful and carried on meeting about quarterly for over 2 years. What started as a post-course action group became an information-exchange support group as they came to understand their changing roles better.

Example

Jonathon attended a management course on handling conflict. The course was structured as a 4-day course followed by a further day 4 months later. He found that whilst he learned a lot on the course itself and had plenty of support back on the job, still the follow-up day was time well spent. He had a chance to learn how other people had applied the same lessons. Together the delegates explored the different ways and outcomes of handling conflict within their organizations. The training team gave insight into why the delegates had such different experiences, helping them to recognize the different organizational contexts involved. Jonathon felt better equipped to predict the outcomes of handling conflict within his own sphere of influence.

Example

A group of graduates joined the IT department as trainees at about the same time. Each was assigned to a more experienced colleague who would be their "buddy", partly for job skills coaching and partly to help them integrate into their teams and to make the transition from being a student to being an IT professional. The group were also invited to get together informally with members of the management team approximately quarterly for their first year. Most of the trainees found this useful to get to know people outside their immediate teams, and to get together and compare notes with other trainees. After about 9 or 10 months, they all felt they didn't need this form of support group anymore as they had integrated fully within their respective teams.

5.7 Summary

In this chapter I have looked at various aspects of learner support, both formal and informal. Learner support takes many forms and occurs at many points in time:

- Pre-training briefing, when the main learning objectives are discussed and the delegate considers what he expects from the course or training material.
- Post-training debriefing, when the actual learning points are reviewed and the delegate considers what was gained from the course or training material.
- Follow-up coaching, in which the lessons learnt are applied to the day-to-day job.
- Action groups for mutual support within a group of people learning similar things.

In the next chapter I look at evaluating the training that has taken place, and consider when to evaluate and what to look for.

6. *Evaluation: Was It Worth It?*

■ ■

6.1 Introduction

In this chapter I look at various ways to evaluate the training provided to individuals. The important questions are Did the training meet the learners' needs, and Was it worth the effort? In answering these questions we validate our decisions in choosing the training in the first place, strengthening the decisions we make next time.

First I briefly clarify the reasons why team leaders should evaluate training at all. I also discuss what their purpose should be in doing so. Next I describe three points in time when evaluation is useful, and some practical tools and ways to carry it out. For each tool I give a description and discuss what it tells you and what it doesn't tell you. I then suggest some remedies or steps that can be taken when the training has not lived up to expectations and there is more work to be done. Finally, I discuss whether it is worth evaluating at all.

6.2 Main Points of this Chapter

- Why evaluate: what evaluation is for
- When and how to evaluate
- Remedies when training didn't work
- Is it worth evaluating?

■ ■

6.3 Why Evaluate : What Evaluation is For

Why should a team leader evaluate training? Isn't that the trainers' job? So runs a common perception of team leaders who see themselves as users of training services (with the exception of on-the-job training, which team leaders typically provide themselves). At one level, this perception is quite right – it *is* the training supplier's job to evaluate the effectiveness of what they provide.

Yet at a different level, it is important that the team leader carries out some evaluation from his own point of view, to ensure that the training met the requirements of his people. This is a different question from the training provider's evaluation of whether the training exercise met its stated objectives and provided all delegates with the possibility of learning the skill. As team leader, we are interested in whether delegates actually did learn the skill, and we can answer this question from the workplace perspective.

6.3.1 Confirm Training Value

A major reason for the team leader to evaluate training, then, is to ensure that the training was worthwhile. Did the training work? Did we achieve what we set out to achieve? This part of the evaluation links back to the reasons for seeking the training in the first place. It then considers whether the desired skill was developed as required. A tricky but important part of this question includes deciding how much the training contributed to the skill development process. We can then see if the training worked satisfactorily.

A second part of ensuring that the training was worthwhile is to consider the effort we put into it and weigh that up against the skill development. Was the result worth the effort? As team leader, we can see the result of the training in terms of the delegate's use of the new skill within the job context. We can also see how much effort has gone into the skill development process, not just by the delegate but also by the rest of the team and other colleagues. Has the developed skill been worth the combined effort of developing it? Has the skill been developed?

6.3.2 Confirm Training Decisions

A second major reason to evaluate the training provided to our people is to check out our training decisions. By looking back at the delegate's training needs and learning objectives, we can see whether the needs were met by the training process. We can look back at the training options available at the time and briefly consider whether we made good decisions or whether, in hindsight, some other option would have been preferable.

Here is the feedback loop back to the set of criteria we used when choosing the training method and format. Do we need to refine the criteria? Can we better understand our people and their learning styles and approaches? Do we need to improve the ways in which we support our people after training while they are practising and developing the skill on the job? Evaluation gives a chance to focus, however briefly, on improving our support to learners.

6.3.3 Confirm Training Estimates

A third major reason to evaluate is to lend support for future estimates or requests for training budget provision. Whatever form of training is used, it will cost something, whether as an internal charge, external spend or simply time spent. It can be difficult to estimate the amount to set aside for training; evaluation of previous training, particularly comparing different types of training, can help to some extent and can give some confidence in the estimates. Understanding what time and money was required to meet previous training needs can help when estimating future training solutions, for example when beginning a new project or when a new member of staff joins the team.

The training budget is often an easy target, one of the first to be cut when corporate finances or deadlines get tight. By evaluating the training provided to your people you can develop confidence in your estimates and so better defend your training budget and time requirements.

Evaluation experience will also help you to refine your budget requirements by using less-expensive training methods where appropriate – but not throwing money away by using cheaper training methods where they are not appropriate. Sometimes the more expensive training method is also the quicker and more cost-effective, and evaluation can help you make that choice.

6.3.4 Confirm Training Solutions

Throughout the discussion so far I have alluded to the fourth major reason for evaluation: to enable future recommendations for training solutions to learning objectives. This will be true not only of people you know well but also of people who you don't know well yet, for example new members of the team. It is not likely that a team leader sits down and consciously asks himself what's different and what's similar between the new team member and his existing people, and therefore what training that worked for the team will also work for this new person. Rather, the experience of making and checking training decisions will underpin future training decisions, providing a foundation on which to make new judgements.

6.3.5 The Need to Evaluate

One final point to make before describing the various evaluation techniques is that evaluation can be as formal or as informal as you need it to be. In some organizations training is entirely the responsibility of the team leader and he is left to get on with it on his own; here, evaluation is for the team leader's own benefit and can be very informal. In other organizations a central department oversees training both internal and external, and often requires some formal evaluation to be recorded. This helps them to refine their training decisions at a corporate level, and to understand training provision within the organization.

Again, some team leaders are well experienced in choosing training for their people and really need to do little formal evaluation; they are likely to be doing a lot of informal – almost subconscious – evaluation of the effectiveness of the training solutions chosen for and with their people. Other team leaders are not so experienced and need to evaluate their solutions rather more explicitly at first.

All of the evaluation tools described in the next section can be used as formally or as informally as is necessary in the circumstances of the individual situation. Most of them are also relevant to the evaluation of on-the-job training, whether provided by the team leader or by another colleague.

6.4 When and How to Evaluate

After the training has been carried out, there are three points in time when evaluation is sensible:

- Short-term, just after the training has been completed.
- Medium-term, 3 to 6 months later.
- Long-term, 9 to 12 months after the training.

At each of these evaluation points there are relevant questions that can be answered to try to discover whether the training worked, and there are evaluation tools to guide the evaluation process.

6.4.1 Short-term Evaluation – Post-Course Questionnaire

In the short term, within the first week or so of the training having been completed, there are two techniques that can be used: the post-course questionnaire and the post-training debriefing.

The post-course questionnaire is probably the best-known form of training evaluation. As the name implies, it is used primarily for taught courses but is also sometimes used after computer-based study in an organization's learning centre, and after individual modules of degree courses. It is not really relevant to on-the-job training or to stand-alone self-study methods, nor to mentoring schemes. For these the relevant short-term evaluation tool is the post-training debriefing, described later.

The main purpose of the post-course questionnaire is to aid the training provider (i.e. the supplier, learning centre manager, or lecturer) in his evaluation of the course or material. The questions are thus directed at the training provision. They are designed to find out if all delegates had a learning opportunity and whether the material was fit for purpose and met its stated objectives. However, sometimes the team leader does get sent a copy of the post-course questionnaire and it can help in evaluating from his perspective.

There is no single standard post-course questionnaire; however an example can be found in Fig. 6.1. The format of the questionnaire is a set of questions, sometimes with yes/no answers and sometimes with scaled answers for example "very satisfied" to "very dissatisfied". The questions usually cover several aspects of the training provided, including venue, refreshments, administration, equipment, instructor, materials and course content. Some of the questions, notably those about the venue and equipment, assess whether the delegate had a learning opportunity. If he was uncomfortable or a PC was necessary but unavailable, then his learning may have been hampered. This may provide early warning that further work will need to be done back at the office to ensure that he picks up anything he missed while on the course. Some of the questions, particularly those about administration and training objectives being explained, are primarily aimed at finding out whether the training provider did everything possible to ensure that the course ran smoothly.

The questions most relevant to a team leader's evaluation are those on course instructor, content and materials. Here the delegate is assessing the quality of the

Institute of IT Training

Course Feedback

Name:	Date:
Company:	
Course:	Tutor(s):

Please will you take a few minutes to fill in this form as we are always looking to improve the courses that we offer and your feedback is valued by the Institute.

Have you had any previous formal training in –   Presentation Skills ☐   Training Skills ☐

Please circle relevant number for each point below

Capabilities of the Tutor   ☺   ☹

	☺					☹
1. Course objectives covered effectively	6	5	4	3	2	1
2. Personal objectives covered effectively	6	5	4	3	2	1
3. Terms/theory clearly explained	6	5	4	3	2	1
4. Interested in whether I learnt or not	6	5	4	3	2	1
5. Listened and dealt with all my questions	6	5	4	3	2	1
6. Was supportive and encouraged my learning	6	5	4	3	2	1
7. Created a conducive learning environment	6	5	4	3	2	1
8. Was available when I needed help or feedback	6	5	4	3	2	1

Please comment -

Overall Impression of the Course   ☺   ☹

	☺					☹
1. Length of the course	6	5	4	3	2	1
2. Pace of the course	6	5	4	3	2	1
3. Level of the content	6	5	4	3	2	1
4. Usefulness of content	6	5	4	3	2	1

Please comment -

Training Facilities/Accommodation   ☺   ☹

	☺				☹
1. Joining instructions	5	4	3	2	1
2. Training facilities	5	4	3	2	1
3. Refreshments and lunch	5	4	3	2	1
4. Accommodation	5	4	3	2	1

Please comment -

Please use reverse side for extra comments if required.
The Institute reserves the right to use any delegate comments recorded on this form, unless indicated ☐

Fig. 6.1 Course feedback form. *Source:* Institute of IT Training. Reproduced with permission.

training he has just experienced. He is typically asked whether the course materials supported the instruction, whether any visual aids used supported the course content. He also can comment on the pace of the course, whether too fast or too slow, and on the course content. A delegate on a training course is rarely in a position to know whether the syllabus left out any topics that should have been included, but he *is* in a position to know whether the whole syllabus was covered during the course. He can also comment on the amount of material to be covered in the time.

It is important that the delegate's own learning objectives are heard and related to the course training objectives by the instructor. If any of the delegates' objectives are not included in the syllabus, then the instructor should at least relate the learning objectives to things that *are* covered in the course even if there is not time to devise a training session on that topic. Where a post-course questionnaire is evaluating a self-study course, any questions about training objectives will refer to the question of whether the course objectives were (a) set out in the material and (b) met by the learning modules presented.

The post-course questionnaire, then, tells us a few things about the training that has taken place. It tells us whether it provided a learning opportunity as opposed to being a complete waste of time. It tells us whether we can expect the individual to be able to build and develop the skills, or whether further training is needed in some (probably different) format. It tells us whether this training method and approach worked for the individual (did his learning process begin), as opposed to being unsuitable for him. Taken together, these things help us ensure that the training worked for the individual.

What the post-course questionnaire does not tell us is anything about the rest of the learner's skill development process. The questionnaire is filled out immediately after the event, so there is no information on long-term learning, nor on how much of the information the delegate received he will actually retain. Neither is it able to assess how the training supports the individual in performing job tasks, as the training assessed by this tool is done in isolation away from the job. It is rare for a post-course questionnaire to measure any further skill development that might be needed; this requires a different sort of test and is beyond the scope of the questionnaire. Being a short-term view, the post-course questionnaire cannot really tell us whether the course was worthwhile: at this early stage in skill development it is impossible to say categorically that the training has worked, let alone that it was worth the effort.

The post-course questionnaire thus cannot tell us everything we need to know to evaluate a training course from the team leader's perspective, but it can highlight some areas for attention.

6.4.2 Short-term Evaluation – Post-Training Debriefing

The other short-term evaluation technique to use is the post-training debriefing. We have seen the details of this discussion in Chapter 5; here I summarize the main points and highlight some of the ways in which it works as an evaluation tool.

The post-training debriefing, you may recall, is held sometime in the first couple of weeks after a training event. It is a suitable evaluation tool for any of the training methods, both short-term and long-term; it can be used periodically during the course of a long-term training course or programme. It is also suitable for evaluating on-the-job training.

The debriefing consists of a short discussion about the merits of the training and how it will relate to the job tasks; an example can be found in Fig. 5.5. The discussion centres on the training and whether it met the individual's learning objectives. It also allows some discussion of how much of the training content is proving to be useful in the work context, although at this early stage that may not be clear as yet. In the debriefing the delegate and team leader also discuss how much more effective he is at carrying out the job tasks as a result of the training. In some cases the individual could not carry out the tasks at all before the training and now can; in other cases the training has provided a foundation on which skill development will build with practice on the job.

What does the post-training debriefing tell us as an evaluation tool? As with the post-course questionnaire, it tells us whether there was a learning opportunity for this individual, and whether he has been able to start the skill development process. Again, it tells us whether this was a suitable training method for this person. In addition, the debriefing session also gives some pointers to the relevance of the training to the job tasks and to the reasons for arranging the training in the first place. It also begins to assess the difference in performance which the training is triggering.

What the post-training debriefing does not tell us, as with the post-course questionnaire, is the longer-term picture. We cannot see at this point anything of the learner's future skill development, nor whether the training will support job tasks in the way we now expect them to. The debriefing cannot measure how much of the learning will be retained, as it is too early to tell. Sometimes you can tell at a post-training debriefing what further training will be needed; usually at this stage it is necessary to wait and see how the individual's skill develops on the job. Thus it is also too early to tell if the training has been worthwhile, although we can get an early indication one way or the other.

6.4.3 Medium-term Evaluation – Post-Experience Questionnaire

Medium-term evaluation can help to address some of the questions that cannot be answered by short-term evaluation. The major tool here is the post-experience questionnaire. Similar in some ways to a post-training debriefing sheet, this questionnaire is filled in some time after the training event, say three to six months after. By this time, the delegate has had a chance to build on the skill foundation laid by the training event and to gain some experience in its use. He has had a chance to make some mistakes and to put them right – to really consolidate his learning and integrate it into work tasks. Now he is likely to be in a better position to comment on the effectiveness of the training exercise and the part it played in his skill development. He is also likely to be able to comment on any gaps in his knowledge left by the training and how the gaps were filled; more specifically, could the training have been expected to cover those topics?

In Fig. 6.2 we see an example of such a post-experience questionnaire. It asks many of the "How effective was the training" questions that we need to answer.

Name: Training Event: Course Date: Supplier: Evaluation Date:
Please take a few minutes to fill in this questionnaire. Your views are important and will be used to improve the training we arrange.
To what extent have you been able to put into practice the skills learned in your training? Fully ☐ ☐ ☐ ☐ Not at all Comments:
Do you consider that there were skills learned that you were unable to put into practice? Yes ☐   No ☐ If yes, please comment:
Do you consider that there were skills not covered which you would have wished included? Yes ☐   No ☐ If yes, please comment:
To what extent were your training objectives met? Fully ☐ ☐ ☐ ☐ Not at all Comments:
To what extent were you effectively de-briefed by appropriate Management/ Supervisory staff immediately following the training? Fully ☐ ☐ ☐ ☐ Not at all Comments:
Following your training, to what extent have you received appropriate support within your work environment?   Fully ☐ ☐ ☐ ☐ Not at all Comments:
Do you feel that follow-up training is required?   Yes ☐   No ☐ If yes, please suggest appropriate training format:
Would you recommend this training event to others?   Yes ☐   No ☐ Comments:
Would you wish to attend another training event in the same format? Yes ☐   No ☐ If no, please comment:
Overall how much more effective are you since receiving the training? Fully ☐ ☐ ☐ ☐ Not at all Comments:
We would welcome any additional comments you may wish to make.

Fig. 6.2 Training evaluation form.

The questionnaire is useful as an *aide-mémoire* if just the delegate fills it out; if the team leader discusses it with him then it becomes an evaluation tool as well as reinforcing the learning points. The delegate is asked to consider how much he has been able to use the skills gained in training. To some extent this is a measure of the effectiveness of the training; to some extent it is a measure of the relevance of the training to the job tasks. If there were skills learned that could not be put into practice then the delegate and team leader need to explore why that was and rectify any problems that might be highlighted: the training may have been in-adequate, or the job role may have changed in the meantime so that the skill is not needed at the moment. Again, if there were things missing from the training then they are likely to have shown up six months after the training. With the experience of having developed the skill further since the training the delegate may be able to comment more knowledgeably on the coverage of topics within the training he received.

The delegate is encouraged to think back to the training event and consider whether his learning objectives were largely met, not only by the training itself but also by the follow-up support and experience he has had since. If an individual is trying to develop a skill but for some reason the workplace isn't conducive to this, then that fact must be included in the evaluation of the training's effectiveness. In this situation, the training can hardly be blamed if the skill development was slow or non-existent. There are all sorts of legitimate reasons for the training and skill development not being supported, for example the work pattern or organizational structure may have changed since the training. In most cases the lack of skill development will not be a problem for anyone (although the delegate will have to work harder to remember the training when he does eventually come to use the skill).

If, having undergone some training and gained some experience, it is felt the delegate requires further training, then consideration of this present training and its effectiveness – or otherwise – can help to decide the format of the follow-up training. Will it be more of a similar training format or something completely different? Will it be to remedy shortfalls in the previous training method or to develop more advanced skill in the same topic?

The delegate and team leader are asked to consider whether they would recommend the training to other people and if not why not. Does the training method work, would they use it again, would they use another course or set of materials from the same supplier? Negative responses to these questions can be very instructive and form an important part of the feedback to future training decisions. Finally the delegate and team leader are asked to consider how much the training has helped in the job context: how much more effective has the training made him?

The post-experience questionnaire, then, poses many of the evaluation questions but from the vantage point of some experience in using the skill. It measures the effectiveness of the training not just as an experience or a learning opportunity but as a learning enabler. Was the delegate enabled to develop the skill? If not, what got in the way – could the training have influenced the obstacles? I have found the post-experience questionnaire to be a useful evaluation tool, incorporating both training and experience. It can be hard to distinguish skill development as a result of training from skill development as a result of experience – but in the last analysis, what matters is skill developed for use in the workplace. Training doesn't happen in a vacuum, it starts a skill development process that is continued in the context of job tasks and team interactions. What we are trying to evaluate is roughly how much the training contributed to this individual's skill development and whether we could realistically expect the same contribution to another individual's skill development from the same type of training.

Medium-term evaluation, then, as measured by a post-experience questionnaire, can tell us whether the individual has met his learning objectives. It can tell us roughly how effective the training was as a spur to develop the skill(s) intended. It can highlight whether further development is needed at this stage, although it is likely to be a matter of gaining experience in applying the skill to different situations. It can also tell us whether the training was relevant – is the skill actually in use, and did the training enable the individual to learn it?

However, the post-experience questionnaire cannot tell us everything we need to know. It cannot tell us about immediate reactions to the training experience, so it does not replace the short-term evaluation tools, merely augments them. The post-experience questionnaire cannot say much about further development needed, unless the training was not effective. (If the training was not effective, then we are really talking about remedying the situation, which I will discuss shortly.) By "further development" I mean more than just further experience, I mean learning more advanced topics about the skills, perhaps taking the individual from a basic understanding to a more expert or in-depth understanding. At this mid-term stage in the individual's development, it is likely to be too early to say at what point he will benefit from advanced training exercises in the same topic.

Neither can the post-experience questionnaire comment very much on how this skill fits with others needed for the job. The post-experience questionnaire is primarily aimed at working out how effective this training has been, and does not really take an overall view of the job and skill set as a whole. The post-experience questionnaire does not relate this training event to any other training the individual may be doing on different subjects – it treats each piece of training in isolation. Of course, it is possible in the medium term to link the various skills together to see how they relate to the whole job; quarterly or interim development reviews would be the vehicle for this. But the post-experience questionnaire by itself does not fulfil this function.

6.4.4 Long-term Evaluation – Performance Review

Long-term evaluation, as part of the annual performance review or appraisal, does address the whole-job overall questions. As an evaluation tool, the appraisal measures the effectiveness of the training as a catalyst for skill development within the context of the job. This periodic discussion examines the individual's performance on the job and any areas for improvement or further development. An evaluation as part of this review discussion will necessarily be an informal evaluation yet it provides a useful opportunity to review the training within the context of the development of the individual as a whole person. It provides a point at which to evaluate whether the training did in fact aid the development of a skill, and whether the skill did in fact aid the completion of work tasks.

At this stage we are not so much measuring satisfaction with a training exercise as an exercise in its own right, rather we are measuring satisfaction with the training as a springboard for skill development. The relevant questions here are: Did the training work? Did it help the skill development process? Would you take the same approach the next time you need to develop a skill or understanding? And if not, why not? Did the training exercise put obstacles in the way? Did the approach taken this time fail to address particular issues? Did it fail to ignite the learner's interest? What can we learn from the experience so we don't hinder skill development the next time?

Evaluation of training events, whether individually or as a continuum, is a small part of the performance review, which rightly concentrates on achievement of job tasks and responsibilities. But it is a useful discussion point and can help both the individual and the team leader to see job performance from a different perspective.

A typical performance review consists of looking at the individual's view of how the year has gone, how he performed overall in the job as a whole. Moving on to specific tasks and responsibilities, the discussion usually includes what was achieved, what got in the way, what development happened to overcome obstacles – in short, what progress has been made in each area. Sometimes the review includes a review of all the training and skill development undertaken over the review period, and how the performance improved as a result. At this point you can consider individual training exercises as well as skill development as a continuous process, looking at the individual's skill set in the wider context of the job and his aspirations. The review often continues with a discussion of career aspirations and how they might be achieved in realistic timescales.

Long-term evaluation of training, then, can tell us about the development of a particular skill within the context of the whole job and the whole person. It can compare different training events and examine the relative merits of different types of training, different events and different methods. Long-term evaluation, however, cannot deal with specific details of any single event. These are best evaluated at the time of the event by debriefing or questionnaire. It is possible to combine the medium- and long-term evaluations, although this can divert the discussion too far away from the main point of an appraisal, the consideration of performance in the job.

6.4.5 Interpreting Evaluation Responses

So far I have discussed the evaluation of training for a particular individual. A team leader develops the skills of several people at once; it can be useful to evaluate their training as a group as well as individually. There are two major aspects to such evaluation: a group of people doing the same training at the same time, and several people developing the same skill set at different times, perhaps in different ways. In either case, we will be comparing evaluation responses of different people to the same event or type of event. In making the comparison, we must remember that different individuals will have different perceptions of the same event. They may have had different experiences of the event as a learning opportunity, as a social occasion, as a break from routine, as an interruption to normal work. All these factors will influence an individual's perception, often without the individual being aware at a conscious level.

It must also be borne in mind that there will be differences in people's approach to evaluation. Some people are more generous with praise than others and will tend to mark highly on all questions; others are less effusive and will tend to use more "middle ground" responses, even if both are equally satisfied with the event. It is also important to remember that the different individuals have different styles and rates of learning. They will have had different levels of previous experience and so will relate to different aspects of the new skill or topic. For these reasons they may understand the new topics in different ways – and this may be reflected in their evaluations of the training they receive.

If we are evaluating the training of several people doing the same training at the same time, say the same internal training course or the same piece of self-study material, then we can use post-course questionnaires to make the short-term assessment. Often in this situation, a questionnaire is designed for the specific event, reflecting the particular circumstances of that training and the evaluation aspects that are of particular importance. The short-term view is especially useful if the same event is being run at intervals, as changes can be made to subsequent events to address problems highlighted by earlier delegates.

The post-experience questionnaire can be used to gain the medium-term evaluation picture. Major differences in evaluation opinion at this stage are likely to reflect different rates of assimilation among the learners, or different levels of support given to them in applying the new skill. They could also reflect different aspects of using the skill in their roles – so that for example a training event that emphasizes analysis issues will be more relevant to those carrying out analysis tasks and less relevant to those carrying out other tasks. A comparison of the medium-term responses provides an evaluation of the training in the wider sense of skill development within the job context. It can also provide confirmation of the rightness of the training decision.

If we are evaluating the training of a group of people developing similar skill sets over a longer period of time, perhaps using different training methods, then the same tools are used but with different emphasis. As we are not comparing different perceptions of the same event, the short term view by itself is not so relevant to the comparison. It still tells us whether the individuals all had a learning opportunity, but we are not looking for feedback on the details of the training.

What is more important in this comparison is to ensure that all delegates were able to develop the skill set required. For this the medium-term post-experience questionnaire is more relevant, taking the wider perspective of skill development in the job role. Feedback here includes an indication of which training methods work in which circumstances and for which individuals. Now a comparison can be made of the characteristics of any particular successful training plan: what was the training style and how did it match the learning style? What was the training format and how did it match the delegates' circumstances? By looking at success factors for several people's training schemes, we can gain an insight into the many influences on training and can hone our training selection criteria.

Example

In her early days as a team leader, Sue evaluated all the training she arranged for her people. She was not able to come up with training success factors but used post-course questionnaires and post-training debriefing sessions to find out whether there was a learning opportunity and whether each delegate actually received instruction in the fundamentals of whichever skill they were developing. She used post-experience questionnaires to find out how her people's perceptions changed as they gained more experience applying the skills, and she reviewed their skill development and performance improvement at their performance reviews. With her own team leader she assessed the qualitative value of the training she had arranged and built up her own understanding of the skill development process. She soon found that she didn't need to use the formal questionnaires and debriefing sheets but could glean the same information from less formal chats at the relevant time intervals after training events.

Example

An IT department embarked upon a large training programme in a new system design methodology. Forty people were to be trained and the department chose one supplier to develop and deliver all the training over a six-month period. As there was a sizeable investment in manpower and in financial commitment, formal evaluation methods were used to ensure that all delegates received consistent and adequate instruction. Post-course questionnaires were used to ensure that delegates had a learning opportunity; adjustments were made to the training room in light of comments made, and some amendments were made to the mix of instruction and practical exercises. Post-experience questionnaires were used to check that training messages were retained and that delegates were given the opportunity to use the new skills and that they had the relevant support in applying those skills. The responses also triggered a change to the work practices to build in time for experiment with the new methodology; no major changes were needed to the training course itself although an *aide-mémoire* was produced and distributed by the training team. The department felt that as the new methodology was understood and put into use within the six months of the training programme the investment had paid off. Using the methodology correctly produced high quality system designs within the required timescales and with the projected manpower levels.

Example

Jim had a team of technical experts specializing in mainframe database support. Turnover on the team meant that he was training up one new person every year; once trained it was important that all team members kept their knowledge of database systems up to date. Jim thus used a few tried and tested training suppliers to provide the training. Evaluation was kept to an informal minimum, as Jim knew that any problems would have been highlighted and ironed out on the course. He only needed a quick chat as people returned from each course to ensure that training was effective. He made sure that each team member had ample opportunity to practise the new skill on their return to the office.

Example

Several new entrants to IT systems development attended a five-week course on programming in Cobol. Every two weeks the instructors evaluated the students' performance on the course, highlighting any problem areas. Two individuals had significant difficulties with programming concepts at various times in the course. When they arrived back at the office and started to put their new skills to use, they had post-course debriefings with their team leaders when they discussed the course reports. All the delegates and team leaders reported that the evaluation process was worthwhile, as it gave them an opportunity to discuss any problems and put remedies in place. As a result, the two people who had had trouble on the course received extra coaching at work. Their post-experience questionnaires showed that this had been a valuable addition to their training plans. The team leaders in particular were glad they had had the chance to do both short-term and medium-term evaluations and so prevent further problems integrating their trainees into their new roles in IT.

6.5 Remedies When Training Did Not Work

Sometimes the evaluations tell you that the training exercise was not a success. This will usually come to light either in the short term or the medium term. The delegate may realize very quickly that the training is not what he expected and is not giving the necessary foundation for skill development. Or the deficiency may not become apparent until he tries to apply the training to his work tasks and finds that the gap is too wide, that what was taught is not appropriate to what is needed.

6.5.1 Check the Circumstances

The first thing to do if the training did not work is to figure out why that was. Find out what went wrong. Look again at the individual's learning objectives and the training objectives for the instruction that was used. Is there a mismatch that is obvious with hindsight? Compare the training objectives with what was delivered by the training event. Did the training fail to live up to its objectives? Look again at the reason for choosing the training that was undertaken: have any of the individual's circumstances changed, and would they alter the training decision? Look at the skill gap that still exists: did any skill development take place at all? Has the individual been able to start to understand the topic and how it relates to job tasks, or are we back at square one so to speak? Do we have to repeat the training altogether or can we see some benefit from part of the training exercise? Armed with this analysis, we can then decide what to do next, depending on what kind of training was undertaken.

6.5.2 Remedies with External Training

External professional training suppliers work very hard to ensure that all delegates have a learning opportunity from courses and training materials they provide. On taught courses, the trainers usually check out each student's learning objectives and relate them to the training objectives of the course being delivered. A good trainer will periodically check the stated objectives of both the students and the course to ensure that any mismatches are brought to light as early as possible.

However, life doesn't always go according to plan and training mistakes do happen occasionally. If a delegate returns to the office having got little or nothing from a course, what can you do? The first thing is to discuss the situation with the delegate and work out what went wrong. Then you can discuss the course with the training company or trainer. They may have some solutions already, particularly if the whole course was a disaster.

At this stage there are three options: to request that the course be rerun, to request a refund of the cost of the course, or to request a different course. Whether a refund or discount is appropriate, and if so how much, depends largely on the circumstances. If for example the anticipated trainer was incapacitated and the course had to be changed at short notice then the training supplier is quite likely to offer a full or partial refund immediately. If, however, the delegate chose the wrong course or failed to carry out course prerequisites, then the supplier may not be at fault. Again, if a delegate became ill in the middle of a course and had to return home, most suppliers are sympathetic and offer a place on a future course at little or no extra cost.

Whether to request a repeat of the training also depends on circumstances and on the reason for the training not working. If the training objectives still match the learning objectives, and no learning took place, then a repeat is probably indicated. If some learning took place but not as much as could reasonably be expected, and if the individual has enough of a start to be able to put the new skill to good use, then a repeat is not likely to be effective (extra coaching from the team leader or another team member would be useful). If it turns out that the course is inappropriate, contrary to the course descriptions, and a different course would be better, then attendance on a different course is probably an option worth considering.

6.5.3 Remedies with Internal Training

Most of the points made for external training suppliers also apply if an internal course didn't meet expectations. You would still discuss the situation with the instructor to see what went wrong and how they would remedy the situation. With internal training, however, there is likely to be more scope for reassessing the skill gap in the context of the organization and the particular job tasks. It is less likely that a repeat of the course can be arranged at short notice, but an internal trainer is likely to able to provide individual training or tutoring to help to make up the shortfall of the original training. With an internal training supplier the question of refund or discount is less likely to be relevant than with an external supplier. Thus the remedy for internal training is likely to be to carry out further instruction or training exercises but in a slightly different format from the original training event, tailored to meet the specific needs of the situation.

6.5.4 Remedies with Learner-Driven Training

If a self-study course or long-term training programme fails to deliver results, there is a variety of factors that could be at work. The first thing to check is the individual's motivation: has his interest flagged? Is he still able to devote the requisite amount of time and energy to his studies?

If motivation is not the issue, then check the suitability of the training to the needs of the job. In effect, this means ensuring that the learning objectives have not changed while no-one was looking, ie while the training was in progress. Is the individual pursuing a course that is no longer appropriate? With a short-term self-study programme, it is unlikely that the training is suddenly inappropriate. But long-term training methods are prey to changing requirements. To some extent, the broad spectrum and general non-vocational nature of an academic degree course for example guard against the course becoming unsuitable. Such courses seek to broaden the individual's horizons and so will remain appropriate to the career aspirations if not to the specific job tasks. Sometimes an individual finds that he is following the wrong self-study course materials. In this case, the solution is to switch to another set of materials that more closely matches the actual learning objectives as opposed to the perceived learning objectives.

Sometimes the material itself is poor or inadequate. In this case, as with a taught course, the provider of the material can be contacted to see what they suggest; there may be an updated version available that addresses some of the problems. Or it may be that the main difficulty lies in the fact that self-study material offers no social interaction for the student. The solution here may be to find someone he can discuss the topic with, such as a coach or fellow-learner, or to try a different training method altogether, one which allows some discussion and exploration of the learning topics. He may also need someone to help him relate the learning to the job tasks, reinforcing the learning points from the materials.

Whatever the situation, there are a number of options that can be considered. Some training needs are difficult to fill, but none is impossible!

6.6 Is it Worth Evaluating?

So, is it worth evaluating? The short answer is: Yes, it is, but only to the extent that you gain useful information from the process. If you have little experience of making training decisions, or if you are undertaking a large training programme, then formal evaluation of chosen solutions will help to clarify the issues that need to be addressed and will give confidence to the training decisions. When you are more familiar with the skill development process or the training programme is proceeding smoothly, then a less formal evaluation approach will do. It is of course highly likely that some training decisions will have to be evaluated more rigorously than others being made at the same time, for example if embarking on a training method you haven't used before. I would argue that it is always worth doing some form of evaluation, if only to keep all interested parties aware that training and skill development are issues you take seriously.

6.7 Summary

In this chapter, we have looked at evaluation of training from the team leader's point of view:

- Why evaluate? To ensure training has worked satisfactorily and individuals have developed the required skills and to validate training decisions.
- When to evaluate and how:
  - In the short term – using the post-course questionnaire and post-training debriefing, checking that there was a learning opportunity.
  - In the medium term – using the post-experience questionnaire, checking that skill development has continued in the job context.
  - In the long term – using the annual performance review, checking that the skills are relevant and useful within the job context, checking for any further training needs.
  - Interpreting the responses – taking into account that responses to evaluation questions must be considered in context.
- Remedies when training didn't work – check out what went wrong and why, look at options for going forward with skill development, including retraining or different formats of training in the same topic.
- Is it worth evaluating? It is but only to the extent that it is useful to you.

In the next chapter I look at continuous development within the job context, considering the use of different tasks and roles to help further an individual's career.

7. *Career Development*

■ ■

7.1 Introduction

So far in this book we have looked at individual training needs and how to meet them. In this chapter I turn to the longer-term development that occurs as a person moves from task to task or project to project within his career. How can the team leader help his staff to develop their potential and achieve their ambitions? Here we are thinking not so much about specific skill sets as about the ability to put the skills to good use. We are thinking about a member of staff developing the perspective that comes from wider experiences, as well as the learning that comes from making mistakes. How can we help our people to learn from their experiences, and how can we help them seek those experiences?

First, I briefly consider experience as a development method, looking at ways the team leader helps his people to expand their understanding. I look next at defining the various tasks, responsibilities and skills within a job role. I then discuss how an individual expands his skill set as he moves from role to role in his career. Next I briefly describe some useful activities for development within a role. Finally, I look at some of the support available from professional societies.

7.2 Main Points of this Chapter

- Experience as a development method
- Defining job roles
- Moving from role to role
- Developing within a role
- Support from professional societies

■ ■

7.3 Experience as a Development Method

We saw in Chapter 1 that as adults, we learn by experience. Yet the learning process is not automatic, we often have to work at it to recognize learning points and actually develop our understanding and our skill. As team leaders, or as colleagues, we can help each other to reflect on the outcome of a learning experience and what it tells us. By instilling a habit of sitting back for a bit and taking the wider view, we can help our people to establish a pattern of identifying what is new in a given situation and what could be applicable in another situation. We help them learn to learn.

Learning doesn't just come from picking out new results and predicting where else it might come in handy. Learning also comes from gaining experience as we continue to use a skill. In one sense we develop a mental library of how the skill or tool can be used in a wide variety of situations and examples. Experience works as a training method because we use a skill set in roughly the same way every time we use it, consolidating our understanding or fluency where we are doing what we know well. For example, an experienced programmer will have built up his skill set and expertise by developing many program modules in several projects or systems over a period of time. He will have developed his skills by using them over and over again. Each project or system will have differed from the others in some way; using his skills to meet the different requirements will have developed his understanding.

Another important aspect of using experience to develop our people is to ask them to do something that is outside their usual sphere of expertise. This presents a challenge to the learner, as he will have to find out how to do the task. He will also have to carry out an unfamiliar piece of work. Perhaps he will find that he enjoys the challenge and can expand both his skill set and his sphere of expertise. Perhaps this challenge is too hard at present. At the very least we will have opened possible new avenues for him to explore in future.

One way of capturing the learning points from a task, piece of work or other experience is to use a learning log. The individual usually keeps his own log of learning points, but as team leaders we can certainly encourage their use. A sample log sheet is shown in Fig. 7.1. The idea is to make brief reminder notes of what it was you learned from, what you had expected to happen and what actually happened. The learning points are then listed and described, sometimes with a note of what might be done differently another time. Some people keep a daily learning diary, others prefer to keep it weekly. Some people find they keep a fairly detailed learning log while they are developing a new or existing skill, and keep a more general or infrequent log at other times.

Example

As May developed her skills in writing REXX routines, she kept a log of her learning points. Figure 7.2 shows a page of her log. When she had unexpected results, she made a note of why that was. She learned something new about the language constructs. She also reminded herself to take care when amending existing routines.

So how does a team leader help his people to continue to learn from their experiences? Keeping an open attitude to learning is a good start, recognizing that we are all learning all the time, from each other and from experience. We can encourage and allow our people to have the quick chat that says: How did it go?

| Name: Date: |
Subject/Skill:
Experience (brief description of what you did)
Expectation (brief description of what you expected to happen)
Outcome (brief description of what actually did happen)
Learning Points (brief description or bullet points of what you learned from the exercise)

Fig. 7.1 Learning log.

What did you learn? Did it work? What made it work or not work? What might we do differently next time? It is useful to do this as a team sometimes too, perhaps after finishing a major piece of work or implementing a system. A "lessons learnt" session focuses on what went well and should be continued as good practice, as well as on what didn't go well and should be modified in some way. The important thing is to reach conclusions and go forward. Experience is a good teacher – but only if we listen to its lessons.

| Name: May   Date: 10 Aug 98 |
| Subject/Skill: REXX programming |

Experience (brief description of what you did)
REXX routine failed to work properly after adding some additional
code to test a parameter value

Expectation (brief description of what you expected to happen)
Testing would show parameter in use

Outcome (brief description of what actually did happen)
Routine failed to recognize the parameter as input

Learning Points (brief description or bullet points of what you learned from the exercise)
· The differences between different REXX input commands
· How to use arguments and the stack
· How REXX uses and assigns variable names
· Difference between local and global variables
· Always check that a variable name hasn't been used anywhere else
  in a REXX routine

Fig. 7.2 Learning log – example.

7.4 Defining Job Roles

I have referred several times to the skill set for a job. But how do we go about
defining the skill set for a job? There are two essential steps: identifying the tasks
and responsibilities to be carried out, and deciding the skills and competencies
that are needed to perform the tasks. This definition can be done in isolation for
one job, or it can be done for a number of roles within say a team or department.

Figure 7.3 shows a sample job or role definition sheet. The first two sections
give the title and major purpose of the job role. In the third section, the tasks and
responsibilities are noted; these can be spelt out in as much or as little detail as
necessary to describe the role to be undertaken. Sometimes it helps to indicate the

Role Title:
Purpose:
Tasks/Responsibilities: (priorities can be indicated if relevant)
Skills and competencies used: (required proficiency levels can be indicated if relevant)

Fig. 7.3 Role definition sheet.

main priority areas of the role, as this shows which tasks are more important or more frequent. Some jobs are very diverse, with many different types of responsibility; others are more focused, concentrating in one or two areas. The final section of the definition lists the various skills and competencies that are needed to perform the tasks and carry out the responsibilities. The skills listed generally relate to the more important aspects of the job. Sometimes a skill level is also indicated, giving the required proficiency at each skill. Again, the skill set will reflect the diversity or focus of the tasks and responsibilities. Typically, a highly-focused role will require higher levels of competence within a smaller skill set than a more diverse role which has a commensurately wider skill set.

The defined skill set or role profile is then used to discuss individual training needs and to determine the real training need as we saw in Chapter 2.

Example

Figure 7.4 shows an example role definition, for a senior programmer who leads a team of programmers. The prime responsibilities are to lead the team and produce the program specifications; secondary tasks include maintaining standards and procedures. The jobholder is also expected to be able to develop and test code if necessary to develop particularly complex routines. The skills involved in these tasks might include programming and specification skills, as well as understanding existing systems. It is also important to have team leadership skills, including interpersonal skills such as delegation and communication, to successfully carry out the responsibilities.

The British Computer Society (BCS) has developed a set of role definitions that covers most if not all roles within the information systems industry. Their Industry Structure Model (ISM) collates over 250 job roles, grouped into nine functional areas such as system development, service delivery, technical advice and customer relations. The roles are arranged in ten levels of responsibility, from unskilled trainees to senior managers. Role definitions are written and maintained by practitioners and academics in each area of expertise, thus reflecting best practice as well as computing management theory. The model is held in electronic format giving a clear and easy-to-use presentation. An extract from the current model can be found on the internet, using the reference in the Bibliography. (British Computer Society, 2000a)

The role definitions are arranged in a matrix such that roles from one functional grouping can be compared to roles in a similar responsibility level from another grouping; this can aid career development discussions about moving between different roles. Within each definition, the model sets out the prerequisites for the role, indicating the appropriate educational background and any assumed previous experience, prior knowledge or existing skill levels. The tasks and responsibilities are described in some detail, with an indication of which tasks are likely to be mandatory and which optional. The skills definition lists technical knowledge and skills, behavioural skills and competencies, and other related skills necessary to carrying out the tasks. For each skill, a proficiency level is indicated from Aware to Expert. The model also gives likely training requirements for a person entering the role with the assumed previous experience. Suggested professional development activities are listed for each role, as well as relevant qualifications.

Either the ISM or your own organization's set of role definitions can be used to identify and clarify the training needs for an individual, team or department. They can also be used to understand the different roles and to discuss an individual's career aspirations and possible moves between roles and between functional groupings.

Role Title: `Senior Programmer`

Purpose:
To provide technical leadership to a team of programmers, building
and testing systems to meet specified business needs.

Tasks/Responsibilities: (priorities can be indicated if relevant)
- Produce program specifications and test plans (1)
- Develop and test program code as necessary (3)
- Understand application systems which support product marketing
  functions (2)
- Resolve technical issues and problems that arise (1)
- Oversee and train team of 4-6 programming staff (1)
- Plan work to be done and allocate to team members (1)
- Coach trainees on the team (1)
- Maintain best practice for program preparation procedures and
  standards (2)

Skills and competencies used: (required proficiency levels can be indicated if relevant)
- Cobol programming in mainframe environment
- Organisational standards for program documentation
- Program specification, coding and testing techniques
- Team leadership
- Motivating staff
- Coaching
- Communication
- Delegation
- Written communication
- Project planning and monitoring techniques

Fig. 7.4 Role definition sheet – example.

7.5 Moving From Role to Role

As an individual's career unfolds, as he moves from role to role, so his skill set
expands and he broadens the range of tasks he can perform. A set of role definitions is useful in exploring career options; this exploration can be done by the
individual alone or with his team leader. Perhaps the individual can find the options
that appeal to him and then discuss his aspirations with his team leader at a development review.

The starting point is the individual's current role. What are the major tasks and
responsibilities involved, and what is the skill set that underpins the role? Which
aspects of the role does the individual most enjoy? Even if these are not his highest

priority tasks, they point the way for a future direction. What is it about those tasks and responsibilities that are so appealing to him? Is there scope for expanding his activities in those responsibilities, is there scope for extending his use of those skills? Looking at the other tasks within the role, things which are perhaps not so much a part of his role or don't come as naturally to him, is there scope for expanding or developing his skill set to support those tasks? Is there scope for growing into the rest of the skill set? Where the individual enjoys the basic role and wants to develop within it, he will be aiming for depth of experience, retaining a similar focus to his present role.

Where the individual is ready for a move to a different role, where he aims for diversity or breadth of experience, here we start to compare different roles to find similarities and differences. Having looked at the individual's current role and identified the kind of tasks and responsibilities he would like to build on, we can look at other role definitions to find suitable next steps. What we are looking for here are roles with a few aspects which are similar to the current one but also some that are new to the individual. Perhaps he wants the challenge of doing new kinds of things, learning new skills. By considering the major aspects of a series of different roles, he can find one or several that he might like to try. Of course, he might not be able to take up a new role immediately, if he is currently engaged on a long-running piece of work or if no suitable vacancy exists within the department, but looking forward is an important part of career development.

Understanding the different roles helps him to recognize and take advantage of opportunities as they arise. It also helps the individual to prepare for planned moves or likely options, partly by being aware of the skills needed for a possible future role and partly by identifying skill development that could start before a move was made.

Example

Dave had been a programmer for many years and vaguely felt it was time for something different. However he enjoyed his work and did not really want to change. He and his team leader looked at his role definition and realized that what Dave wanted was to be able to concentrate on the technical parts of the job, as he had built up extensive knowledge of the business area he concentrated on. He took on a role of senior programmer and agreed to pass on his business knowledge. Instead of leading a team of programmers, he documented his business understanding in a series of papers that explained the business functions that were supported by the various programs the teams had developed. Dave thus built on his expertise and retained his technical focus.

Example

Sue had also been a programmer for many years and also felt it was time for something a little different. However she felt ready for a new challenge. She looked at her current role and what she enjoyed about it. She found that whilst she had always enjoyed getting a program working quickly, what she now enjoyed most was helping other team members to achieve their goals. She looked at other role definitions and liked the look of the team leader role. She was not able to move to a new role immediately but it gave her the chance to start developing her skills in that area. She began to take note of how her team leader operated, how he led meetings, how he got people to do things, how he kept them all motivated. She borrowed a few things from the training library that gave her valuable background information about leadership and also some new insights. When the time came for her to move into a leadership role, she felt ready to attend the required training and to take on the role.

7.6 Developing Within a Role

There are many ways to help someone develop within their current role. The individual may not need any further training, but a different kind of experience might bring a new insight. Here I bring together a range of development activities, many of which take the individual outside his usual sphere of influence. Some of the activities are individual, others involve working with colleagues; some are within the organization, others take place in a wider arena.

Reading around the subject – researching a topic of interest within the individual's role, for example a new technique or methodology that is not in use within the organization but which might be a good thing to adopt. The research might include reading journal articles, finding information on the internet, talking to people in other organizations or suppliers, contacting a university known to be researching the field. The findings can be presented to the rest of the individual's team, with a discussion of how the topic might be relevant or useful to the team's work. Finding that a new technique would not be relevant is an equally valid result!

Attending seminars or conferences – there are many seminars and conferences which discuss and explore technical subjects. Hearing about new approaches can encourage the delegates to reconsider the approaches taken in their own organizations. Talking to other delegates from different organizations helps to put one's own experience into perspective. It also gives the individual a chance to see his work from a distance, to come back to it with a fresh insight.

Extra responsibilities – it is often possible to develop one's skills by taking on extra responsibilities, for example taking part in monitoring a project, or managing a larger project. Sometimes an extra set of tasks with a different focus can provide a fresh challenge, for example providing a business explanation for the technical systems being developed.

Coaching other people – whether providing instruction or acting as resident expert, coaching other people is a good way of developing one's understanding of the subject. Another individual will have a different perspective on the topic of discussion, and will have different experiences of putting the subject to work. The coaching can be within the same organization or outside it; external coaching arrangements are often made through a professional body or industry-based society.

Writing technical articles – there are many topics which might be of general interest within a technical department or industry, and one way of developing an individual is to ask him to write about a subject he knows well. Of course, writing an article can also be a good way of disseminating what was discovered in researching a new topic. Technical articles can be published internally, say in a newsletter or intranet site, or externally in a journal or the trade press.

Professional society membership – joining a professional society often entails demonstrating proficiency in a relevant range of skills and experience, some of which might be developed in the application process. The individual may discover new skills and new perspectives, thus broadening his horizons.

Participation in a professional society – active membership of a professional society can take many forms. The individual could contribute to the work of a local branch, project, special interest group or working party. He could be an officer or committee member at one of these groups. In this way, the individual not only develops his own interests and outlook but also puts something back into the industry or profession. There is a wide variety of ways in which individuals participate in their societies, whether publicly or in the background.

Being a mentor – participating in a mentoring scheme can help the individual to develop his career without changing his main role. One can be a mentor for new entrants into a professional society, for example, or to students in local secondary schools, or to the teaching profession in local schools or colleges. One could also provide industry-based support for academic courses at a local university or college, as a mentor or guest lecturer or speaker for example. Some schools and colleges ask local information systems practitioners to help assess student projects and to help with teaching students about industry.

Speaking at conferences – there are many conferences run by different technical groups and user groups. If an individual has a particular expertise in a subject of interest, for example perhaps he has experience of using a software product in a particular environment, he might also be able to present a paper to a relevant forum of interested parties, for example a user group conference. In this way he develops his own understanding and his communication skills while describing his organization's experience of the topic or product and its applications.

There are many other activities that could be used as career development opportunities; some activities are peculiar to one part of the IT industry, others are more generally relevant. Clearly, it is not necessary to change roles in order to develop one's career.

7.7 Support From Professional Societies

There are several professional societies relevant to people in the IT industry. Many of them provide some kind of career development support, often in the form of guidance in developing professional skills. These societies provide a standardized, centrally-maintained set of relevant professional skills and role definitions.

Professional development schemes offer a way of structuring an individual's training and development in the specific skills needed to carry out the profession. Many societies offer such schemes to individual members as part of the membership package; some also offer structured training schemes to member organizations. For example, the British Computer Society (BCS) runs a continuing professional development (CPD) scheme for individual members; the Society and the Institute for the Management of Information Systems (IDPM) jointly run a Professional Development Scheme for organizations.

The CPD scheme run by the BCS is aimed at individual members and provides a way of planning, recording and evaluating the various development activities undertaken by the individual. Without being overly bureaucratic, it provides a useful prompt to ensure that professional development is not lost in the press of day-to-day tasks and deadlines.

The first essential step in any professional development is to carry out a skills analysis, using the skill set as defined for the role. The skill set can come from the Industry Structure Model (ISM) as discussed earlier, or from the organization's own role definitions. The individual's current skill levels are compared with this skill set and any development needs identified. The second step is to plan the activities that will be used to carry out the required development. These could include some of the development activities we saw in the previous section, and it could include training using any of the training methods we saw in Chapters 3 and 4. As the training and development activities take place, the individual records the completion and his assessment of each activity. At the end of the year, the individual looks back over each of the development activities and reassesses what he learned from each one and which were more valuable to his development. The record or log of development activities can be sent in to the professional society; development undertaken by members can be recorded and accredited by the society. This provides evidence and confirmation that the individual does indeed take a professional approach to his own skill development. By carrying out this process each year, the individual is continually developing his professional skills. (British Computer Society, 1998)

At an organizational level, the Professional Development Scheme (PDS), run by the BCS and IDPM jointly, provides a similar process on a larger scale. It can be used by large organizations with their own internal training departments, or by small organizations with no dedicated training services. Designed to fit in with whatever training and development arrangements are already in place within an organization, the PDS can also provide a complete training planning solution if required. (British Computer Society, 2000b)

The PDS consists of four essential elements. The first element is the Industry Structure Model which we saw earlier, giving role definitions and skill sets. The second element is a set of individual career development plans, one for each member of staff included in the scheme. The individual's development plan sets out training and development objectives and planned activities for the year. The plans are carried out and experiences noted as for any other training activity. The third key element of the PDS is a validation exercise. Carried out by a trained PDS supervisor from within the organization, this validation reviews the development activities and checks both the accuracy of the record-keeping and the attainment of the standards indicated in the role definition. A further level of validation is given to the organization by an annual inspection of the scheme by the BCS, checking that the scheme is being run properly. The fourth key element of the PDS is the individual log book; this holds an individual's development plans as well as career history, qualifications and other items. As the completed development plans are validated, this builds into a portfolio of achievement and proven career development.

The professional societies strive to help practitioners in the information industries to understand their roles and the work they carry out. They encourage the adoption of best practice and codes of conduct. They also help practitioners to keep abreast of latest developments in their chosen branch of the industry, and to keep them informed of the implications of recent legislation on ethical issues such as data protection. The professional societies also act as industry advisors to government and the media and hence to the general public.

7.8 Summary

In this chapter we have looked at various aspects of career development:

- Experience as a training method, both learning from experience and seeking new and different ways of working with existing skills.
- Defining jobs and roles, in which we set out the tasks and responsibilities for a role and then list the skills needed to perform them.
- Moving from role to role, whether to provide depth of experience in the same role or to provide breadth of experience by moving to a different role.
- Developing within a role, finding many different kinds of development activity that can be carried out within any role.
- Support from professional societies, who keep centrally-maintained industry-wide standards for continuous professional development and can accredit the development activities for members whether individual or organizational.

In the next chapter I look at skill assessment and the various ways of working out an individual's level of expertise in different types of skill.

8. *Skill Assessment*

■ ■

8.1 Introduction

Part of identifying a training need or analysing a skill gap is the assessment of an individual's current level of expertise in a given skill. There are several ways of making this assessment, ranging from simple observations over a period of time to written tests in particular skills. Skill assessment can be done for both technical and non-technical skills as required. Some assessment methods give a long-term view of developments and tendencies; other methods give a snapshot view of performance on a single occasion. Some methods are suited to assessing single skills for individuals, others lend themselves to assessing skills or skill sets for groups of people. If we are embarking on a training programme to improve the skills of a group of people, for example, we might start with an assessment of the current skill levels before designing the training programme.

In this chapter I look first at various forms of technical testing, for single skills and sets of skills. I consider briefly the skill assessment aspects of the performance appraisal in all its forms. Psychometric tests provide a test of an individual's reasoning skills in general terms; I discuss the format of these tests and what we can learn from them. Finally I briefly look at assessment centres as a way of demonstrating people's skill levels in interpersonal skills and other intangibles.

8.2 Main Points of this Chapter

- Technical testing
- Performance appraisal
- Psychometric testing
- Assessment centres and development centres

■ ■

8.3 Technical Testing

Technical testing takes many forms. In measuring someone's technical ability in a job context, we usually assess specific skills within that context.

8.3.1 Skill Types

Technical skills can be grouped into three different types: specific tools or languages; disciplines or techniques; and simple or complex tasks.

In the first group I include all those tools and languages in use in IT today. There are languages for design, programming, data manipulation, graphics definitions, application building, data and process modelling, and a host of others. There are operating systems and families of application packages. There are communications protocols, network hardware and network software. There are architectures and standards to be adhered to. In short, there is a wide range of tools and languages. For specific skills, we expect to use tests designed to measure understanding of that skill on its own, with little or no reference to other skills. For example, we would not expect a test on one programming language to include questions about another language.

In the second group, disciplines or techniques, I include things like programming or network design. In many ways these disciplines map to job roles and to skill sets. For example, programming includes many skills: the ability to describe a process to carry out an automated task, to translate that process into a suitable programming language, to derive suitable module tests and test conditions, to carry out planned tests until the module works correctly, to prepare the module for operation outside the test environment and to document the module, its requirements and its effects.

We would expect a test of ability in a discipline to make reference to all of the skills involved. We also expect it to make cross-references between the skills to some extent. Testing a discipline is likely to include testing in some widely-used tool or language; for example many programming tests actually test ability to program in Cobol or ability to program in C. But this is not necessary; there are programming tests that devise their own language as part of the test.

My third group of skills is actually the application of a tool or group of tools to a specific task, to solve a particular problem. An example here might be in creating and maintaining files for word-processed documents; another example might be in setting up a local area network. These are very much practical skills and we would expect to use a test method that calls on the learner to demonstrate practical ability.

8.3.2 Testing Methods

All of these skill types require that the individual have some theoretical knowledge. He requires an understanding of the background and purpose of the skill as well as a good grasp of the various underlying concepts. We also expect him to be able to demonstrate mastery of the various components of the tool or discipline as well as some degree of practical skill in using it to solve a problem or achieve a goal.

We therefore expect any testing methods to examine the individual's conceptual understanding of the skill being tested. This should include both the high-level background and concepts and the more detailed aspects of the skill, the constructs and building blocks that make up the tool or technique. We also expect to see some form of putting the knowledge to practical use, either by giving example problems to solve, or by giving sample solutions to correct or to highlight deliberate mistakes.

Technical testing methods can be grouped into three major types: short written tests, longer written exams and practical tests.

Short written tests are generally up to an hour long. They may be specific to a particular situation or set of people, or they may be more general-purpose and generic. Specially-written tests may be designed to test the use of a skill in a particular application or environment, or within a particular company.

Generic tests are designed to demonstrate the use of a skill in a typical situation or in a range of likely scenarios. We can write our own tests within our particular organization, or we can use a specialized testing company to write our tests, or we can use one of the many skill tests available on the commercial market. Externally provided tests are sometimes presented in multiple-choice format to facilitate marking and to allow automated scoring methods. Some test providers will also mark the tests and report the results.

There are short mastery tests included with many self-study courses, particularly, it seems, on computer-based courses. These follow the same pattern of multiple-choice single-response questions. They are marked by the course software and the result is displayed to the student. In some implementations, an administration package records the results for each student, for review by a learning centre manager or similar. Some taught courses also include an optional test or exam at the end of the course, to test and reinforce the learning that took place.

The second type of technical test in common use is the longer written examination. These are generally longer in duration and more comprehensive in their content. They are typically used not so much to give a quick assessment of skill level, as to demonstrate mastery of a skill or skill set. They are often the assessment method for proprietary certifications or professional qualifications.

Exams tend to require a period of preparation, of studying to a syllabus. Similar to an academic exam format, many of the professional exams consist of several papers each on a different part of the exam syllabus. Typically lasting 2–3 hours, these test the candidate's grasp of theory as much as his ability to apply the theory to practical problems. The different papers can be spread over a few days or some longer period of time, depending on circumstances and requirements.

For example, many of the proprietary exams consist of several papers or sections. The candidate registers with an examination centre for the exam to be taken. As he is ready for each part of the exam, he attends the centre and takes each part. When he has passed them all, he is able to receive the qualification or accreditation. Such an exam registration generally has a 12- to 18-month validity; if a student can't complete all the papers in that time the earlier ones may be out of date and have to be retaken.

In another example, the British Computer Society's Professional Examination covers a wide range of topics within the information systems industry. There are three levels within the exam syllabus, each consisting of three or four modules, with a project at the second and third levels. The modules generally include both theory and practice and some study is usually required. Within the levels, each module is assessed by a 2-hour exam paper. The different papers can be taken in different years. Each level provides a level of qualification on its own, and also counts towards professional membership of the society (British Computer Society, 1999a).

The third type of technical test in common use for skill assessment is the practical test. Typically run on PCs in an examination centre or learning centre, the practical test checks that the candidate is familiar with the equipment or software needed to carry out the task(s) and is able to put it to good use. Computer-based practical tests simulate the real situation in which the task is to be carried out. The tests are marked by the test software and the results presented to an administrator for recording. In some test software, the assessment is done as the candidate answers the questions; the software then decides how much or how little probing must be done on any particular topic being tested. Thus a confident candidate who is doing well will be presented with the difficult questions whereas a less confident candidate is presented with a larger number of easier questions, in order to build a picture of the candidate's ability with the skill.

I have seen three major applications of practical tests: as part of a larger exam set, as a standardized test of skill level, and as a test of mastery of an application system. As part of a larger exam set, practical tests are often used in gaining a proprietary qualification or in the use of specific systems for specific purposes. For example, a qualification which includes setting up and maintaining a local area network (LAN) would typically have a practical test for configuring the network connections and another for ensuring that the PC is correctly set up for the LAN connection. These tests do not really stand on their own but form an integral part of an exam set.

As a standardized test of skill level, practical tests are useful for tasks that cannot be tested without carrying out the task, for example PC skills. A good example of this is the European Computer Driving Licence (ECDL), co-ordinated in the UK by the BCS. This tests candidates' current level of expertise with application packages such as word processing and spreadsheets. Candidates are issued with a logbook showing their level of attainment in the various applications tested. When all parts of the qualification are completed, a certificate is issued to the candidate (British Computer Society, 1999b).

Some organizations also use practical tests to ensure that staff who need to use a particular application system are proficient in its use. Such tests are often given following a period of training on the system concerned, but may also be used as a periodic check that staff skill levels are maintained. For example, call centre staff may have to pass a practical test after their training to ensure that they are able to use the systems and equipment correctly.

8.3.3 Uses of Technical Testing

There are, then, several ways in which to do technical testing. Some are administered by the candidate's own organization, some are administered by an outside body of one kind or another. As with all training solutions, testing takes time and resources but it can be very useful.

Technical testing can be used as an analysis tool in finding a skill gap and working out what training is needed. It is also helpful in situations where a large number of staff need varying amounts of training on a particular topic. If, for example, a system development area is to adopt a new methodology that some staff have used previously, some form of technical testing can be used to help form a training needs analysis and work out who needs what training.

Technical tests are sometimes used when recruiting new staff, to ensure that any training need is picked up early and the individual can be given training if necessary. Some companies use technical tests as part of the selection process in a recruitment exercise, to ensure that the applicant's understanding of a topic is up to the required level.

In deciding whether and when to use technical testing, there is a need to balance the need and reason for testing against the cost, time and inconvenience of running the tests.

8.4 Performance Appraisals

The performance appraisal or development review provides another type of skill assessment, for both technical skills and the harder-to-pin-down non-technical skills. There are several different viewpoints to be taken into account in gaining an accurate picture of an individual's skills levels. This type of skill assessment necessarily consists of observations rather than tests results, and these observations can give a valid insight into the individual's current capabilities.

8.4.1 Different Viewpoints

The main players in a performance appraisal are the individual and his team leader. The discussion usually begins with an overall assessment of the work as a whole, paying particular attention to the individual's opinion of his own efforts and contribution to the work of the team, before moving on to a more detailed discussion of the major tasks or pieces of work covered in the appraisal period, appraising both performance in the past period and expectations for the future period, and highlighting any development needs that arise. While the appraisal focuses on the work that was done and what was achieved, an informal assessment of the individual's competence at the various skills involved addresses the related issue of how well the work was achieved. The individual will have a good understanding of the difficulties he faced and how he overcame them. He will also have a good understanding of his own skill levels relative to the tasks to be carried out – he is well aware of how easy or difficult he finds the various tasks that make up the job. Many technical people set themselves high standards and are their own worst critic! Most adults are aware of their own shortcomings and welcome the chance to improve their skills. The performance appraisal offers the opportunity to discuss those shortcomings and find ways of improving the relevant skills.

Individuals who work as part of a team may also be aware of how their skills stack up against those of the rest of the team. The various team members will have different strengths that are called upon for various tasks in the work of the team as a whole. The individuals may or may not have a clear picture of where their particular skill sets fit with the skill sets of the rest of the team and with the work being done by each of them. The team leader does have this perspective and can help the individual to understand his own position in the team's skill set. The team leader is also in a position to benchmark the performance – and hence the skill levels – of the team members against the work to be done.

The team leader, then, is the other key player in the performance appraisal discussion. The team leader's opinion of the individual's performance and skill levels is very important, both to the individual for confirmation of how well he is doing and to the team leader himself for confirmation of how well the team is doing. The team leader has a good idea of the direction in which the team is growing and developing. As team leaders, it is our assessment of the current skill levels of each of our team members that helps us to develop our people in line with business needs. As team leaders, we are almost unconsciously assessing the skill levels of our people as they carry out their work. The performance appraisal gives us a chance to harness that assessment of capability.

There are two other sets of people involved in the performance appraisal process – an individual's peers and their customers, those people whose work is impacted by the work of the individual. In some organizations there are formal processes in place to record these viewpoints, using peer review among colleagues and satisfaction surveys to gain customer feedback. Then there is a 360-degree appraisal which puts all of the views together, from self, boss, peers and customers. Where there are no formal processes in place, the team leader is likely to have talked to the peers and customers at some point to gain an idea of their views of the individual's performance and skill levels. Some caution must be exercised, however, as peers and customers may have an indirect view of an individual's skill level, seeing only the results of using the skills in the finished product or service. These people do not always see the individual in action. They cannot see his thought processes nor how much or little he struggles to achieve his results. However, a performance appraisal is incomplete without their views, and they may have some insights into the individual's skill levels as well.

8.4.2 Observations of Performance

The skill assessment that comes from a performance appraisal necessarily consists of observations rather than, say, test scores. What are we able to observe?

The first thing we observe is results. What was achieved? Is the product fit for purpose, is the service satisfactory to the client? If the result of applying a skill is not satisfactory, then we know immediately that there may be a lack of skill, or the skill level may be inadequate. Of course, we also need to look at other factors like inadequate tools to carry out the job, or too many conflicting priorities, or poor understanding of the requirements. If an individual has the technical skill required but still produces poor results, then there may be a lack of some other skill such as time management or communication. This is very common in the world of IT where technicians take pride in their technical skills (rightly) but give little credence to their non-technical skills, feeling (mistakenly) that such "airy-fairy stuff" is not important. Poor results, then, may indicate a lack of skill but a little more analysis is needed to see which skills are lacking.

The second thing we as team leaders can observe is the process of applying skills to carry out work. Does the individual find it easy or hard to apply the skill and do the work? We cannot see the individual's brain working, but we can see how comfortable he is with the various tasks. We can see how readily he tackles the work – or how much time and effort he puts into setting out the materials for the work without actually getting down to it. We can see how he operates in meetings or in encounters with other team members. We can see how much confidence he brings to the work, or how much he hesitates and lets other people take over. We can see how fast he is at producing the results and how accurate he has been. If he is slow and methodical but always accurate then experience is what is needed. If he is slow and methodical and also inaccurate then his skill development should include further instruction. If he is fast and inaccurate then he needs an awareness of the inaccuracies and their impact, and possibly some instruction if there are gaps in his skill level. If he is fast and accurate then the problem is elsewhere!

The third thing we can observe is the level of support needed from other people. As team leaders, we know how much each individual has asked us for help and guidance. We are able to compare the help needed by the different team members and to make a judgement of their different skill levels – does this individual seem to have a problem applying any particular skills? (Again, there may be other factors in operation – perhaps there is a great deal of uncertainty within the organization and people's skill levels are actually fine.) People work together within a team, but it may be that one individual relies more heavily on the others, whether for guidance or help or to finish off things he can't complete in the timescales. This would indicate a need for further development with the skill; if not addressed, this sort of skill development need can lead to resentment as team members find they are always having to help people who "should have learned by now".

There are, then, several things we can observe and use to assess the level of competence the individual has in the skills required to do the job. The key thing to remember here is that we are observing and assessing current capabilities. We see the results of an individual's current level of skill and must remember that skills can develop – they are only the starting point for the development that will take place during the next appraisal period. Wherever our people start from in their levels of expertise, they can always continue to grow.

Example

The members of an IT help desk team realized that they needed to know how their customers saw the service they provided. They devised a customer satisfaction survey that provided feedback on the operators' technical knowledge, personal approach and ability to understand the caller's problem. The results of the feedback were then used in the operators' individual appraisals to assess development needs. The different operators needed to develop different skills and were able to provide a much-improved and more consistent service as a result.

Example

Sara was a trainee programmer and had been on several courses in programming skills and the language and tools she was using. John, her team leader, encouraged her to seek help and guidance from him and from any of the rest of the team. He saw that Sara needed less and less support as she gained more experience and confidence in using her programming skills. He mentioned this at her quarterly reviews and it reinforced her own confidence in her programming.

Example

Jonathon was carrying out his programming and testing tasks well enough but very slowly, needing to ask colleagues and double-check his work at every stage. His team leader, Sam, noticed this and raised it at a performance appraisal; Jonathon was glad the topic had been raised and admitted some difficulty in seeing how all the different aspects of the test bed actually worked. Sam asked Jonathon to do a little investigation and then explain to him how the test bed did work. After he'd explained it to Sam, Jonathon found he could understand the process much better and his productivity improved greatly. Note that Sam did not just explain the test bed to Jonathon, but got Jonathon to find out for himself and then explain it back. We learn best what we teach someone else.

8.5 Psychometric Testing

8.5.1 Description

Psychometric tests are used as a way of assessing people's reasoning skills. Some tests are general and measure how well the individual reasons in a variety of everyday situations; others are more specific and measure reasoning within the context of a particular profession or type of work. Most psychometric tests are timed, to simulate the normal pressures found in the work place – there is never enough time to give every task the whole day. Typically lasting about half an hour to an hour, the tests contain a number of questions, deliberately too many to complete in the time if one were to pore over every question and work very carefully. In some psychometric tests, the questions are all self-contained, with the problem and its context all in the same question. This format is frequently used to test aspects of perception and pattern recognition. In other tests, the test presents several question blocks, each containing a passage of text or a table of results plus several questions about the contents and judgements that can be made from the information. This format tests the individual's understanding and ability to spot trends in data of different kinds.

The questions are multiple-choice with the student filling in an answer sheet; this aids an automated or semi-automated marking process. The tests are scored – the answer choices are designed so that one answer is right and the others, although close, are not. The tests are scored on the number of correct answers given against the number attempted in the time allowed. This gives a picture of the individual's basic approach: have they attempted only a few and got them all right – are they slow and methodical? Or have they attempted everything but got them all wrong – are they hasty? Or have they attempted a reasonable percentage of the test and got it mostly right – are they considered in their approach but not overly anxious about mistakes?

The raw scores on their own do not tell us much. The real benefit is in putting the scores against a set of relevant benchmarks. To understand the benchmarking it is necessary to know a little bit about how the tests are constructed. Tests are designed and supplied by companies specializing in occupational psychology. These suppliers carry out extensive research and rigorously test their tests to ensure that they remain fair and consistent in the changing world of work. The test suppliers train their client organizations in the use of the tests and grant licences to use their tests; in this way they ensure that the tests are used fairly and consistently and are not misused.

Part of the package of test materials is a comprehensive set of scoring benchmarks called norm groups. These show typical scores for people in the same type of work, say junior managers and supervisors, or analysts and programmers, or senior managers. The individual's scores are then matched up against the relevant norm group to arrive at a percentile figure, which indicates where that test result sits within that benchmark. For example, a person scoring in the 80th percentile of a management norm group on a verbal reasoning test demonstrated verbal reasoning at the same level as the top fifth of management: 20 per cent did better than him and 80 per cent did less well on that test. Psychometric test scores thus give an indication of an individual's ability in a type of reasoning relative to other people in a similar position. They indicate how well someone can apply reasoning skills in a pressured environment.

8.5.2 Reasoning Skills

Psychometric tests are used to demonstrate skills that are neither technical nor behavioural. These are the various kinds of reasoning that lie behind an individual's other skills. The most common types of test are for verbal reasoning and numerical reasoning, as these are relevant to most jobs in some way and at some level. Very few jobs do not require people to read and understand reports, journals, books, memos, reference manuals, instructions or some other form of written material. The ability to digest the information contained in these is tested by verbal reasoning tests. Again, most jobs involve numeracy in some way, not just adding up but understanding what a graph or spreadsheet is saying, whether for financial accounting, productivity figures, system throughput or whatever.

Other psychometric tests are more tuned to specific jobs or specific aspects of some kind of work, for example spatial reasoning and diagrammatic reasoning, two tests commonly used for computer programming potential. Diagrammatic reasoning is the ability to break a problem down into its constituent parts and to see a logical flow between the different steps in an algorithm. This includes being able to recognize the rules used within a flowchart or language, and to apply those rules to specific examples. Spatial reasoning is the ability to see what fits together and in what ways in a spatial context. It helps the individual to visualise shapes and patterns in three dimensions even when working from a diagram in two dimensions.

8.5.3 Uses for Psychometric Tests

How are psychometric tests used? They should always be used in conjunction with other assessments, for example with observations of actual performance and behaviour. Psychometric tests are often used as part of a selection process, for example for entry to a management development programme. In this case a threshold is set and applicants must score above the threshold to be considered for the programme. The selection process would also include some form of interview with the applicant, an analysis of performance and potential as evidenced by performance appraisals, observations from simulated management tasks, or a combination of these activities. Psychometric tests are also widely used for recruitment purposes, and many individuals seek to improve their ability to take the tests. Indeed, test scores can contribute to an assessment of an individual's development needs, although you wouldn't usually run psychometric tests just for analysing training needs.

The test scores can be used in two ways – to discover a need for improvement against a benchmark and to analyse an individual's approach to working with that skill. If an individual has scored poorly compared to other people in a similar position on a reasoning test, for example below the 30th percentile in a relevant norm group, then that individual would probably benefit from some training, development or practice in using that form of reasoning. Perhaps a technician took a psychometric test as part of a recruitment process but did not score very highly. He might then wish to further develop his abilities in that form of reasoning, either by instruction or through experience. The test has shown him a development need.

The other way to use test scores in developing an individual's potential is by looking at the scores themselves – the number correct against the number attempted. Do these indicate that the individual needs to temper his approach, perhaps to be less dogged or to be less hasty? Here the test results themselves are not the important thing, the individual won't retake the test just to get a higher score. The important thing is to use the test score as an indicator of possible problems in applying his skills to job tasks, and to improve his overall performance.

8.5.4 Room for Improvement

All of this begs the question, "Can you improve your test scores by studying?" As psychometric tests are not based on a body of knowledge or facts, you cannot cram for a psychometric test. No amount of extra reading the night before is going to help. However, you can improve your reasoning skills by practising reasoning exercises – and this improvement is often the major objective. An individual can read a newspaper or journal article and summarize the main points. He can look at financial or productivity reports and analyse the underlying trends. He can also practise taking similar tests, using self-help books available at most bookshops; if an individual is reasonably familiar with the format of psychometric tests then he is more likely to be comfortable with taking them and not freeze or panic during the actual test.

Example

Paul was concerned that he had not done very well at a range of psychometric tests designed to test aptitude for jobs in IT, as he wanted to become a programmer. He practised doing logic puzzles and summarizing journal articles. He found that he was getting better at solving the logic puzzles and that he had improved his logical thinking generally. A few months later he passed the IT aptitude test and joined the IT department. His work on logic paid off as he understood the concepts more easily than he would have, much to his surprise.

Example

Jane seemed to have all the right skills for her job as a technical support analyst. Yet she struggled to carry out the tasks in the timescales required. She happened to take a psychometric test after applying for a place on a development programme. The test results showed that she got all the questions right that she tried, but that she only attempted a third of the questions on the paper. This careful methodical approach was holding her back in her work, too. She built up her confidence in working quickly and also learned to judge when to press on for 100 per cent right and when she could safely settle for "good enough but not perfect". She found that she could now manage the workload. The poor test result had helped her skill development.

8.6 Assessment Centres and Development Centres

Assessment centres are another way of assessing skills, and are used for behavioural and interpersonal skills. The principle of an assessment centre is that the participants are given simulated work tasks and are observed by a team of observers and assessors as they carry out the tasks. A development centre is similar but lacks any element of competition or comparison between participants. Some organizations use these centres as part of a wider development programme, sometimes for people in a particular role. An assessment centre can also be used to identify the actual training needs before designing a training programme for a specific group of people.

The observation team are specially trained to be objective and fair and to make their judgements based on behaviour they see on the day rather than basing judgements on prior knowledge of the individuals. The tasks for the delegates might include: conducting a meeting in which the delegates together must make a policy recommendation, or individually analyse some material and present their findings, or present their individual view of the issues in a project, or conduct a recruitment interview, or gather the requirements for a new system. The possibilities are endless but are usually relevant to the purpose of the assessment centre. There may be only one or two exercises in a half-day centre or there might be, say, five or six exercises over 2 days. The exercises used will give all delegates an opportunity to demonstrate their use of the different behavioural competencies or interpersonal skills being observed.

The result is a set of observations, summarized by the assessment team, and a set of scores relative to a benchmark of average or expected performance; these results are common to both development centres and assessment centres. In an assessment centre, a further result is that the scores for the delegates are compared to each other; this is often necessary to select a small number from the total number of delegates.

For skill assessment purposes, the observations are the most important result. These point to the individual's particular strengths in the skills assessed and indicate possible development areas. An assessment centre observes performance in a variety of behavioural and interpersonal skills. The different exercises are each designed to focus on one or two key skills. For example, although a presentation can demonstrate a range of skills including communication, analytical ability, conceptual thinking, persuasion, strategic vision and taking ownership, an assessment team might make and record observations only about communication and persuasion. A group exercise simulating a planning meeting can demonstrate such things as leadership, communication, analytical ability, persuasion, interpersonal sensitivity and team work; an assessment team might concentrate on leadership and interpersonal sensitivity in that exercise.

The skills to be assessed in an assessment centre are the ones that are relevant to the purpose of the assessment centre. If you are looking for management potential you look for things like leadership and planning, if you are looking for analysts you look for things like analytical ability, conceptual thinking and personal organization.

Example

An IT department wanted to find and develop leadership. An assessment centre was designed including a group exercise, a presentation of the individual's ideas for improving productivity in the department, and a structured interview focusing on teamwork, resilience and drive to succeed. Each individual's profile of observations was discussed with him and summarized for his team leader. Many of the individuals developed their skills by training, coaching and experience and many became effective leaders within the department, gaining responsibility and developing their skills in the process.

Example

There was a need to improve the way a group of business analysts understood their role, and to develop their skills so they could carry out the role. First the role was clearly defined and then an assessment centre was run to assess the analysts' expertise in the skills identified for the role. The assessment centre consisted of a group exercise simulating a group of business users with conflicting priorities, and an extensive fact-finding exercise in which no single person had all the answers but the requirements for a new system were all available from various sources throughout the exercise. Each individual briefly outlined his view of the system requirements and presented it to the others. The results of the assessment centre were used to design a training program including the particular skills of analysing business requirements, as well as some training in interviewing skills and presentation skills. The training program was very successful and all the analysts were equally effective in their new role.

8.7 Summary

In this chapter, we have looked at four methods of assessing people's current skill levels:

- Technical testing – various tests which are used to assess expertise and ability to apply skills in technical topics.
- Performance appraisals – using observations made in assessing a person's performance to indicate skill gaps and hence long-term development needs.
- Psychometric testing – using well-constructed tests to assess reasoning skills in, for example, verbal and numerical judgements from data.
- Assessment centres and development centres – using simulation exercises to observe current capability in a range of behavioural and interpersonal skills.

In the next chapter I consider non-technical skills in some depth, in particular the possibility of teaching non-technical skills.

9. *Soft Skills – Can They Be Taught?*

9.1   Introduction

It goes without saying that technical skills are key to the success of technical projects and support groups. What is perhaps not so obvious is the importance of non-technical skills, the so-called "soft skills". People working together on a project to develop a new product, or within a group providing a support service, must be able to work together effectively. For some this will be easy, for others it may be a challenge to wait for and trust other people. The IT industry in particular seems to attract technically minded individuals who value their individuality and take great pride in their technical skills. Engineers and technicians thrive on problem solving and many of them prefer to do this by themselves, without reference to other people. As an industry we have a reputation for preferring things to people, preferring cold hard facts to warm gooey feelings. Yet we cannot operate in isolation – the success of our work depends not only on our individual efforts but on the combined efforts of many individuals. It is the use of "soft" behavioural and interpersonal skills that make the difference between success and failure, between a great result and a mediocre one, between consistent success and one-off achievement.

In this chapter I look first at the distinction between skills and competencies – what are we talking about anyway? I then consider which soft skills are important, for individuals and for teams. There is some debate about whether soft skills can be taught at all and I consider some of the issues within this question. Finally I look at some of the challenges we face in encouraging people to develop their non-technical skills, and how we might meet the challenge.

9.2   Main Points of this Chapter

- What are soft skills?
- Which ones are important?
- Developing soft skills
- Challenges we face

9.3 What Are Soft Skills?

What are we talking about here? What's a skill and what's a competency – and is there really a difference between them?

9.3.1 Definitions

The dictionary defines skill as a practical ability, a facility in carrying out an action (*Pocket Oxford Dictionary*, 1984). Competencies are often defined as the underlying attitudes and mental abilities that govern how an individual interacts with the world. Skills can be seen in action in the way someone carries out a task or technique; competencies are hidden inside the person but influence how he uses his skills. There is a distinction to be drawn between skills, which have an external manifestation of a person's abilities, and competencies, which are internal but drive the skills.

We need to be aware of the distinction because people develop their skills and their competencies in different ways. It is relatively easy to learn a new skill based on background knowledge and new activities. It is much harder to realign one's attitudes and approach to life in order to build one's ability in a particular competency. In this chapter I am dealing primarily with interpersonal skills and behavioural competencies, as opposed to technical skills and manual or mechanical competence.

When we think about interpersonal skills we are actually thinking in terms of skill sets which we use to carry out tasks and techniques. For example, giving presentations is commonly seen as an interpersonal skill. Yet the process of creating and delivering a presentation or technical briefing calls on several abilities:

- Conceptual thinking and analytical ability in deciding what to include.
- Planning and communication in ordering the contents.
- Some kind of design skills in creating the supporting visual aids for the presentation or briefing.
- Communication in delivering the material.
- Reading body language in gauging audience reaction.
- Active listening and quick thinking in answering questions.

When we talk about presentation skills we are really talking about the ability to marshal all these capabilities and perform the steps involved in presenting material to an audience. We are talking about the ability to use various techniques such as structuring ideas or working with visual aids, as well as the ability to relate to people such as the audience and any co-presenters.

It is because non-technical skills are so closely bound up with people, whose reactions are unpredictable and whose feelings defy modelling techniques, that they have become known as soft skills. But there is nothing soft about conducting a negotiation or presenting to a large or hostile audience. Soft skills pose their own particular challenges, and we meet the challenges by calling on our behavioural competencies.

Behavioural competence stems from our own individual attitudes and experiences, which shape our reactions to the world around us. Some people are much more effective than others in the way they carry out their work; usually what differentiates them is the way they display and use behavioural competencies. Many organizations have tried to encapsulate the various competencies involved in carrying out the work to be done, and have developed lists and descriptions of those behaviours. Often collected into a competency framework or dictionary, each competency is described by a definition supported by a series of descriptions of behaviour corresponding to high or low levels of performance in that competency. Figure 9.1 shows an example of a competency definition, in this case developing others.

9.3.2 Using Competencies

In terms of skill development, we can look at behavioural competencies as a starting point for understanding interpersonal skills and how they fit into technical jobs. We can then use the competencies to begin developing the required interpersonal skills.

To continue with the earlier example of presentation skills, we see that this includes several competencies:

- Conceptual thinking and analytical ability for working out what needs to be done.
- Decision-making and taking ownership for making it happen.
- Personal organization, self-confidence and adaptability for carrying it through.
- Communication, interpersonal sensitivity and influencing for working with other people.

Behavioural competencies can be used to analyse behavioural skills. This analysis is very useful when we need to figure out how an individual needs to develop in his use of a behavioural skill. By using a set of competencies that underpins any particular skill that is proving problematic, and working out how the individual performs in those competencies, we will gain some insight into the specific things he needs to learn to do differently. Again using the example of presentation skills, if he is having difficulty turning his ideas into visual support materials, then some development in the skills of creating visual aids might be needed. If he is having trouble talking to an audience then development in communication or self-confidence might be called for. If he is more concerned about making his point persuasively then some work on influencing would be indicated.

Another use for behavioural competencies is to help with job performance as a whole. To do this, we can use a role definition to discuss the tasks, roles and responsibilities with the individual to see what competencies are used in the job. There will be a lot of them, perhaps the entire list of competencies included in a framework. (After all, if a competency is not important in a work environment, it will not appear in the dictionary for that environment.) Then we pick out the half dozen or so most important competencies. This can be done in one of three ways: either from the job as a whole, or from the competencies that are needed for the

Competency: Developing Others

Summary: The ability to encourage other people to learn and to guide them in the identification of development needs. Involves giving feedback, conducting performance reviews, mentoring and giving support.

Level	Behavioural Indicators
1	Has to be asked to develop others or delegate tasks. • Only deals with pressing training and development needs • Leaves things as they are • Delegates mundane work only • Ignores interpersonal skill development needs • Sends people on courses but does not follow them up
2	Identifies training needs • Sees coaching and developing people as key to team success • Regularly meets with staff to agree training needs • Considers training needs to include both technical and non-technical skills • Encourages under-performers to identify training needs • Gives priority to immediate technical skill development needs
3	Helps others to learn and develop • Delegates activities as part of individuals' development • Helps people to work through problems • Acts as a sounding board/mentor • Gives and encourages on-going feedback on performance • Recognizes that interpersonal skills are the key to using technical skills successfully
4	Supports and encourages self-development • Allows team to learn from their mistakes • Does not interfere in day-to-day running unless needed • Encourages experimentation • Allows individuals to develop career-related technical and non-technical skills • Encourages the sharing of best practice across the team and with other teams

Fig. 9.1 Competency definition – example.

most important or most frequent tasks, or from those needed for the largest number of tasks.

When you have a group of six or eight key competencies, you can look at the competencies with the individual and discuss how well he currently performs on those behaviours. How easy does he find them – do they come naturally? Each of us finds that some competencies are second nature while others are quite hard work and maybe we shy away from them. We prefer to use what is for us a more natural approach to the task (i.e. to use some different competency) or to let someone else do that part of the task, someone to whom that competency does come naturally. Any uncomfortable competencies thus identified indicate possible development needs – a further discussion will decide whether the individual wants to develop that competency or use some other coping mechanism. Perhaps a reshuffle of responsibilities will allow the team to play to individual strengths while still getting all the work done effectively.

9.3.3 Room for Improvement

It is of course possible to improve our performance on behavioural competencies. But because they reflect a person's underlying attitudes and immediate reactions, changing behaviours can be a little daunting. It is important to remember that what we are trying to alter is not our personality but only our behaviour in certain circumstances. We are trying to change the way we perceive a situation – to turn an instinctive reaction into a considered and appropriate response, within the context of a workplace task.

Interpersonal skills and behavioural competencies, then, are different ways of describing the way we do the things we do. By looking at our interpersonal skills and the competencies that support them, we can understand why we perform the way we do and how we interact with our colleagues. As team leaders, we can help our people to understand themselves better and we can work with them to improve the way the work gets done.

9.4 Which Ones are Important?

There are a large number of interpersonal skills and of behavioural competencies. How can we tell which ones to concentrate on? The purpose or context for using a skill is just as important for interpersonal skills as it is for technical skills. Clearly we need to ensure that we develop the skills that are needed rather than those that are not needed within the job. Analysing the job is the starting point, working out what skills and competencies are used in carrying out the requirements of the job.

The tasks that technical people carry out fall into three rough groupings: those done primarily as individuals, those done primarily with other people and those done primarily as leaders of the team. Each grouping gives rise to a different type of interaction and thus a different set of interpersonal skills.

The work we do as individuals is largely focused on the work itself, on the tasks to be carried out. Thus we use technical skills and analytical skills. Working independently, we have little need to interact with other people. We concentrate on the requirements of the task, the objectives to be met and the tools we use to meet the objectives. Perhaps the only interpersonal skills we use are in reporting progress to our team leader or sponsor. Most of the soft skills we use are therefore internal ones, planning the work, finding the necessary support materials, selecting the appropriate tools. We also use a number of competencies, such as conceptual and analytical thinking, planning and organization, taking ownership, attention to detail.

The work we do with other people is slightly more complex. We still have our individual tasks within the group, but now we have to interact with others in the group to get the larger task completed. The others in the group may be our team members, or they might be our customers or suppliers outside the immediate team. We need to be aware of how the work we are doing impacts and is impacted by the work the others are doing. Some of our tasks may involve other people directly, for example gathering user requirements for a new system feature. We need to be aware of how the different tasks fit together to accomplish the overall goal, and to realize that we could not achieve the goal as effectively on our own. So in addition to our internal skills we call upon our interpersonal skills such as working with other people, taking part in meetings, keeping each other informed. The competencies we bring to these interpersonal skills are things like team working, influencing, communication, customer focus.

The work we do as leaders of a team or group of people add yet another layer of complexity. We may have delegated most of our technical tasks to other people, but we have picked up the managerial tasks of co-ordinating the team and developing the people. We now need to use interpersonal skills almost exclusively – things like delegation, setting targets, planning the work for now and the future, sharing a vision. The competencies we add to the picture include communication, persuasion, developing others, delegation, leadership, providing direction. Some of the competencies we relied on for individual work are not so important in the leadership role – attention to detail for example. Some others are still important for our individual tasks but not so key to leading the team effort, for example information acquisition or goal orientation.

Thus the individual's job requirements drive the interpersonal skills and behavioural competencies that he needs. As we saw in Chapter 7, the job requirements can be summarized in a role definition, including the various skills and competencies needed to support the job tasks.

As a general guideline, I have found that most roles in the largely technical world of IT require some fluency in the following competencies. The list is not intended to be exhaustive!

- Analytical ability – breaking the problem into constituent parts; analysing the relationships between the parts; finding the logical flow of control or data; suggesting solutions and seeing how they address the problem.

- Conceptual thinking – seeing the "big picture"; finding patterns and trends; seeing how solutions to parts of a problem can be put together into an overall solution; understanding abstract models, theories and designs.

- Communication – explaining the analysis results; explaining complex ideas, by building them up from simpler concepts; keeping people informed appropriately.

- Self-development – acquiring relevant new skills, driven by the individual.

- Adaptability – willing and able to try new approaches, new skills, new styles, new methods; letting go of things no longer useful.

- Initiative – seeing what needs to be done and getting it done, without needing to be told by someone else; using the solution to one problem to help solve another.

Developing these competencies will enhance the individual's ability to apply his technical skills.

By identifying the key competencies for the work on the one hand and on the other hand any areas where individual job performance needs to improve, we arrive at a set of competencies to develop. It is a good idea to single out no more than one or possibly two competencies to change at any one time, lest the individual be overwhelmed and the development process falter. We must also keep in mind that no one person can be brilliant at everything, we cannot expect to perform perfectly at all competencies.

Example

A group of software testers got together to analyse the interpersonal skills and competencies required for their role. They found that their role included interpersonal tasks such as keeping each other informed of progress against test plans, discussing problem modules with the developers, reviewing their own and each others' work, and working together as a team. The competencies they identified for these tasks were communication, teamwork and interpersonal sensitivity. Their technical tasks of designing, building and executing suitable tests of new modules and reporting on the results were supported by the internal competencies of analytical thinking, information acquisition, persistence, attention to detail and written communication.

9.5 Developing Soft Skills

Can soft skills be taught or do they have to be learned? They are like any other skills – we can teach the techniques but the individual must learn the skill for himself, he must develop familiarity and ease with the techniques, he must adapt his own behaviour to give appropriate responses to new situations.

We can teach the techniques associated with most interpersonal skills. There is instruction available in a wide range of soft skills, using many of the training methods described earlier in Chapters 3 and 4. Some individuals will benefit from taught courses in which they have a chance to try out the techniques for themselves in role-plays and group work. These courses provide both instruction and practice, within an environment that encourages experimentation and allows everyone to make a real mess of it at first. The learning comes from analysing the mistakes and trying a different approach, seeing what happens if a different method is used. Courses in interpersonal skills should be carefully chosen to ensure that there is extensive opportunity to try the new skill in practical ways during the course. The instructors on such courses encourage delegates to seek feedback from each other on how they did, what it felt like and what could be done differently. Often the delegates learn as much from each other as they do from the instructor – this is very healthy and indicates that the instructor has created an atmosphere of trust and constructive criticism. Most courses also point out that developing interpersonal skills takes some effort. Good instructors will get the delegates to work out what they will do differently back in the office and when, to help them relate their learning to the workplace. The process of assimilating a new soft skill into the work role is often harder than assimilating a technical skill. Most instructors give guidance to their delegates on getting over this hurdle.

However much these courses provide a safe learning environment, some people are not comfortable learning something very new in front of other people – they are afraid they will make a fool of themselves. (Self-development and the ability to make mistakes and learn from them is a competency in its own right, and can be developed like any other competency.) These individuals may prefer to start with some form of self-study material to learn about the concepts and maybe practise them in private before they plunge into the maelstrom of a taught course or even the team at work. There is a great deal of very good self-study material on interpersonal skills, including books and workbooks as well as interactive PC-based material. These can be very effective; they present the concepts and give some practice at identifying options in various scenarios. The individual progresses through self-study material at his own pace; this can be crucial for someone who is not comfortable with some aspect of interpersonal interactions. Self-study materials can be used on their own, or in conjunction with coaching, or as an introduction before attendance on a taught course.

In Chapter 8 we looked at the use of development centres and assessment centres, as a tool for assessing non-technical skills. A development centre can also be used as a training ground – the observation team often tell the participants what they are looking for, and encourage the participants to try different approaches if they find their natural approach is not working. Indeed, some development centres also include instruction in some interpersonal techniques such as active listening. The development centre then acts as a starting point for learning about interpersonal skills. The participants are able to see how other people relate to each other when carrying out a task, and they can experiment with new ways of doing things, such as delivering a project briefing.

Whatever training methods are used, the team leader plays a key role in supporting the individual during and after training, as he tries to put his new skills into practice. We can help the individual to identify situations where the new skill can be used, and to anticipate how it might be applied and predict what the results might be. By continuing to analyse the outcomes and getting the individual to consider different aspects of the skill and how it worked, we can keep the learning process going and help the individual to develop his facility with the new techniques. This is where the real learning takes place, where the individual not only gains experience from using the new skill in lots of different situations, but also gains insight from reflecting on each experience and what was learned from it – what worked, what was different, what was similar. He learns to see any new perspectives fairly readily, he gets comfortable with the new techniques and viewpoints until they come naturally to him.

If a role model can be found, someone who displays a natural gift for the particular skill being developed, then that can also help. The individual can observe this person in action and can see what it looks like to use the skill – he has an example of the kind of behaviour that is exhibited when putting the skill to use. A good way to learn negotiating, for example, is to be part of a negotiating team for a while, watching the other more experienced negotiators and discussing afterwards why they made the moves they made, what were the intermediate and eventual outcomes, and how they understood the interactions during the negoti-ation. The individual then has an idea of what negotiating looks like, which he can later try to emulate, and an insight into the thought processes that go on during the negotiation.

"Practice makes perfect", as the saying goes. When learning new interpersonal skills or when trying to develop a behavioural competency, it can feel artificial, very much like play-acting. This is a natural reaction. After all, if we are trying to change the way we do things then we are trying to learn an approach that is somewhat alien to the way we currently do things. In fact it's a good way of getting started, to think oneself into a role in order to see what the new behaviour feels like. Using the new skill feels awkward at first, we have to think about it consciously. But with practice, it begins to get easier and more natural as we truly learn the new skill and we become unconsciously competent. We begin to understand the new perspectives and take them into account automatically. As team leaders, we help our people through this process by supporting them, believing in them and their ability to develop, and by sometimes talking them through what they are learning and how it helps them do their work within the team.

Example

Ann needed to improve her presentation skills, so that she could really influ-ence her audience's thinking. In talking with her team leader Sue, she realized that she was giving a presentation but not really addressing the audience. Ann and Sue discussed the need to think about the audience. Ann found a course on giving persuasive presentations. She learned how to figure out – or find out – the audience's current assumptions and ideas of the subject, to "put herself in their shoes", and to build her talk around their concerns and interests. At first she found it quite difficult to predict their starting points and their reactions. It felt very strange to pretend she was someone else when she worked out how to say what she wanted to tell them. But she found that her audiences reacted favourably when she took their views into account and she found it easier to do each time. Sue also helped by talking over one or two presentations with Ann to help her to understand the different views of the topics. These discussions also helped Ann to anticipate questions and to be ready to answer them. Ann also had Sue's support in trying to develop her competencies of customer focus and influencing. Ann was successful in improving her interpersonal skills, by using instruction and team leader support to aid her learning process. She was able to get agreement from the people she presented to, whether they were system developers or the business users. As a result, her projects went more smoothly, with fewer hold-ups due to lack of under-standing or commitment.

Example

Paul would shortly be taking over responsibility for negotiating contracts with PC support suppliers. He attended a course on negotiations but realized he had a lot to learn about dealing with suppliers as people – up to now he'd seen them as faceless companies. It was different now he would have to deal with them himself. He joined the existing negotiating team for several of their meetings, both before and during the negotiations. He gained a lot of insight from watching Tim and Mark, the current negotiators, discussing the contracts and issues beforehand. Watching them conduct the meetings with the prospective suppliers, Paul began to see the point of understanding the other negotiating team as individuals. He saw Tim and Mark use somewhat different approaches with the negotiating teams from the different suppliers, although he noticed that the conditions and criteria discussed in the meetings were exactly the same for all suppliers. He discussed this with Tim and Mark afterwards and they confirmed his observations. They gave Paul a lot of background information on the different suppliers they had dealt with. Having seen the process in action, Paul understood the relevance of the seemingly irrelevant details they passed on to him. He went on to continue the negotiations very effectively when he took over, earning himself a reputation for driving a hard bargain, based on realistic expectations and building strong relationships with his suppliers. He had learned his negotiating skills partly from instruction and mostly from having good role models who were willing to help him through his learning curve.

Example

Sarah was working as a programmer within a system development team. Her work was very good, always accurate and on time. However, she found it difficult to work within the team and there was a lot of tension between her and her teammates. Her team leader helped her to see that although she was very comfortable with the internal competencies of conceptual thinking, analytical ability and planning, she did also have to be aware of other people as their work impacted hers and her work impacted theirs. Sarah worked on understanding the nature of teamwork and thought about how it related to her. She worked through an interactive PC-based course on working with other people and read some books on body language and active listening. Her team leader encouraged her to watch the way people operated as they did their work, and in weekly chats helped her to understand why people reacted the way they did. After a while, Sarah found there was less tension and she began to really enjoy working with the people around her.

Example

John had been a senior analyst for a few years, gaining more experience and coaching new people on the team. He found he enjoyed this aspect of his work and decided to move into team leadership. He attended a training course on leading teams and discovered a host of interpersonal skills that would be used in the new role. Although he had to develop the new skills rather quickly once he returned to the office, he found the experience exhilarating and soon grew into the team leadership role. Every now and then he reviewed his course notes to further develop his leadership skills.

9.6 Challenges We Face

In helping our people to develop their interpersonal skills and behavioural competencies, there are a few challenges to be met. It is not always easy to find a suitable role model, nor to choose an appropriate training method. Allowing people to change and supporting their development can also prove harder to do than to say.

9.6.1 Finding a Role Model

Sometimes it is easy to find a good role model for someone trying to learn a new soft skill. Sometimes the role model is not only known to the individual and his team leader, but is also glad to help the learning process by talking to the individual about how the skill is used in real life. But this happy state of affairs is not always present. By discussing various possible role models, people who demonstrate the skill to some extent but not perfectly, the individual and his team leader sometimes identify not just a role model but also what might be learned by watching him in action.

Sometimes you may have to contrive a way of watching a role model in action – do they carry out the skill in a semi-public setting, for example chairing a forum that any member of the department can attend, or giving a presentation open to anyone in the company? Or you might introduce the individual to the potential role model and arrange some coaching sessions, or a work shadow when the individual sits with the person for a day or so, observing and discussing how he operates. Many people also use public figures as role models, watching them on television or in public engagements. In this case you can rarely discuss observations with the role model himself, but the team leader can help to tease out what can be learned from watching someone in action.

There are many training videos that highlight a particular interpersonal skill, showing a role model demonstrating the skill both badly and well. Such videos then compare the good and bad performances and emphasize what makes the good performance good and showing the viewer what it looks like in practice. Again, the team leader can help the individual to relate what he saw to his own situation as he tries to understand and develop the skill.

9.6.2 Choosing a Training Method

Another challenge is in choosing a suitable training method for the individual. We do not want to put him off ever developing a soft skill again, so we try to ensure that the training method will work for the individual. This is largely a question of understanding the individual, his learning style and any unique circumstances that affect his acceptance of training. We need to ensure that we find a training method that lays a foundation for learning the skill and allows the individual

to build his skill from there – it needs to be only as basic or advanced as the individual needs. If at all possible, we need to ensure that the individual will have a chance
to exercise his own learning style but also take part in all stages of the learning
cycle. He needs a chance to try things out for himself, especially with interpersonal
skills. He also needs a chance to observe the results and reflect on what can be
learned from them, then to think what to do differently and to try again.

The training method should if possible include points of relating the learning
to the workplace, to ensure that the individual can continue to develop the new
skill within the context of the job. We continue to get the individual to relate his
learning to the workplace by occasionally getting him to talk through what he has
learned and how he is applying the skill to his tasks.

One training method that warrants special attention is the "outward-bound"
adventure course to teach leadership and teamworking. These courses aim to
combine teaching and learning by practical experience, in an "in at the deep end"
fashion. They have a strong outdoor element, where individuals are put into groups
and given some adventurous challenge such as build a raft to cross a river. The
groups must work out for themselves what needs to be done and then carry it out.
Sometimes the groups are in competition with each other, to add an element of
pressure. After the challenge, the groups look back on the experience to see what
lessons arise from what they did and how they worked together. Many outward-
bound courses are excellent and successfully combine instruction, new experience
and reflection on what was learned from the experience. This is especially true
where the instructor can help the delegates to relate the learning to the job tasks
both during the course and back in the work place.

Many people have enjoyed outward-bound courses and learned a great deal
from them, both about themselves and about leadership and teamwork processes.
But these courses must be used with great care. Every participant must feel
comfortable with outdoor pursuits – if an individual is reluctant to attend, find
out the reason. For many people who have indoor jobs, outdoor activities are off-
limits for work purposes of any kind. We need to respect their feelings and fears.
If an individual is forced to attend a course, he will not be receptive to its lessons;
if he is forced to do outdoor activities against his will, he will be tense and anxious
and probably not able to meet the challenge in safety. Adventure courses are not
for everyone.

9.6.3 Allowing Change

The final challenge is to allow people to change. An individual who is learning a
new skill, especially an interpersonal one, needs to be supported sympathetically.
He is very likely to be unsure of himself for a while and he needs reassurance that
even though he's finding it hard while he learns, that he will develop the skills and
find it comes easier as he progresses. We as team leaders need to be careful to
respond positively to his attempts at using the new skill or changing his behaviour in relevant situations. We also sometimes need to temper the responses of the
rest of the team, so that he isn't continually derided for early mistakes. Part of this
challenge arises when several or all the team members are learning new behavioural skills at the same time, although in this situation they may be more

empathetic as they all go through similar learning processes together. Reminding them of their strengths and allowing them to use existing skills will boost their confidence and allow them to develop new skills. It should be possible for any individual to use or develop any behavioural skill or competency, although some behaviours will come more naturally to him than others.

9.7 Summary

In this chapter, I have looked at non-technical skills, the so-called soft skills that govern the way we do the things we do:

- What soft skills are – interpersonal skills are supported by behavioural competencies which describe what good performance looks like.
- Which ones are important – skills and competencies are related to the tasks and roles within a job and the most important ones highlighted.
- Developing soft skills – skills and competencies can be developed by anyone. We can teach the techniques but the individual must learn and develop the skills and behaviours for himself, with our support.
- Challenges – helping our people to develop behavioural skills poses some challenges in finding role models, choosing training methods that suit the individual, and in allowing them to change.

In the next chapter I look at the wider organizational context for training and how organizational structure affects the training issues we face.

10. *Wider Organizational Picture*

10.1 Introduction

So far in this book we have been looking at training from an individual point of view, dealing mostly with the training needs of individual members of our teams. Now it is time to look at the wider organizational picture, to put training into the context of the project team or IT department as a whole. There are several ways of organizing the system development and support functions; what are the implications for training and skill development? How do we go about training large numbers of people and giving them the opportunity to use and develop the new skills?

In this chapter I discuss these issues. First I outline some of the more common ways of structuring an IT department, discussing the impact each structure has on training. Next I describe how to organize large training programmes, including how to set up a single course for many people. Finally I look at training in the context of a small IT department where large training programmes may not be relevant.

I must point out at the outset of this chapter that there are no hard and fast rules governing the structure of a workgroup. Neither are there firm predictions to be made about the training needs or relevant training solutions for the group or its members. Several factors play a part, including size of the workgroup, organizational culture, size of the workgroup's task, amount of creativity needed, timescales, product volatility, and of course the size of any training budget that may be available. However, it is true that some structures are more conducive to long-term skill and people development than others. I will give some ideas for guidance and illustrate them with examples.

10.2 Main Points of this Chapter

- Organizational structures and impact on training
- About large training programmes
- Setting up large training programmes
- Training in smaller IT departments

143

10.3 Organizational Structure and Impact on Training

In my system development experience and in researching this book I have come across four major ways to structure an IT department (Barton, 1995; Humphrey, 1997; Keen, 1981; Parkin, 1980):

- Traditional structure derived from system development phases.
- Project-based structure.
- Matrix structure combining projects and development activities.
- Hybrid structure combining project or matrix structure with specialist support teams.

How do these operate and what are the implications for training?

Most of the discussion and examples that follow are based around software systems development. The engineering approach involves the steps of analysis, design, construction, testing and implementation. This approach applies equally well to the development of other types of IT product, sometimes with iterations through one or more steps. Thus I would expect this discussion of structure and training to have some relevance in any IT department, not just those devoted to developing software systems.

10.3.1 Traditional Structure

In a traditional hierarchy structure, people are organized into teams around the major parts of a system development plan; the system development life cycle typically looks like Fig. 10.1. Thus we might have for example a team of business analysts that carries out feasibility studies; a team of system analysts that design systems to solve business problems; a team of system designers that turns the system design into a detailed system specification; a team of programmers that specify, build and test the modules within the system the analysts specified; a team of system testers that ensure the modules work together coherently; a team of acceptance testers that ensure the system meets the business requirements; a team of implementation staff who convert the system from test to production; a team of operations staff who operate the system in test and/or live production environments; a team of maintenance staff who develop, test and implement enhancements and corrections.

There are many variations on this theme. One typical structure is illustrated in Fig. 10.2. In this type of structure, projects or pieces of work are passed from one team to another as the different phases are completed. There may be several teams working on different parts of the same system at once, for example several programming teams coordinated by a single person. Thus the team leader is typically also the project leader for the phase of work being done, looking after his staff's welfare and their work progress.

What are the implications for training? Clearly, the team leader is the one who oversees training needs and arranges suitable training solutions for his people. He is in a good position to understand both the project-related skill requirements and the career-related soft skill development needs of all his people. Often however

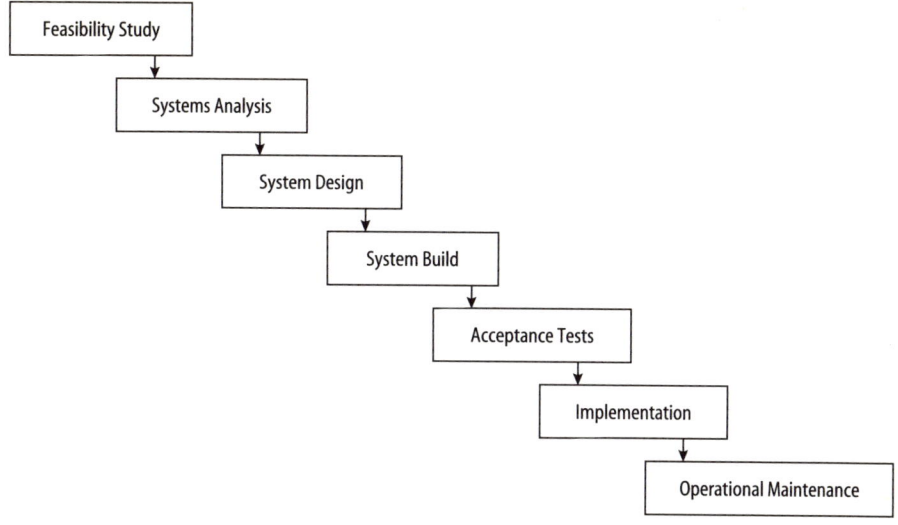

Fig. 10.1 Typical software system development life cycle.

the main drive is to get project work finished on time. Thus the task-focused project skills come to have priority over longer-term career-related skills. The tendency is to concentrate on the former and neglect the latter, although this outcome is by no means inevitable. Skill development is centred around the roles carried out within the team, for example business analysis or programming skills, and generally includes many soft skills necessary to the role. What can be overlooked is any development of skills for other roles an individual may wish to move to. Typically, any training required for a new role is given if and when the individual takes up that role.

Thus in a traditional structure based on the system development life cycle, training is driven by the team leader and tends to be focused on the roles carried out by his people.

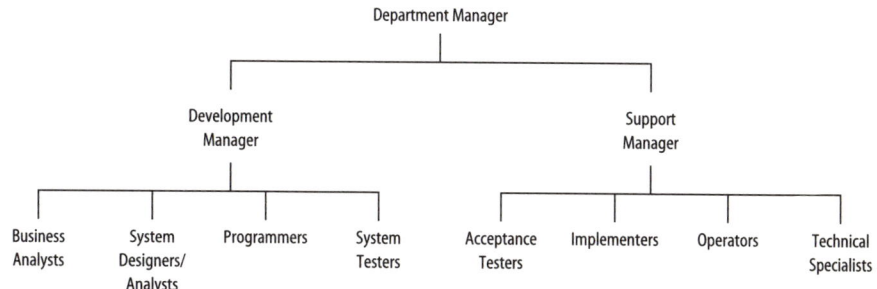

Fig. 10.2 Example of traditional department structure.

10.3.2 Project-based Structure

A second structure grew up from the need to manage large projects as single entities rather than as a production line. In a project-based structure, the department is still divided into teams but now they are grouped into project areas. Thus a department might have separate teams for distinct projects, for example one for each software product being developed. In organizations where projects tend to be of short duration or manned by small teams, often the project teams will be grouped according to system type or business user being supported. Figure 10.3 illustrates this structure. The different project teams may or may not have the same internal structure, but most will contain analysts, programmers and testing staff, to cover the development of the system from start to finish, i.e. from feasibility study to implementation. In some teams, all the staff carry out all of these roles, without specializing. In some departments, support staff including implementers, acceptance testers, operators and technical specialists are contained in a separate pseudo-project; in other organizations these people form a separate department of their own.

The implications of the project-based structure for training are somewhat different. Here, the project leader is also the line manager for his people. Although his primary concern is getting the project delivered on time, he must also look after the welfare of his staff and this includes training. Due to the project-focused nature of his main concerns there is a tendency to concentrate solely on project-related skills to the detriment of non-project-related skills. Thus career-related training needs are frequently postponed to a later date, with the danger that tomorrow never comes. However, a project leader has greater scope for allowing his people to learn something of the other roles within a development project, should they wish to do so.

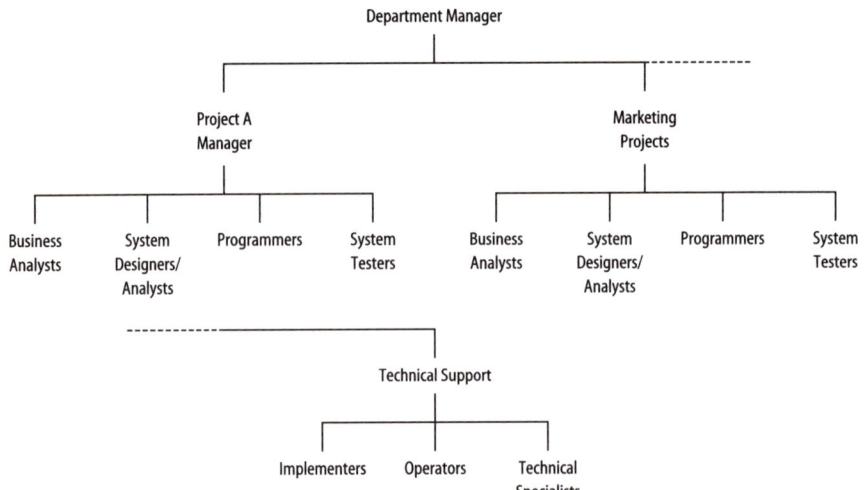

Fig. 10.3 Example of project-based department structure.

One of the problems with training in a department structured into distinct project teams is that of fragmentation. In this structure, each project typically has its own training budget to spend as required. The difficulty arises if one project finds it needs to organize more training than it had budgeted for (to cater for unexpected staff turnover for example, or a new set of software tools) while another project needs less training than it had planned. The result is an inefficient use of the department's overall training budget. It can also lead to staff being left inadequately trained on some volatile project teams, a situation that adversely affects productivity as the project staff must take time training each other and learning by trial and error. Another problem that can arise is that of a new project starting up between budget cycles. The new project can end up with no training budget at the start of the project, exactly the time when we would expect to be training our staff.

Thus in a project-based structure, training is driven by the project leader and tends to be focused on the specific skills needed to complete the project.

10.3.3 Matrix Structure

A third structure evolved to allow IT departments to concentrate both on project deliverables and on staff utilisation and development. In a matrix structure, staff are organized and managed along development activity or functional lines. Project teams are brought together using people from the various functional areas, according to the changing needs of the project. Functional lines and project lines are diametrically opposed, with very different day-to-day concerns, but the matrix structure allows both sets of concerns to be addressed. In a matrix structure, the line manager is the person in charge of the functional area, for example the Analyst Manager is line manager for the analysts. He ensures that his people are productively engaged in project teams, and looks after both their skill development and career planning. The project manager is free to concentrate on project matters and ensures that project tasks are completed and deliverable deadlines are met. An example matrix structure can be seen in Fig. 10.4. In this example, Project A currently includes business analysts, analysts and programmers. Project B is at a later stage of development, including analysts, programmers, testers and implementation staff. The production systems area is treated as a pseudo-project and includes some people from the development functions to maintain and enhance existing systems, as well as the support staff necessary to keep production systems going. A matrix structure lends itself to the allocation of staff to projects for only the time they are needed.

What are the implications of a matrix structure for training? First and foremost, the line manager is not running a project and thus is able to concentrate on people development issues. This includes allocation of staff to requests from project leaders; it also includes skill development. Here, the line manager is usually able to place people on projects that will give them scope to develop their careers and wider skills sets, using project assignments as a development tool. The line manager also develops the skill sets both of the individuals, through individual training planning, and of the function as a whole, through a role-related training

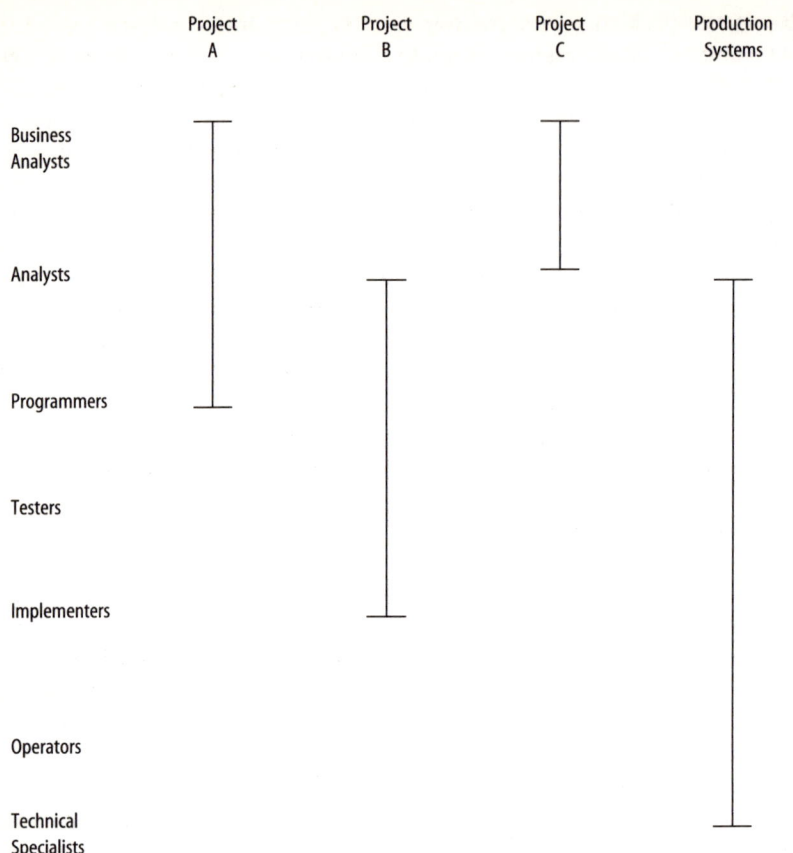

Fig. 10.4 Example of matrix structure.

curriculum. He can ensure that his people have the skills to carry out various aspects of the role and also the experience to develop those skills in different project contexts.

A matrix structure thus lends itself to skill development within a context of career development. One danger is that it can sometimes be hard for individuals to move to a different role, particularly if there is great demand for staff in the current role. One advantage, however, is that the function manager can evolve the skill set of the function. He can also track individual progress through the skill set. Training is arranged by the function manager and often includes the use of skill mentors, people from within the function who can act as role models or resident experts in the various skills used within the function.

A skill mentor is typically someone who is well-versed in the skill in question, with experience of using that skill in a variety of settings. Just as there are a number of skills in use in a functional area – for example a range of analysis skills plus a design language plus a methodology – so there may be a number of mentors for the different skills, some concentrating on just one skill, others covering several. Skill mentors get involved in skill development in a number of ways depending on local requirements. He might select appropriate training events, or he might do the training himself. He might provide expert advice, or he might tutor individual staff. He might select topics for training and then liase with a training supplier to provide suitable training events or materials. He might arrange training and monitor individual progress through the skill development process. The skill mentor(s) work with the function manager to develop the people in that function.

The function manager can often arrange training for a relatively large number of people at a time, thus obtaining economies of scale and maximising the use of the training resources. However, this cannot always be the case particularly if people within the function are at different levels of expertise with their skills. Conflicting project schedules may also prevent the use of simultaneous training for a large number of delegates within the same function.

Thus in a matrix structure the team leader or function manager is able to address staff development issues in some isolation from project delivery problems.

10.3.4 Hybrid Structure

A fourth structure is a combination of the matrix and the traditional structures, and recognizes that support staff do not naturally fit into a matrix structure. In this hybrid structure, system development staff are organized in a matrix structure while the technical support staff are organized in specialist groups. Projects can call upon the services of technical specialists as internal consultants, without the need to formally assign them to projects. Figure 10.5 shows one way of illustrating this structure.

The training implications of this hybrid structure are that the specialists and the developers are treated according to their needs. Thus project staff are assigned to projects to carry out their work but still have function managers looking after their skill and career development needs. Function leaders are still able to arrange role-specific training for all their people; project leaders are still free to concentrate on project deliverable issues. Specialists, on the other hand, are treated as a central resource available to all projects and to the production systems currently in operation. Their training is arranged by their various team leaders and is specific to the skills they need to carry out their specialist tasks. Individual and career development needs can be catered for by the specialist team leaders more readily than it could be by the traditional project team leaders. This is partly because specialist teams are usually smaller than project teams and partly because specialist careers are frequently less diverse than those found across a project team.

Thus in a hybrid structure the different types of IT staff are organized and developed in different ways according to their needs.

Matrix and hybrid structures are best suited to medium- to large-sized IT departments. With fewer than about 30 staff and more than one project to support, there aren't enough people to both do the work and keep the functions and project leadership roles separate. There is a danger of having too many people organizing the work and not enough people doing it. Small IT departments generally require a greater degree of flexibility than a matrix or hybrid structure provides. Of necessity, smaller departments tend to be made up of multi-skilled teams; I return to this topic at the end of this chapter.

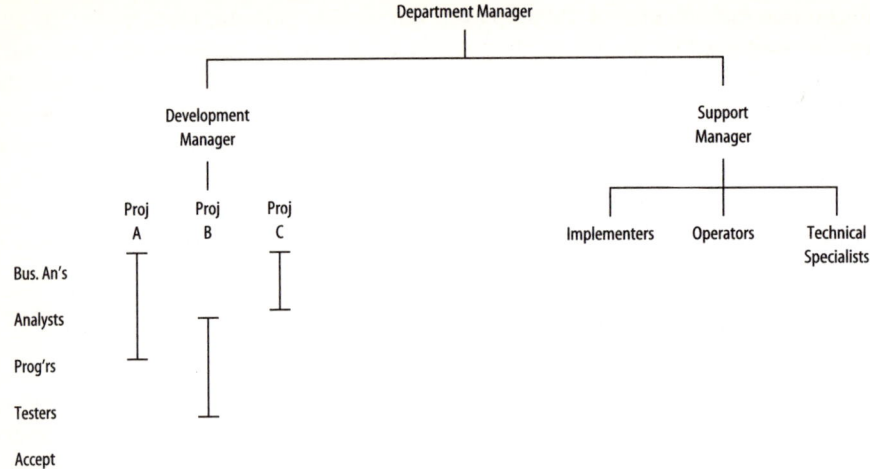

Fig. 10.5 Example of hybrid department structure.

10.4 About Large Training Programmes

There are several types of large training programme that are relevant to IT staff. I will describe four of them, assuming that the delegates all come from an IT background:

- Same skill set, many people.
- Same people, large skill set.
- Large in numbers.
- Large in time.

In this discussion I do not include those training programmes that are specifically linked to an accreditation, although these are perfectly valid ways of training large groups of people to the same standard skill set and level of competence; see Chapter 4 for a discussion of accreditation as a training method.

10.4.1 Three Elements

The four types of large training programme that are most relevant to IT team leaders centre around three elements: a set of specific skills, a group of people and a timeframe. The skill set can include all technical skills, all soft skills, or a mixture of the two. Typically, these skills are all part of the required skill set for some aspect of the work they are carrying out, whether part of the role in general or part of a project they are undertaking. The group of people may be small (one team of three or four for example) or large (100 people on a large project for example). The timeframe may be short (all training to take place in one week, say) or long (we have 6 months in which to train the delegates). Large training programmes can of course use any of the training methods discussed earlier in Chapters 3 and 4, although it is more usual and easier to manage if the training programme restricts itself to the short-term training methods seen in Chapter 3. Typical methods include taught courses and self-study materials, possibly augmented by on-the-job training and coaching. The details will of course depend on the circumstances.

10.4.2 Same Skills, Many People

My first type of training programme covers one skill or skill set and delivers the same training to many people. Depending on the number of delegates involved, this may entail one run of the training (be it a single course, series of different courses, or the use of self-study materials) or it may mean a repetition of the training provided. It may mean delivering all the training at once or it may mean spreading the training out over several weeks or months.

The major principle with this type of training programme is that the training should be uniform for all delegates as far as possible. This is one instance where evaluation of the training being undertaken can help provide instant feedback to the training team, ensuring that early problems are solved and avoided in later training sessions on the same programme. Earlier delegates will have a chance to experiment with the new skill(s) and can become mentors for later delegates. Clearly those who will need to use the skills earlier should be among the earlier delegates if the programme is likely to be protracted.

10.4.3 Same People, Many Skills

My second type of training programme covers a large set of skills for a single group of people. Here the different parts of the programme have different training objectives and contents. This type of programme often includes a variety of courses or self-study materials, sometimes including some on-the-job experimentation. Again, the training may be delivered all at once or it may be spread out over several weeks. In this type of programme, if the skills are tightly related then the training can usually happen all at once; if the skills are more diverse then the delegates will need time to assimilate and practise each skill so a longer time scale is probably indicated.

This type of programme is often used to train or retrain a group of people in the various skills for their role, and some form of action group or continuing discussion forum can be included as a training method within the programme. This type of programme is also often used if a team of people is moving from one set of software tools to another, in which case the training should be delivered as the new tools become available for everyday use. The idea is to minimise the time delay between getting the training and being able to put it into practice.

10.4.4 Large in Numbers

My third type of training programme is for large numbers of delegates. This type of programme can encompass both of the previous types. The major issues here include making sure that the training given is consistent across many groups of delegates. This can be difficult to ensure, particularly if the training team itself is large. If the training includes the use of self-study materials, sufficient copies or access points to the material must be provided. Another issue is the size of the administrative task in ensuring that each delegate has received the required training and has had a chance to put it into practice and consolidate his learning.

A third issue is that of different requirements. Some delegates may find that not all of the training is required when actually putting the skill(s) to use, perhaps because their team or work context is not the same as the majority; for example technical specialists may need a different understanding of a development tool compared to the programmers using the same tool. This should be written back into the training being delivered if possible, so that the training is relevant to all delegates. Indeed, one of the issues with training large numbers is how much the training can be tailored to the needs of the individuals without sacrificing the needs of the training audience as a whole. Generally speaking, it is best left to the instructor to relate specific needs of the individual delegates to the course content. If you are using self-study material then the team leader or skill mentor can help individual delegates to relate the content to their work.

10.4.5 Large in Time

My fourth type of training programme is large in terms of time, spanning several weeks, months or even years. Again, this type of training programme can encompass both of the first two types. Here, the major issues again include ensuring that the delivered training is consistent. This can be difficult to achieve particularly if the training team changes a lot during the programme. Again, the issue of administration is not trivial, as it is a big task to ensure that all delegates have received the training and put it into practice. There is likely to be some staff turnover during the course of a long programme and newcomers also need the relevant training.

Here, a third issue is one of changing requirements. Over a lengthy training programme, the work content may change enough to require amendments to the training, perhaps in the way a new tool is to be used. Where the delivered training needs to be altered, you must also consider whether earlier delegates need to be told of the new approach or whether they will have found out for themselves in the course of their work. The issue of individual delegates' requirements is still best left to the training team to address on the day and to the team leader or skill mentor to discuss with delegates in applying the training to their work tasks.

10.4.6 Other Training Programmes

I have mentioned four types of training programme commonly used in IT departments. Other types of training programme do exist, of course. For example, many organizations run training programmes for the development of future managers within their organization. These cover management topics within the context of the organization's culture and values, for example relating leadership techniques to particular business drivers. They also include people from all over the organization; thus the delegates are from a variety of backgrounds and disciplines. Generally speaking, these training programmes have more than one purpose. Not only do they aim to develop specific skills, they also aim to present corporate aims and objectives. In many cases, these training programmes also instil a sense of group identity and common understanding in the delegates, who will often all be working together as managers at some time in the company's future. Organizational training programmes are usually arranged by a central group such as a training or personnel function; the IT team leader is seldom called upon to arrange this type of programme, although we are sometimes asked to participate as speakers, observers, or in some other way.

10.5 Setting up Large Training Programmes

The IT team leader may well need to drive a large training programme within his department or project. I start by describing how to set up a single training session, then go on to describe how to create a series of such sessions. There are several tasks to be carried out; these tasks can be assigned in whatever way suits your resources. Some administrative assistance is very helpful but not obligatory.

Setting up a single training session involves several major steps. First, we need to plan what the training will consist of, what are its objectives and contents. We also need to think about who needs to receive the training. Next the event needs to be organized in detail. After the training event has been held, the team leader needs to ensure that all delegates have a chance to put the training into practice on the job.

10.5.1 Training Requirements

Deciding the detailed training requirements is often fairly straightforward. In Fig. 10.6 we see an *aide-mémoire* for outlining the details of a new training event. In many cases, the overall objective is very simple and a standard course from some training supplier will fit the requirement very well. If this is the case then the detailed requirements sheet can be used to record the course name and supplier, target date or range of dates for the training to be delivered, likely number of delegates and the main objective of the course. If any special equipment or venue arrangements are needed, they can be recorded on this form to ensure that everything for the event is ready at the appropriate time. The training event might equally well consist of delegates' use of a set of self-study materials, for example a computer-based course delivered on CD-ROM or over the intranet. The detailed requirements can be recorded for this type of event just as for a taught course.

Sometimes the standard syllabus is not entirely sufficient to meet the training requirement. In such cases some tailoring of the course materials will be necessary and the detailed requirements form can be used to record the decisions. Clearly, the training supplier will need to be identified at or before this stage and the requirements discussed with them. Most training professionals are willing to discuss specific training details with their clients and there should be little difficulty in agreeing your requirement for the training event. The training team may come entirely from the training supplier, or it might include internal people who can describe the work context for the training. Thus an IT manager might give a brief presentation on why the training is relevant and how it will be used in the

Course Name: Target Date (or date range):

Supplier: Likely number of delegates:

Overall Objectives:

Taught Course Required : Y / N
    Standard course syllabus to be followed: Y / N
    Specific topics to be added to course, if any:

    Specific topics to be deleted from course, if any:

    Specific requirements for examples or case studies:

Materials for examples / case studies to be provided by
    In-house team : Y / N
    Supplier team : Y / N
Equipment needed / other special requirements:

Self-Study Materials Required : Y / N
    Standard materials to be used: Y / N
    Specific topics to be added to materials, if any:

    Specific topics to be deleted from materials, if any:

    Specific requirements for examples of case studies:

Material for examples / case studies to be provided by
    In-house team : Y / N
    Supplier team : Y / N
Equipment needed / file access requirements:

Follow-up Activities:

Fig. 10.6 Detailed course requirements.

department. There is space on the form for you to note any specific alterations that need to be made to the standard course contents.

Sometimes it is desirable to use training examples and case studies that are based within your organization. This can greatly help the delegates to assimilate the new information into their normal work tasks, and helps the transfer of learning from the training event to the work environment. Sometimes the examples can be provided from within the job context; other times a description of the job context can be given to the training team to develop into their own examples within the course outline. Again, the form caters for a taught course or a set of self-study materials. It can also be used for both at once, for example if a self-study package is to be used to give the facts and the taught course is to expand on the facts and relate them to job tasks.

Although it is not an essential part of the training event itself, identifying any follow-up activities can usefully be done at this early design stage. What will the delegates need to do to consolidate their learning and begin to put the new skill and tools into practice?

10.5.2 Practical Arrangements

Once the training requirements have been identified and discussed with the training team, the next stage is to arrange the practical details of running the event. In Fig. 10.7 we see a sample training event checklist. This gives a list of the relevant tasks and some indication of their relative timings. The checklist can be used both as a reminder of what needs to be done and as a progress sheet to ensure that all tasks are carried out. The first step is to outline the detailed training requirements and get them agreed with the training team.

A dialogue needs to be started with the appropriate supplier to work out practical details. Figure 10.8 shows a sample training events details sheet that can be used to record details as the course arrangements progress. Thus the high-level information about the training event is transferred to the details sheet; as more details such as date, cost and delegate names are agreed, these are added to the sheet. As the overall course arrangements progress then the checklist can be filled in as appropriate.

Most of the items on the checklist and detail sheet are straightforward; some items need a little explanation.

Training venue – one challenge that many organizations have is finding a training venue. This could be a room on your premises, although many companies find space at a premium and impossible to set aside for a training event. Other alternatives are to use a local conference centre or college, or a local hotel, or to hold the event at the suppliers' training centre. Each alternative has advantages and disadvantages. For example, holding the event on-site eliminates extra travel expenses but allows delegates the distraction of popping back to the office. Holding the event at a hotel or training centre may be costly but allows delegates to focus on the new topic. Whatever the venue is to be, it needs to be booked and notified to the training team and the delegates.

Budget support – financial arrangements differ from organization to organization and from course to course. The important thing is to make sure you have

COURSE: DATE:

Step	What	When	When Done
1	Specify the training requirements		
2	Initiate course arrangements with appropriate supplier – including equipment required – and note on Detailed Course Requirement sheet	after 1	
3	Start to fill in Training Event Details sheet	after 2	
4	Identify delegates and fill in names on Training Event Details sheet	after 3	
5	Confirm date(s) and cost with supplier	after 2	
6	Confirm course details with supplier	after 5	
7	Book room or venue for course	after 6	
8	Book equipment – PCs, file access, etc if needed	after 6	
9	Book equipment – OHP etc if needed	after 6	
10	Organize financial arrangements	after 6	
11	Confirm course content with supplier	after 5	
12	Send confirmation letter/joining instructions to delegates	after 7	
13	Check room or venue, software and equipment ready	day before course	
14	Meet trainer, show to room or venue, give expected delegate list	first day of course	
15	Get actual delegate list from trainer, check room or venue	last day of course	
16	Get and discuss feedback from each delegate	week after course	

Fig. 10.7 Training event checklist.

made arrangements for all costs to be met and accounted for. This may entail a pre-training sanction to spend money and post-training settlement of invoices. Again, it is important to remember to carry out whatever training budget processes your organization requires.

Joining instructions – joining instructions are the details sent to delegates informing them of the event details. These typically include the name and supplier of the event (or the access point for self-study materials), as well as the date, time

Course Name:		
Supplier:		No of Delegates:
Date:		Duration:
Venue:		
Cost of Course:		Cost per Delegate:
<u>Name:</u>	<u>Team:</u>	<u>Confirmed Y/N:</u>

Equipment Needed / Special Reqts:

Accomodation for Trainer to be arranged by: In-house / Supplier

Joining Instructions to be produced by: In-house / Supplier

Fig. 10.8 Training event details.

and venue. There may be a list of the training objectives or topics to be covered. There may be a map if the venue is unfamiliar. There may be some reading material to be perused before the start of the event, and this would be included with the joining instructions. Either the organization or the training supplier can produce joining instructions, it depends largely on which of you has both the information and the resources to write them. Again, the important things are to know whose responsibility it is and to get the details to the delegates in good time before the event.

Attendance – the delegate list on the day may be different from the planned delegate list for any particular session. This is common and arises from such things as illness, essential work to be carried out, last-minute delegate substitutions. It is important to link the actual delegate list back to the planned list. This is so that anyone who missed their training can be offered another session or some other alternative way of getting the instruction. It also helps ensure that a delegate who has already attended isn't invited a second time.

Many of the tasks on the checklist can be carried out by a member of the administration staff either from your organization or from the training supplier. How the tasks are allocated to resources will depend on local circumstances and the details of the event. For example, in a typical scenario the training supplier takes care of course details such as joining instructions and reproducing course materials, while the client organization takes care of the venue and delegate lists. In other instances, the training supplier also takes care of delegate lists and venue arrangements. On other occasions, the training supplier delivers the training and the client organization arranges the course and provides the materials.

10.5.3 Evaluation

The final major stage in setting up a training event, after the event itself, is the collection of feedback from delegates and their team leaders. Did the training fulfil its objectives, what problems were there that could or could not be overcome? Here the various evaluation methods come into play, as discussed in Chapter 6, and can give valuable insight into the effectiveness of the training event. This is useful information both for a stand-alone event and for a larger training programme. Immediate feedback is essential if the same event is to be delivered to further delegates particularly if some things require improvement. Short-term feedback can be useful as a health check to make sure that the training as designed and delivered really does meet its objective and really does equip delegates to start their skill development process within the job context.

Example

A large IT department needed to incorporate a new development methodology into its existing work practices. This new methodology included up-to-date ways of working such as rapid development; it also explicitly described contributions from business users and technical specialists within the system development process. The new methodology was fairly complex and some overview training was required. A project team was formed to carry out the training. The first task was to draw up a list of requirements. There were three available courses on the methodology, one of which was close to what was needed. Figure 10.9 shows the detailed course requirements sheet, with the tailoring that was done to the existing course. The project team and the training supplier agreed the changes that would be made; they also agreed that the course would be delivered in half-day sessions by a

Course Name: NIM (New Integrated   Target Date (or date range): 2H1997
                  Methodology)
Supplier: ABC Training Services   Likely number of delegates: 300, in
                                                      groups of 10-15

Overall Objectives: introduce NIM and its terminology and deliverables

Taught Course Required : Y
    Standard course syllabus to be followed: Y with tailoring
    Specific topics to be added to course, if any:
       —introduction relating NIM to existing practices
       —summary stating next actions and when to start
       —correlation between new and old deliverables
    Specific topics to be deleted from course, if any:
       none

    Specific requirements for examples or case studies:
       none

    Materials for examples / case studies to be provided by
       In-house team : n/a
       Supplier team : n/a
    Equipment needed / other special requirements:
       OHP, screen, OHP pens, flipchart x 2
       member of internal team for introduction and summary

Self-Study Materials Required: Y / N – NO
    Standard materials to be used: Y / N
    Specific topics to be added to materials, if any:

    Specific topics to be deleted from materials, if any:

    Specific requirements for examples of case studies:

    Material for examples / case studies to be provided by
       In-house team: Y / N
       Supplier team: Y / N
    Equipment needed / file access requirements:

Follow-up Activities:

Fig. 10.9 Detailed course requirements – example.

trainer from the supplier. Each session would be augmented with a short introduction by a member of the project team to put the new methodology into the context of the IT department and to explain why they were implementing it. A short summary would be given at the end of each session, when delegates would also have a chance to raise any immediate questions with the project team. Figure 10.10 shows one of the training event checklists; each checklist detailed one session. Figure 10.11 shows a typical details sheet for one session. Administratively the biggest challenge was pinning delegates down to their booked sessions. Some delegates were working on

COURSE: NIM (New Integrated Methodology)   DATE: 22 June

Step	What	When	When Done
1	Specify the training requirements		12 Mar
2	Initiate course arrangements with appropriate supplier – including equipment required – and note on Detailed Course Requirement sheet	after 1	14 Mar
3	Start to fill in Training Event Details sheet	after 2	25 Apr
4	Identify delegates and fill in names on Training Event Details sheet	after 3	2 May
5	Confirm date(s) and cost with supplier	after 2	25 Apr
6	Confirm course details with supplier	after 5	16 May
7	Book room or venue for course	after 6	20 Apr
8	Book equipment – PCs, file access, etc if needed	after 6	20 Apr
9	Book equipment – OHP etc if needed	after 6	20 Apr
10	Organize financial arrangements	after 6	20 May
11	Confirm course content with supplier	after 5	25 May
12	Send confirmation letter/joining instructions to delegates	after 7	25 May
13	Check room or venue, software and equipment ready	day before course	21 Jun
14	Meet trainer, show to room or venue, give expected delegate list	first day of course	22 Jun
15	Get actual delegate list from trainer, check room or venue	last day of course	22 Jun
16	Get and discuss feedback from each delegate	week after course	1 Jul

Fig. 10.10 Training event checklist – example.

projects with very tight deadlines and some were in the live system support area; these groups frequently had to cancel their sessions at the last minute. Eventually everyone managed to attend a session.

```
┌────────────────────────────────────────────────────────────────────────┐
│  Course Name:   NIM (New Integrated Methodology)                         │
│                                                                          │
│  Supplier:      ABC Training Services      No of Delegates:   15         │
│                                                                          │
│  Date:          22 June am                 Duration:     half day        │
│                                                                          │
│  Venue:         Training Room 8                                          │
│                                                                          │
│  Cost of Course: £600                      Cost per Delegate: £40        │
│                                                                          │
│  Name:                    Team:                     Confirmed Y/N:       │
│                                                                          │
│  A Black                  Technical Support              Y               │
│  C White                  Analysts                       N               │
│  G Green                  Analysts                       Y               │
│  D Brown                  Programming                    Y               │
│  E Smith                  Programming                    Y               │
│  F Jones                  Analysts                       N               │
│  D Wilson                 Technical Support              Y               │
│  G Davies                 Testing                        Y               │
│  J Patel                  Business Analysts              Y               │
│  P Singh                  System Design                  Y               │
│  W Smith                  Programming                    Y               │
│  B Bloggs                 System Design                  N               │
│  R Doe                    Live System Support            Y               │
│  F Harris                 Live System Support            Y               │
│                                                                          │
│                                                                          │
│                                                                          │
│                                                                          │
│  Equipment Needed / Special Reqts:                                       │
│     ·OHP/screen/pens/flipchart x 2                                       │
│     ·internal team member for this session: P Smith                      │
│                                                                          │
│                                                                          │
│  Accomodation for Trainer to be arranged by:   Supplier                  │
│                                                                          │
│  Joining Instructions to be produced by:  In-house                       │
└────────────────────────────────────────────────────────────────────────┘
```

Fig. 10.11 Training event details – example.

10.5.4 Large Training Programme

Setting up a large training programme consists largely of setting up a series of training events. Starting with a set of overall training objectives including a set of skills to be learned and a group of people to be trained, we identify the options in terms of available courses and materials. If the training programme includes several diverse topics then the options probably include several training suppliers; if not then a single supplier may be able to do the whole programme.

Arranging the programme becomes a co-ordination task, with one checklist for each training event to be run. The checklists may be all for the same event on different dates or for different events, depending on the requirements of the programme. Each checklist may be supported by one or several event detail sheets. If you are using a single supplier or a principal training supplier to deliver the training or materials, they might also be able to administer some or all of the training programme in partnership with you. Such partnerships are often very effective in training large numbers of people in new skill sets. If your organization has an internal training team, they may be able to help with setting up and administering a large training programme.

Evaluation of training in a large programme is important whatever type of programme it is. This is partly to ensure that the delivered training is consistent and relevant all the way through the programme. It is partly to check that all delegates are able to start developing the new skills and to put them into practice on the job. And it is partly to enable a cost-effectiveness analysis to be done at whatever level of detail is required for the programme. A large training programme represents a major investment in the staff of the organization and it is only right to evaluate the effectiveness of the training purchased under that investment. Evaluation also enables us to spot any deficiencies and do something about them at an early stage.

Example

The methodology overview training seen in the previous example was given to all members of the IT department. The department's administration team co-ordinated the delegate lists, dates and joining instructions for 30 sessions of the event. Initial feedback indicated some areas where the message needed to be clarified, and one delegate suggested a one-page summary of the major components and deliverables within the methodology. These changes were made and the summary sheet sent to all previous delegates. The new methodology was successfully integrated into the department's work practices.

Example

When a group of business analysts was to be trained in various aspects of their redesigned role, a series of training events was used. As the topics were not all covered by any single training supplier the department identified and co-ordinated all the events themselves. At times it was very difficult getting all the delegates together at the same time and it became a challenge to avoid double bookings. Evaluations showed that some events were more successful than others, and one event highlighted the need for some background reading in business analysis topics so all delegates had the same starting information. Overall, however, the programme was highly successful, equipping the analysts for their new role.

Example

A large section of an IT department needed to learn about a new communications protocol and networking software. Most people would need to be able to use the new software, while small teams would need to become experts at one or other of the many elements of the communications network. A library of self-study materials was put together, with different courses giving background and introductions to the various components of the network. Short on-site courses were arranged for those people who would need to install and support the various components of the network. All of the delegates were trained to their requirements within a short time scale; the self-study material remained as a reference library and as training material for new recruits to the section.

10.6 Training in the Smaller IT Department

The challenges for training within a small IT department are in some ways similar to the challenges within a large or medium-sized department. The range of skills required is likely to be just as big; new tools, languages and skill requirements arise just as fast and just as frequently. However, the small IT department has the added challenge of small numbers. There is often less scope for using formal training methods such as taught courses, which can be relatively expensive for individual places. The small IT department has little scope for gaining the economies of scale that large departments enjoy when they can make large volume purchases of training places or materials. (Of course, large and medium-sized departments cannot always arrange their training in so methodical a fashion – but the possibility of economies of scale does certainly exist for them.)

One solution to this problem is the use of leased libraries of material for use in self-study training; most of the large suppliers of such material can organize the material into rolling libraries where a small number of titles is swapped for a different set every six months or so. Another of the challenges particularly for a small department or team is that with small numbers of staff, it is often difficult to spare anyone to attend a training course without overburdening those back in the office. The use of self-study materials can help with this challenge also, as the material can be used in small chunks of time which are easier to accommodate in the working week.

However, the small IT department has some advantages that larger departments do not often share. There is much more scope for multi-skilling. By necessity, the people in a small department are more aware of what else is going on in the department and can lend a hand to provide cover or extra help at whatever task needs extra resources. Staff in larger departments often find they are channelled into specializing in one skill set or business area, even if they do not wish to have such a narrow focus. Staff in smaller departments become versatile and adaptable without even realizing it. The small department with its lack of formal specialization and formal hierarchies also has much more scope for informal training methods. There is often a great deal of informal communication about the job tasks being carried out and this includes exchanging hints and tips and ways of doing things.

Thus on-the-job training and informal coaching, while being perhaps the only training methods available to staff in a small department, are also much more natural occurrences in that environment. A typical scenario is for one or two members of a small department to attend a taught course or follow a self-study course and then, while experimenting and learning on the job, also to train the others on the job. Thus the whole team or department learns together and can learn effectively from each other's experiences. This tends not to happen in larger more structured departments.

On the whole, the small IT department is not vastly different from other larger departments. Most of the comments made in this book apply just as well to small departments as to large ones. Whatever the organizational context, skill development is just as important, and we as team leaders have the same role to play in nurturing our people and encouraging them to stretch themselves, develop their skills and learn from their mistakes.

10.7 Summary

In this chapter, we have looked at training from an organizational perspective:

- Organizational structure – which has an impact on the way in which training is organized within the department. Although the impact is largely in terms of roles and responsibilities, the different structures favour different types of skill development.
- About large training programmes – training programmes can be large in terms of skill set, number of delegates, and timescales.
- Setting up large training programmes – how to organize training programmes for large numbers of delegates and/or large skill sets.
- Small IT departments – some of the peculiar challenges we may face in training small numbers of staff.

In Chapter 11 I look at training new entrants to the IT department. What do they need to know? and, How do we tell them?

11. Trainees: New Entrants to IT

█ ■

11.1 Introduction

People enter the IT profession at various stages in their careers. Many young people are attracted to a career in IT because they see it as a fast-moving arena in which they will be rewarded highly for carrying out the technical work they enjoy doing. The intellectual challenge of problem-solving, coupled with the clear result of effort expended, make computing a lot of fun for many young people. This is where they start their working lives, as trainees in some branch of IT. The same challenges also appeal to many people part way through their careers, perhaps after using the more advanced features of application packages such as database manipulation software. Gradually they find themselves more fascinated with the tools they are using than with the tasks they are carrying out, and they want to know more about the computing tools. Many of these mature entrants to IT will educate themselves about the subject, through evening classes, part-time degrees, or just extensive experimentation – buying a package and tinkering about, seeing what they can make it do. Most trainees, then, come into IT with an enquiring mind and a thirst to know more. They know they have a lot to learn and they want to get started – now.

In this chapter I look again at training and skill development, this time focusing on trainees. First I consider what sort of things they need to know especially as they begin. I then examine whether there are any special ways of telling them what they need to know. Sometimes we have a lot of trainees at once, other times only one or two at a time, and I look at the differences in the two circumstances. I look at some of the issues specific to graduate entrants and to mature entrants. Finally, I discuss the importance of encouragement and the various forms it takes. Some of the discussion in this chapter is aimed at a team level, while some of it is more relevant at a departmental level, particularly where there are a large number of trainees at the same time.

11.2 Main Points of this Chapter

- What trainees need to know
- How to develop trainees
- Organizing the training

165

- Graduate entrants
- Mature entrants
- Encouraging trainees

■ ■

11.3   What Trainees Need to Know

When a trainee joins the team, the first thing he needs to know about is the background to the work. At this early stage he doesn't need a lot of background, just enough to make some sense of his initial tasks. Once he has become familiar with his own work within the team, then he is probably ready for a more complete explanation of the background, the context in which his work sits. He will probably go on filling in his understanding of computing as a whole for some time to come, particularly as the field develops over time. He will also build up his understanding as he learns new job-related skills and see things from different perspectives as he gains experience.

To a large extent, the background knowledge that trainees will need to receive depends on their own background. Thus for trainees who have had little exposure to computing, for example mature entrants coming in from a business area, the background might include computer fundamentals. They will need to learn about the components of a computer system, both hardware and software, and what each one contributes to the overall function. They will need to understand some of the terminology in use in IT and to relate it to systems they have seen before and also to their new work. They will need to be given a picture of how systems are developed and tested, as well as an understanding of the separation of files and data from programs and processes.

Trainees who have had some exposure to computing but no experience of business, for example recent IT graduates, will need to be told about the business or commercial background. They will need to know, for example, how a company or organization is divided into business functions and what each function does. They will need to understand the importance of finance, production and distribution, sales and marketing. They will need to be aware of what kind of information is used in their organization and why. Armed with this appreciation of the business arena, they will be better equipped to see where computer solutions fit in and what problems they solve for the users.

All trainees will also need to be given a grounding in the basics of their chosen part of IT and their chosen discipline. Thus a trainee programmer will need an understanding of programming principles and where they fit into the system development process. A trainee network engineer will need an understanding of data communications principles. Whatever the specifics, any consideration of basic computing skills and knowledge is likely to include a look at the hardware involved. For some this will include how to make it work, for others it will mean just an awareness of what hardware is used and how it achieves its purpose within the context of the overall system. Hardware is useless without software, and any consideration of the basics will also include something on the relevant software. Very likely there will be operating system software, to make the hardware do its stuff, as well as application software to provide the end user with a way of giving the computer its input and receiving the outputs in a relevant format.

The basics will also include the organizational context of the trainee's work, in terms of who the users are, where they fit in the organization and what functions they carry out in the business. Thus our trainee programmer will need to be aware of who will use the applications he develops and what part his programs will play in helping them to carry out their functions. Our trainee network engineer will need to know what traffic will be on the networks he supports, whose traffic it is and how those messages relate to the organization's business.

Clearly, trainees will need to be given instruction of some kind in the specific skills needed for the job, as with any of our team members. The major difference with a trainee is that he is likely to need a lot of new skills all at once. Trainees will need to become proficient with the tools used to carry out their work, for example PC skills, language compilers, network administration systems. They will need to develop expertise with the relevant languages, for example programming languages, data manipulation languages, communications protocols, graphics descriptors. They will need a more in-depth understanding of their own part of the job, for example developing and testing program modules or setting up and maintaining communication ports. As team leaders, we need to ensure that our trainees receive training and experience in all the skills they need. Some of these will be apparent at the start, some will not show up until some difficulty arises with job tasks.

The field of IT is huge, the range of skills is vast. As our trainees begin to see just how vast, we need to reassure them that they are not expected to know all there is to know about IT, nor even every aspect of the segment of computing that they are working in. Very often, a trainee's initial picture of computing is somewhat naive and they expect to be able to do it all in a very short time. We need to help them come to terms with the complexity and to accept that each person finds his own specialism within the field of IT.

11.4 How to Develop Trainees

Trainees are generally very receptive to new ideas. They know they have a lot to learn and they are eager to get started. How do we tell them what they want to know? The most important thing is to avoid overloading them with new information, to allow them to assimilate what they have learned before adding to it. Thus we should proceed at a pace that is brisk but not too fast. At the same time, trainees do have to become productive members of the team so we don't want to take too long giving them initial training.

There can be no universal timetable, of course, but most trainees become productive within 3 to 6 months of joining IT, depending partly on what they are expected to do and partly on what technical knowledge they started with. This period generally includes a week or so of induction training, getting to know the team and its organizational context, learning about the fundamentals of computing and the business. Then follows a period of some weeks when the trainee learns about the basics he will need to do his work; this training often includes some of the most important specific skills and tools to be used in the process. The basics are then put into practice for several weeks, while further skills are learned as required. As he begins to get more confident with using his new skills, he gradually moves from being a trainee to being a practitioner, albeit an inexperienced one.

During the trainee's initial training period, any form of instruction can be used. There are public training courses and self-study materials available to provide instruction in all but the organization-specific parts of what the trainee needs to know. Some large organizations also have induction courses or materials designed to introduce trainees to the organization and its business, and to outline the organizational standards and ways of doing things. Some training suppliers specialize in designing and delivering programmes specifically for IT trainees, including courses on IT fundamentals, on business fundamentals, and on various types of basic skill such as programming skills.

Other training methods can be used as well. Some organizations arrange for a personnel officer or a series of business managers to give an overview of the various departments and their functions. Reading the corporate literature can provide organizational background. There are also some books available that give an overview of IT for business managers and these give an excellent introduction to an IT trainee's new career. There are also books written that introduce business concepts and describe the functions of different parts of a business or organization.

Training of some kind should be provided in the fundamentals of computing. Training in the basic skills required for the new role is likely to be fairly lengthy – for example, courses in programming skills typically run for 4 to 6 weeks. They include programming concepts, program design and testing processes and some of the more common skills such as a programming language. These courses include a lot of practical work and often a sizable case study to give plenty of practice. Training in other related skills such as test control processes is likely to be shorter, probably a few days' duration if a course is used. Once the basics are understood, everything else relates to that foundation.

Support for trainees is very important throughout these first few months. We need to help them to relate what they are learning not only to their immediate tasks, but also to their previous experience. By getting them to make connections between what they are learning and what they already know, we can help them to assimilate the new knowledge that much faster. For graduate trainees, this means getting them to relate what they are doing now to what they covered in their degree course; for trainees from a business background it means getting them to relate what they are learning to what they did before or to the user perspective of computer systems.

The trainee needs the support not just of the team leader but also needs the support of the rest of the team. Very often, a more experienced team member will be assigned as a "buddy" or coach. The buddy shows the trainee how the team operates and helps him to understand his role within the team. The buddy also helps to relate the training he is receiving to the tasks to be carried out. The trainee's coach needs to be able to help in a way that allows him to learn for himself but without leaving him to struggle on alone for too long.

It is also important to allow the trainees time to gain experience, time to experiment. They need to be encouraged to try things out, to see what happens when
they use the new tools in different ways. Anyone, but trainees in particular, can be
encouraged to think about what happened and what that tells them about the tool,
its applications and relevant tasks. We as team leaders can give them tasks that
will increase their use of the tools and their understanding of the tool's features.
We can show them different ways of accomplishing the same task, then get them
to try it out and tell us what they found. Do they prefer one technique over another
and if so why? Do they find one tool more applicable to some situations than to
others and if so which ones? As team leaders we can also help them to learn from
their experiences by getting them to recount what happened and how that differed
from what they expected. We can help them to see how much they have learned
by getting them to review the tasks they are now able to do that they could not
do before. We can also help them to look forward to decide what to tackle next.

11.5 Organizing the Training

Some organizations, particularly large companies, have a policy of recruiting
several IT graduates each year to provide a continuous input to the talent pool.
Other organizations, including large and small companies, prefer to recruit IT
graduates for specific trainee posts as they arise. Some organizations find that as
the business and the organization evolve, they have many people changing from
a business career to an IT career, sometimes several at once, sometimes one or
two at a time. There are two major approaches to training people in these different
situations: the training programme and the individual training plan.

11.5.1 Training Programme

If we have a lot of trainees at the same time, we can easily combine their training
needs into a training programme for all of them. The training programme typically consists of a series of taught or self-study courses and many also include one
or more presentations on relevant topics; refer to Chapter 10 for a discussion of
how to organize a training programme. If they are all taking up the same role, for
example all joining as trainee programmers, then all of their training can take
place on the programme. If they are to undertake different roles then some of
their training will be individually-focused. A trainee programme can also include
informal get-togethers to reinforce the fact that they are not alone, to provide some
group identity and to help them build a support network.

Thus a trainee programme might include some organizational background, in
the form of talks given by managers in different parts of the organization for
example. It might include some training on IT fundamentals, possibly in the form
of a course or lecture series delivered on the company premises. It might include
an extended course in the relevant computer basics, say a course in system development, taken at a training supplier's training centre or on-site.

Following their training, the trainees work in their own teams on their own
tasks. Sometimes they have opportunities to meet up and exchange progress notes,

at lunches or get-togethers or talks arranged by the training programme administrator. If all the trainees require it, follow-up courses on specific tools or skills are also arranged as part of the trainee programme. Otherwise, any skill training is organized on an individual basis as the need arises.

11.5.2 Individual Training Plan

If on the other hand we recruit trainees one at a time, or for very specialized roles, then we use individual training plans to organize their training. This is closer to the individual training planning we saw in earlier chapters, but with a wider scope to include background as well as skill training. If we have several trainees on individual training plans who all need the same training in some topic, for example organizational context, then of course we can arrange a training event for all of them to attend at the same time.

Trainees on individual plans, then, might all have the same company induction talks, then split up for basic skills training in different disciplines on different technical topics. The trainees might come together again at informal gatherings once every couple of months, to meet with different team leaders or managers from around the IT department. The trainees might also come together for specific skills training for example on tools in common usage in the department such as project monitoring tools.

11.5.3 Supporting Trainees

Learner support for groups of trainees can include action groups and buddies, as well as the team leader and other team members. If there are several trainees at a time, then they form a mutual support group for each other. In fact, if this is not organized formally then it often happens naturally as the trainees get to hear of other trainees in the department. They often gravitate towards one another, fellow learners in a new environment, and exchange experiences and impressions. If the trainees are pretty well isolated then they can be assigned a "buddy" from within their new team, someone to turn to with questions about the work, new skills or whatever. The buddy can be someone who was new to the department themselves not so long ago, or it can be someone who is fairly experienced already.

11.6 Graduate Entrants

For graduate entrants, this is typically their first full time permanent job. (In discussing graduate entrants, I also include those who do not have a degree as such but have come straight from education of whatever kind. Having said that, recruitment of IT trainees increasingly means recruitment of IT graduates.) They may have had IT jobs before, perhaps in the form of summer or student placement jobs. These young people are learning many things in addition to the technicalities of their new career: they are learning to live independently, they are learning how to fit in to the team, they are learning the discipline of getting to work each morning. For the most part, they learn these life skills by themselves without needing to be taught.

The majority of graduate entrants to IT will have had some exposure to computing on their degree courses. For IT graduates, we can expect them to have had a good grounding in some part of the theory behind computing topics. Most will also have had some practice through course work, projects, case studies and any summer or placement jobs. A summer job is usually for a few months; a placement job is for 6 months or a year, built into the structure of the degree course. They will often have carried out some fairly hefty pieces of work in this time, but sadly this cannot be guaranteed. Thus what they learn in their trainee period will build on the foundation knowledge they bring with them. As team leaders, we can help them to see which aspects of what they are learning now relates to which parts of their degree course. Non-IT graduates are likely to have come across IT in some way during their education, as many degree courses now include some aspects of using IT as a tool.

Graduate entrants to an IT career bring the theory they learned in their studies to the practice they find in their work. Hopefully they will find that the theory informs the practice, explaining some of the reasons why the work is approached in the way it is. Sometimes, however, they find that commercial application of the theory does not keep up with latest trends and research. There are many good reasons for this, not least because what is taught at universities, the new exciting topics, have not been taken up in the industry as yet. Commercial companies, who rely on their IT solutions to support business functions, need to have proven IT solutions that are robust enough for high volumes of traffic and data, and which provide secure computing environments. The new exciting solutions, not yet fully developed, are rarely up to this performance standard. This can be a hard lesson for graduates to learn, and they can become bored with what seems like antiquarian practices. The team leader can help them come to terms with their disappointment and to see the work they do as a useful and valuable contribution to the success of the organization as a whole. We can also ask them to describe the new topics in computing for the rest of the team, who may not be aware of current research. It may well be that other people on the team will want to explore the new topics with the recent graduate and see how they can be applied to current methods. An understanding of new approaches may well help the team to evolve their function and the support they give to their users. The consideration of current research also brings a breath of fresh air to an existing team, encouraging them to look forward as well as dealing with present issues.

Graduate entrants are eager to try new things, to learn as much as they can as quickly as possible. One of our tasks as team leaders is to manage their aspirations and expectations. Many come into an IT career hoping for rapid advancement whether in technical expertise or in career development terms. They are used to having to learn things quickly and prove what they have learned. They are not yet accustomed to having to apply what they have learned to a variety of similar situations. Many get frustrated by the need to keep doing the same thing again and again. Frequent changes to user needs can be particularly irritating for an impatient new entrant, as these are seen to impede progress and hold him back. The team leader needs to be sensitive to these feelings and to help the individual to see beyond the current frustrations, to keep an open mind and to help manage the changes. By giving the new entrant a balance of tasks including some exciting things as well as some boring ones, we can keep his brain from rusting and also help him come to terms with the mundane tasks.

Example

A large systems development department recruits about ten new IT graduates each year. The training programme includes a short induction to the company followed by a six-week course covering programming skills, one computer language and the application development platform in use. The programme thus divides into two parts, one course covering mainframe developments in Cobol and another covering client-server developments in C++ and related Unix-based tools. The training period includes a social event each week, to allow people to get to know each other informally. Team leaders from around the department are invited to meet the trainees, at the social events or during lunch periods. The trainees are initially unassigned; as the course progresses, the trainees and the training and resources managers work out which projects or teams the trainees wish to join and which ones will be suitable for them. By the end of the course, all the trainees have been assigned and they move to their new teams. Over the next few months they come together again on courses about specific skills as required, for example systems testing skills or presentation skills.

Example

In another system development department, graduates are recruited for specific trainee posts, working on very diverse projects. Individual training plans are drawn up for each one, based on the needs of the job and the skill set the individual brings with him. A PC-based induction package was written and all new entrants view the package in their first week. This package outlines the commercial background and history of the company. Each trainee's team leader introduces him to key people in the department and to the team. Many trainees attend a five-week programming skills course based on the application development platform and major language to be used. Others attend a series of shorter courses based on communications networks and how to design and support them. On their return to the office, the trainees are given work tasks to practise their new skills. As they progress, they also attend various shorter courses in specific skills like analysis and design concepts or network maintenance. Their individual training plans are reviewed with the team leader at regular intervals – often monthly to start with, then reverting to quarterly as for the rest of the department.

11.7 Mature Entrants

The mature entrant to IT is usually making a career change at some stage in his life. He may be a recent graduate having been a mature student, or he may be a new entrant direct from a business department. In either case he brings some experience of the world of work, and in many cases he also brings an understanding of the business side of the organization. What he may also bring is some anxiety about the rightness of his change of career. Will he really make the grade? As team leaders we can work with him to ensure that he will indeed be a productive member of the team.

The mature entrant who has come in straight from a business area is likely to need more background in the fundamentals of IT than those who come in from an IT degree. This could take the form of basic introductory training, or it might take the form of time devoted to reading material on the fundamentals of IT. There could also be several chats or discussions about the IT industry in general and the background to the team's work in particular. All of this helps the individual to relate the background to something he knows or is getting to know. Training in the fundamentals does not all have to take place at the start of the trainee's training programme, it can and probably will continue over the first few months, as he finds out new things and picks up more of the pieces of the jigsaw.

As the mature entrant's training progresses, as he gains experience, we need to ensure that he also gains confidence in himself and his abilities. At times, this may mean reassuring him that his progress is satisfactory. Of course, we have to monitor progress to make sure it is satisfactory and to spot any problems in time to correct them. By working with the trainee to overcome any obstacles that arise, we demonstrate that problems are acceptable so long as we find a way forward. We also demonstrate our trust in his ability to overcome the obstacle, thereby building his confidence in his own capability.

The mature entrant, having already had some experience in an earlier part of his career, brings with him a wider understanding of the world at large. He may bring an understanding of the business as a whole, perhaps of the business side of the same organization. He may be able to explain the commercial importance of a specific application system, for example, or to explain the significance of a particular business process. He can thus bring a fresh insight to the team. Perhaps he could explain these insights to the team as a whole, so that they may increase their understanding of the impact of what they do. Perhaps the team's structure lends itself more to informal discussions as the opportunities arise. The chances are that the team members will relish the opportunity to gain a different view of whatever product or services they provide. Sometimes, of course, the mature trainee just wants to forget about what he did before and this view should be respected.

Mature entrants sometimes find that because they have so much to learn, they don't get on or progress through the new material as fast as they'd like. Managing their expectations includes reassuring them that you as team leader do not expect them to be as productive as their more experienced team-mates, at least not in the short term. This might need fairly frequent reiteration to help them overcome their own frustration at not getting up to speed quickly enough. They need to be reassured that their main priority at this early stage is to get a good grounding and a solid understanding of what they are doing. We need to demonstrate that we value their contribution to the work they are learning to do. We also need to demonstrate that, while we value their insights from their previous experience, we will let them move on and develop their new skill set.

Example

Janice came into the IT department when her previous department, an administration function, was merged with another area. She wanted to become a programmer, but her only exposure to computers had been using desktop PC tools. While she worked as an IT administrator, she did some evening classes in computer fundamentals and in basic programming concepts. After about 18 months, she applied again to be a trainee programmer and this time she made it. Her training programme included further training in computer fundamentals within a business context, as well as the basic skills of programming and testing in a client-server application environment. She soon became a valued member of the team, responsible for several small systems. Her ease with administration tasks helped the rest of the team to see admin not as so much burdensome bureaucracy but as necessary tasks to support their work. When the next trainee joined the team, Janice was assigned to help him learn the ropes.

11.8 Encouraging Trainees

Encouraging and supporting trainees is very important, to keep them enthusiastic and to continue the development of their new skill set. Both the team leader and the team members help the trainee to learn new things and apply them appropriately to job tasks. By taking an interest in the trainee and what he is doing, his colleagues show him that his work is important. By welcoming him onto the team, they show him that he is important as one of them. By allowing him to work on his own but always being ready to answer questions and help out, they show him that they trust him to become productive and to make a useful contribution to the work. By asking him about what's going well and what didn't work and why, they can help him to learn from his mistakes; they can also share mistakes they've made and the lessons they gained from the process. Learning from mistakes is an important part of doing the job.

Encouragement, then, takes place at many levels and at several points in time. Day-to-day encouragement happens all the time in the course of normal team interactions. People frequently turn to each other for a fresh perspective on the problem, or to keep each other informed of what they're doing. In some work groups it is necessary for all team members to keep abreast of current progress on support problems for instance, or on system test progress. In other work groups the individuals work largely autonomously on completely separate problems. Whatever the work pattern, keeping people involved supports them in their day-to-day work and this is especially true of trainees who are new to the team.

Another level of support is at the task level. Here, the team leader or another member of the team keeps an eye on progress with specific tasks the trainee is carrying out. We get him to discuss the structure of the task, what tools will be needed to carry it out, and help him devise a plan of action. Having a helping hand readily available often encourages the trainee to make a go of it by himself, reporting back progress and seeking help when it is needed. When the task has been accomplished, we can talk it through with him to explore how else it could have been done or what other tasks could be done in a similar way. The next time he has a similar task, we can draw back and support him from more of a distance, always letting him know that help is at hand should it be required.

The team leader can also provide encouragement at the performance review. Here we look at progress in the job as a whole as well as at significant parts of the job. We can praise what went well and discuss what can be learned from what did not go so well. We can also talk about the challenges that have been met, obstacles that have been overcome. Part of any review is looking forward and deciding what to tackle next. We can help the trainee put things into perspective by relating tasks to one another and showing how learning or doing one task lays the foundations for another set of tasks. At a review we also get the trainee to look back at what he's learned so far and where that learning can be applied. We also get him to look forward to what is the next thing to be tried, what are the next skills that need to be developed and practised.

Part of the encouragement that is so valuable to our trainees is the reassurance that they are not alone, either as trainees – we all had to learn sometime – or as team members – they are part of the team, part of their new profession, and can take pride in that fact.

11.9 Summary

In this chapter, I have discussed some of the points to note in developing trainees, including:

- What they need to know – including computer fundamentals, the basic skills for the job they will do, and specific skills or tools for the job.
- How to develop trainees – trainee training generally lasts for three to six months intensively, using many different training methods and allowing plenty of time to gain experience and experiment with new skills.
- Organizing the training – whether as a general training programme for several trainees or as individual training plans for separate trainees, or some combination of the two approaches, always supported by visible learner support for the trainees.
- Graduate entrants – who bring an understanding of the theory of the subject and new research topics but must learn how to apply the theory in practice.
- Mature entrants – who bring experience of a different kind of work, sometimes the business perspective of IT, but who must learn all about IT and its application in their new job context.
- Encouraging trainees – providing day-to-day and task-based support and encouragement to trainees to help them integrate into the team and become productive in their new role.

In the next chapter I turn to the future and consider the question of planning and preparing for future skill requirements. Is this possible?

12. *Into the Future*

■ ■

12.1 Introduction

I now turn to the future. There are always new tools and techniques being developed. As we gaze into a crystal ball, how do we ensure that our people are equipped to use those new techniques? Is it worth trying to keep one step ahead in the skill development game, or is it better to cross our bridges when we come to them?

In this chapter I look at some of the issues in planning for future skills. Of paramount importance are the business goals and how they can be supported by current and developing technologies. These drive the skill requirements for the IT department; I look at analysing the requirements and planning what training will be needed. Carrying out the training for future skills recalls some aspects of carrying out training for immediate requirements but the time pressures are different. I then discuss ways to support individuals who wish to develop new skills in readiness for future requirements. Finally I take a sideways look at the whole question of future skills: if change is so constant, will the future skills we aim to develop really be the ones we need when we get there?

12.2 Main Points of this Chapter

- Planning for future skills
- Analysing future needs
- Carrying out the training
- Supporting self-development
- Does the future ever come?

■ ■

12.3 Planning for Future Skills

In planning for future skills, the key word is "foreseeable". It is sometimes tempting to see interesting new research results in terms of future computing techniques, but predicting when those new techniques will be in common usage is fraught with difficulties. There can be long development times for turning current research

177

into robust usable systems or techniques that appear on the market. Investment in existing systems is considerable, and it usually takes more than just the availability of a new technology to make companies change their use of IT. A strong business driver needs to be present to change or remake that investment. Understanding the key business drivers and predicting when they will change are thus part of the process of planning for future skills.

It is hard to put a timescale to the word "foreseeable". In periods of high business change, it can be hard to see beyond the next six months. In periods of relative stability you might be able to plan three years ahead. In planning a major change you might be looking at a 5-year span. The important thing is for the IT department to keep in touch with the business goals.

Future skills planning can be done at several levels within the organization. At a high level, strategic planning discussions need to take place regularly between those planning the business direction and those planning the IT solutions that will support the business. Strategic information systems planning is outside the scope of this book, but if we are trying to develop our people to meet future needs, then we need to be aware of the strategic plans for the IT department as a whole. Skills planning can then take place at a departmental level, especially if there is to be a major shift in, say, development methodologies or system delivery platforms. At this level, we are planning future skill needs in order to support the department's strategic direction.

We can also plan future skills at a lower level within the department. For example, a long-term project may know at the outset that its skill requirements will change as required functions are developed using, perhaps, different delivery mechanisms. Early functionality may be developed using existing technology, knowing that later functionality can be delivered better using new technology; while the project develops the early phases, it must also learn the skills required for the later phases. Or the project plan may include provision to recruit and train new project personnel over a number of years, either to allow for staff turnover or to adjust to the differing needs of different project development phases.

Planning for future skills can thus be project-based. It can also be relevant for a technical support team. There are constant advancements both in hardware and in the various software systems that interface the hardware with the applications running on it. Clearly, the support teams need to be skilled in the software systems they maintain. Perhaps less obviously, they also need to keep an eye on new developments so they can be ready to take advantage of new techniques that begin to offer business benefit.

12.4 Analysing Future Needs

The starting point for working on future skill needs is an understanding of the business goals and how they will change. We need to understand the long-term direction the organization wishes to take, at least in outline, and the intermediate goals it sets itself to get there. We must also be aware that the organizational goals may change as its environment changes – perhaps a sharp increase in the amount of competition, perhaps a sharp decrease or increase in customer demand, perhaps a fundamental change in customer requirements, perhaps a takeover or merger of the organization with another. Understanding the business goals is not a once-for-all exercise, it should be an ongoing dialogue.

Just as we need to understand the main drivers for business success, so we need to be aware of new technical developments and what they can and cannot provide. If we are considering taking up a new technology, we must ask some questions. What problems have arisen for other companies when the technology was put into practice? Which of these problems would we be likely to face if we implemented the same thing? More importantly, what types of business problem does the new technology solve and do our business goals contain those problems? When we look at our changing business goals, we also identify the technologies, old and new, required to realize those goals. Then we can analyse the underlying tools, languages and skills we will need in order to implement the technology.

Having made the decision to adopt a new technology, the next stage is to analyse the job roles and skill sets needed in using the new techniques. It is very tempting indeed to skip this step and move straight on to the new tools and languages to be learned, but beware: it really is important to understand how the skills group together. Without grouping skills into skill sets or role profiles, skills planning degenerates into a numbers game you cannot win – knowing how many web page programmers you'll need doesn't help you to identify which people to train; knowing how many people already have each skill doesn't tell you which people they are, nor whether they are already multi-skilled. For example, if we have 50 Cobol programmers and 50 Java programmers, that doesn't tell us whether we have 100 programmers altogether or 50 people with both skills. For manpower planning purposes, role profiles or definitions provide a shorthand for sets of skills. After all, you don't resource your team with isolated skills but with people who have collections of related skills.

We need to work out what sorts of roles we will need people to carry out in implementing and in working with the new technologies. This is one area where a model such as the Industry Structure Model, described in Chapter 7, can help. We need to visualise what it is like to use the new technology and what it means for existing roles. Where there is an aspect of the new world that is not included in any existing job roles, perhaps a new job role is indicated. For example, the traditional analysis and development roles have been augmented by testing and integration roles, reflecting the increased complexity both in business application systems and in the need to interface existing packages and applications rather than always writing new ones. Having identified the broad roles needed in the future, we can further analyse them into the sets of skills involved in carrying out the roles. This will include both technical skills and non-technical skills. Existing roles and skill sets should not be discarded, unless we intend also to discard all of our existing tools and techniques, which is in the short term highly unlikely.

Now that we know the sort of things we'd like to be doing in the future, and the kind of things we're doing now, we need to work out where we are and where we need to be. Working out where we are means recording what role profile or skill set each member of our teams is currently working in. This is ideally done with the people themselves, individually or working as a team. Choosing a role profile or skill set may be simple and straightforward, or it may end up rather complex. Difficulty mapping to role profiles may indicate the need for a new role profile, or it may indicate that future needs are significantly different from present needs. Once the mapping is done, it is a simple matter to find out how many people we have in each role profile or skill set. This tells us where we are.

Working out where we need to be takes us back to the future again. We need to make some prediction about how many people will be needed in each future role profile. Even a rough idea is helpful at this stage; if we cannot tie ourselves down to numbers perhaps we can figure out whether we will need more or fewer than we have now in each role profile. Again, we need to visualise what it will be like to use the new techniques in our own working context and try to turn that into a sort of unstructured organization chart. Often it is easier to subdivide the department into smaller chunks for planning purposes, and work out the required size of each chunk. This is frequently an iterative process: the more we look at it, the better we understand it and the better we can refine our estimates. This tells us where we need to be.

We now see a skill gap, the chasm between where we are and where we need to be. We also have an idea of the time we have to get there, reflected in how long we have until we will need the new technologies to be in place. If at this stage we don't see a skill gap, then we are ideally placed already to use the new technology. If that assessment seems wide of the mark, do we need to move people around to make best use of their talents? Perhaps training in the new tools is all we are lacking.

How are we to bridge the gap? At this point we start to analyse the skill gap in terms of skill sets. Sometimes it helps to make a diagram of the role profiles we want, with current and future numbers superimposed. Then we can see the problem as a whole and identify any areas of particular concern. Is all the retraining needed in one part of the department? Is it best to plan retraining by team rather than for the department as a whole? Where we do not have enough people with a given skill set, what do we have and how close is it to the requirements – are our people short of just a tool or two or is the existing skill set vastly different from the new one? It can help if we work out which existing skill sets lead naturally to which new ones, and which new skill sets represent a completely new way of working. If the new ways of working are very different from the existing ways, then competencies and attitudes to change are going to be as important as the technical skills an individual possesses. Some people will be able to change their approaches more readily than others; some will take longer about it or might see change as a threat rather than an opportunity.

At this stage we must decide who to train for what. This is actually quite tricky and is best done in conjunction with the people themselves. One way of doing this is to publicise the new skills and what they'll be used for, i.e. the new technologies and how we intend to use them in the future. We need to let people know what the future looks like, in terms of role profiles and skill sets, and also give an indication of expected numbers in each. We must give as much information as we can about the skills and tools that will be involved, then let people decide for themselves what they'd like to train for. One might think that everyone will want to train for the newest, most marketable skills. But in practice I have found that, while some people do indeed want to stay in the forefront of technology, many people prefer to remain with their current skill set and build up their expertise in that area.

In this way, we take people's aspirations into account as well as their experience. We let them develop themselves for the future having given them an insight into what that future may look like.

12.5 Carrying Out the Training

When we are thinking about training for future skill requirements, as opposed to immediate skill requirements, we are working with longer time scales. We have the luxury of plenty of time in which to lay the foundations for the new skills and to develop what may be a new way of looking at IT solutions. However, the long time scale also removes any sense of urgency from the training exercise. The skill requirement is not immediate and may fall victim to other priorities. It is important to realize at the outset that long-term training is not the same as training for the short term. Not only should we as team leaders understand the differences, we must also tell our people that training for the long term is both an opportunity and a challenge to keep on developing a skill that won't be used for a while.

12.5.1 Building the Training Programme

The training programme will have several different elements. Some form of introductory material or training will need to be provided, to introduce the new topic and approach. This will help people to understand the terminology of the new skills and will get them thinking in terms of the new approach. More detailed in-depth training will be needed in the specific tools, languages and other things that will be involved; this training will be delivered nearer to the time people need to start using the new skills. There should also be some provision for experimentation, preferably using a real environment that includes the new hardware and software. Depending on how long it will be before the new technology is actually in use, there may need to be some refresher training or *aide-mémoire* provided to help people remember what they learned.

As we saw in Chapter 10, there are a few options for putting the training programme together. Which option to choose will depend partly on how many people need the training and what organizational training resources are available, and partly on how much instruction is needed and how diverse the topics will be.

One option is to co-ordinate it yourself from within the organization, arranging training courses from different training suppliers and running them for your staff on or near your premises. This works fine if you have a lot of diverse skills to prepare for, have not too many people to train in each skill, and have some administration staff you can dedicate to the training programme.

Another option is to choose a training supplier to work with you in partnership on the training programme. In this case, the training supplier would be expected to formulate the programme and co-ordinate all the elements of it. In some training partnerships the supplier does all the administration as well as all the training. In other partnerships the supplier provides the training while the organizaton co-ordinates who attends each session.

A third option, useful if no single supplier can be found to do all the training, is for the organization to co-ordinate a series of smaller training programmes. These might be centred around different skill sets needed for different roles to be carried out, or they might be centred around different tools from different manufacturers. Either way, the organization needs to do some of the co-ordination at an overall level while the various training suppliers can be expected to organize their own parts of the programme.

The first part of the training programme itself, after the outline planning has been done, is to provide the introductory instruction. We need to ensure that our people understand the terminology of the new skills, and to give them time to get familiar with the new jargon. Introductory training can take many forms. It can easily be provided by self-study methods, perhaps PC-based training packages giving the fundamentals and an overview of the topic. A library of such material can be used by many people at once, each using a different package; several copies of each can be provided, or the material can be delivered over an intranet. Many suppliers of PC-based study material can arrange a corporate library of materials over long periods. Self-study introductory material can be used either in the office, in a learning centre equipped with PCs for the purpose, or even at home if people so choose. Any option should be available; people should be allowed to do their training in company time regardless of where they choose to use the material.

Another form of introductory training is to arrange a series of short talks on different aspects of the new topics. This has some advantages; the delegates are able to discuss the new topics as they learn about them and this can reinforce the lessons. A series of short talks minimises the disruption to existing work, as people are away from their desks for a short time, perhaps an hour or two each time. If the talks are reasonably frequent then the learning is reinforced each time and the new topic stays fresh in the mind. Of course, a series of short talks represents a large number of sessions to be administered.

A third form of introductory material is to arrange taught courses to introduce the topics and train in the fundamentals. The delegate can concentrate on the new skills during the course and can gain a good understanding in the time. The courses can be co-ordinated by the training partner delivering the training. Some form of reference material can be provided to support the learners when they come to use the new skill or attend more in-depth training later.

The next stage in the training programme is the detailed in-depth training. Here the delegates learn more about the tools and skills and how to put them to good use. In-depth training is typically delivered as taught courses run by an appropriate training supplier, your training partner if you have one. The instructors act as experts not only in teaching the details of the topic but also in giving advice on using the skill in practice. Most in-depth training will also give the delegates a chance to practise using the new skill or tool in a variety of situations. If the training supplier can integrate some likely scenarios from your own organization's use of the tool then so much the better. The delegates will be able to relate easily to familiar examples and they will be able to visualise the new tool in use that much faster, aiding not only the learning but also the eventual implementation process.

The in-depth training usually includes some form of experience with the new technology. Equally important is the opportunity to experiment with using the new tool or skill. Experimenting is likely to be carried out as an adjunct to the normal work, but time should be allowed for it and people need to be encouraged to use the time to test out different aspects of the new skills. Can they make it work? Can they make it fail? These provide excellent learning points, especially before the pressure of working to deadlines comes along with implementation. If there is a training partner, perhaps the training can include some case study or project work that will encourage and direct the experimentation.

Detailed in-depth training can also be provided using PC-based self-study material. If this option is chosen, I would recommend that learner support should be very strong. Delegates will need to be able to ask questions and get advice from someone who is already familiar with the new skills. Learner support then might take the form of action groups so people can experiment together and exchange notes on what they have found. It might include having a resident expert for a while until they are proficient with the new skills.

12.5.2 Evaluation of Training Progress

As the training programme progresses, you will need to do some evaluation of how it is going. The evaluations serve to reinforce learning points as delegates review what they have learned and possibly how they might apply the new technology. The evaluations also highlight any problems or difficulties that arise, either with the instruction or with the administration. The findings of the evaluations are fed back into the design of the training programme as necessary, ensuring that all delegates have learning opportunities whatever their learning style. Some will prefer more experimentation, others will prefer more instruction before they start to put it into practice. Evaluations may also highlight necessary changes in the timing of the training, to ensure that people have a chance to assimilate the fundamentals before moving to more advanced material.

12.5.3 Follow-up Training

If the training for future skills is taking place a long time before they are to be used, or if the implementation of the new technology is significantly delayed, then some form of refresher training should be considered. This might be another taught course, or it might be a review of self-study material. It could also take the form of a case study or small project using the new tools. Or it might be a series of short presentations to follow up the training and remind people of what the technology is and how to use it. It could also take the form of reference sheets or *aide-mémoire* to briefly recap on the major components of the new technology and how it is used.

12.6 Supporting Self Development

Individuals may wish to train for future skills independently of a training programme. Perhaps there has been no formal future skills planning done by the department or team. Perhaps the individual is outside the scope of the future skills training programme. Perhaps the individual is just keen to develop new skills. Whatever the motivation, individual self-development is to be encouraged.

We can provide introductory materials easily through a departmental training library stocked with self-study books and PC-based training packages. These are made available to anyone in the department who wishes to find out more about topics they are not familiar with. People should be allowed to use the material in the office or at home but generally in their own time if it is not directly relevant to current or known future skill requirements. Another popular method of developing skills for the future is for individuals to embark on part-time study through a degree course, with the Open University for example. This is a fairly long-term but perfectly acceptable method of keeping oneself up to date with new technology in the fast-moving world of IT. Many organizations give financial support to employees taking relevant education courses. Another long-term training method that is gaining in popularity is the online university, an amalgam of computer-based self-study delivered through the internet with tutorial support. Again, students work at their own pace learning about new skills that interest them and that will be useful to their future directions.

We as team leaders can certainly support and encourage our people's desires to develop themselves in new directions. We can harness that development by asking them to investigate the suitability of a new technique for current problems. It may be that some aspects of a new technology can be put to good use in a small way without requiring major investment or disruption. Finding out about this and reporting back to the team will help the individual to learn more about the new techniques and helps the team to look forward in their work. We can also ask the individual to give a brief overview of the new technology to the rest of the team, perhaps motivating them to find out more about the subject or a related one.

In supporting individuals who wish to develop new skills, we must be realistic and honest about the prospects for using both current and future skill sets. Skill development shouldn't be undertaken just for its own sake but in order to get a different perspective on what needs to be done, and to get a different set of approaches to use as each becomes relevant. But if we know that there are not likely to be any opportunities to use new skills, then we must be honest about it. We must be open about the likely direction of our work at a team or department level. People can decide for themselves what they wish to develop, but they can only decide if they have the whole picture, if we communicate our long term plans to them.

12.7 Does the Future Ever Come?

IT skills planning can be a vicious circle: we can't use the new technology until we have the right skills, but by the time we have developed the skills, the technology has changed again. Preparing for the future can be frustrating if the predicted skill sets have changed by the time we get there, having done all that training, or if the predicted skill sets are still valid but the organizational requirements have changed in the meantime. Faced with all this uncertainty, many IT departments shy away from planning for future skill requirements. It can be very hard to justify the investment whether in terms of money or time. Where there is a clear business driver giving a clear need for change then the investment can be justified, but in this situation it is not likely to be future skills we need to develop so much as nearly immediate ones. The business users cannot wait for us to retrain as well as to develop a new solution to support their changing requirements. This is a gloomy picture but unfortunately one that is all too common in reality.

In the absence of any clear direction for future skills, probably the best we can do is to develop adaptability and business awareness. We can develop our people so they are able to relate to many different approaches to IT solutions. This means giving them introductory training in many of the techniques and tools not currently in use on our teams. We would like them to be able to relate to a new approach so that they can learn about it quickly when the time comes. We don't need them to be multi-skilled so much as multi-aware, willing and able to develop new skills readily. We also need to encourage business awareness among our IT people. They need to be able to understand the pressures and difficulties faced by their customers. If our people have some understanding of the business problems their users face, then they will be better equipped to understand the changing requirements of the business over time, and to provide solutions that solve the new problems.

12.8 Summary

In this chapter, we have looked at the problems of planning for future skill requirements:

- Planning for future skills – we must plan for the foreseeable future. We can plan at a department level or at a team or project level.
- Analysing future needs – starting with the business goals and relating these to new technology trends, analysing job roles and related skill sets, and deciding which people to train in what new skills.
- Carrying out the training – devising a training programme that includes introductory as well as in-depth training, working as an organization or with a training partner to deliver the training programme.
- Supporting self-development – recognizing that some individuals will want to develop their own skills for the future and supporting and encouraging them in that desire.
- Does the future ever come? – recognizing that although it is not always appropriate to plan for specific future skills, still we can lay the foundations by developing our people's adaptability and business awareness.

In this book I have outlined some of the things that we as team leaders can do to support our people in their skill development. The most important thing we can do is to encourage their quest for new ways of doing things. We can help them to learn to learn, to find the lessons to be found in mistakes and apparent failures. As team leaders we strive to develop our people into skilled individuals who can learn for themselves and from each other, able to meet whatever challenges the future brings.

Bibliography

References

Barton, D. (1995) Organization Design and On-the-Job Learning: their Relationship in the Software Industry, *Centre for Labour Market Studies Annual Research Conference Session 5 – 3rd September 1995*. University of Leicester, Leicester.

British Computer Society (1998) Continuing Professional Development. British Computer Society, Swindon, `http://www.bcs.org.uk`

British Computer Society (1999a) British Computer Society, Swindon, `http://www.bcs.org.uk`

British Computer Society (1999b) European Computer Driving Licence (ECDL). British Computer Society, Swindon, `http://www.bcs.org.uk`

British Computer Society (1999c) Information Systems Examinations Board (ISEB). British Computer Society, Swindon, `http://www.bcs.org.uk`

British Computer Society (1999d) Professional Membership (Qualified Grades). British Computer Society, Swindon, `http://www.bcs.org.uk`

British Computer Society (2000a) Industry Structure Model. British Computer Society, Swindon, `http://www.bcs.org.uk`

British Computer Society (2000b) Professional Development Scheme (PDS). British Computer Society, Swindon, `http://www.bcs.org.uk`

Honey, P. and Mumford, A. (1992) *The Manual of Learning Styles*. Peter Honey Publications Ltd, Maidenhead, `http://www.peterhoney.co.uk`

Humphrey, W. S. (1997) *Managing Technical People*. Addison-Wesley Longman Inc, Reading, MA.

Kalinauckas, P. and King, H. (1994) *Coaching: realizing the potential*. Institute of Personnel and Development, London.

Keen, J. (1981) *Managing Systems Development*. John Wiley & Sons, Chichester.

Kolb, D. (1984) *Experiential Learning*. Prentice Hall, Englewood Cliffs, NJ.

Lovell, R. B. (1980) Learning Skills, Chapter 5 in P. J. Hills (ed.) *Adult Learning*. Halsted Press, a division of John Wiley & Sons, Chichester.

Open University (2000) Open University, Milton Keynes, `http://www.open.ac.uk`

Parkin, A. (1980) *Systems Management*. Edward Arnold, London.

Soat, D. M. (1996) *Managing Engineers and Technical Employees*. Artech House, Norwood, MA.

Background Material – Training Theory

The training literature is vast, but written from the point of view of the training profession. The following publications have informed my experience and discussions:

Anderson, R. E. (1994) Matrix Redux, *Business Horizons,* 37(6): 6–10.

Bartlett, C. A. and Ghoshal, S. (1990) Matrix Management: Not a Structure, a Frame of Mind, *Harvard Business Review,* 72(4): 138–145.

Buckley, R. and Caple, J. (1995) *The Theory and Practice of Training,* Third Edition. Kogan Page Ltd, London.

Centre for Labour Market Studies (1993–94) *MSc in Training Course Materials,* Modules 1–3. University of Leicester, Leicester.

Dangot-Simpson, G. (1991) Making Matrix Management a Success, *Supervisory Management,* American Management Association, 36(11): 1–2.

Kearns, P. and Miller, T. (1996) *Measuring the Impact of Training and Development on the Bottom Line – an Evaluation Toolkit to Make Training Pay.* Technical Communications (Publishing) Ltd, Hitchin.

Phillips, J. (1991) *Handbook of Training Evaluation and Measurement Methods,* Second Edition. Kogan Page Ltd, London with Gulf Publishing Co. (Book Division), Houston.

Rae, L. (1991) *How to Measure Training Effectiveness,* Second Edition. Gower Press, Aldershot.

Reid, M. A., Barrington, H. and Kenney, J. (1991) *Training Interventions,* Third Edition. Kogan Page Ltd, London.

Robbins, S. P. (1990) *Organization Theory – Structure, Design and Applications,* Third Edition. Prentice-Hall Inc, Englewood Cliffs, NJ.

Robinson, K. R. (1988) *A Handbook of Training Management,* revised second edition. Kogan Page Ltd, London.

Wood, W. (1988), *Continuous Development, the Path to Improved Performance.* Institute of Personnel and Development, London.

Background Material – Technical Focus

The following publications, some of which have been cited above, are written about management topics from the point of view of a manager of technical people. Some are specific to training and some are specific to the computing industry:

Association for Project Management (2000) Association for Project Management, High Wycombe, http://www.apm.org.uk

Barton, D. (1995) Organization Design and On-the-Job Learning: their Relationship in the Software Industry, *Centre for Labour Market Studies Annual Research Conference Session 5 – 3rd September 1995.* University of Leicester, Leicester.

Bellinger, A. (2000) Lotus Everything, *IT Training,* Feb. 2000.

Eager, A. (2000) The Return of the Apprentice, *IT Training,* Feb. 2000.

Earl, M. J. (1989) *Management Strategies for Information Technology.* Prentice Hall International (UK) Ltd, Hemel Hempstead.

Hiscock, J. (2000) Unipart's Online University, *IT Training,* June 2000.

Humphrey, W. S. (1997) *Managing Technical People.* Addison-Wesley Longman Inc, Reading, MA.

Institute of IT Training (2000) Institute of IT Training, Coventry, http://www.iitt.org.uk.

Institute for the Management of Information Systems (1997) http://is/lse.ac.uk/iswnet/profact/idpmhome.htm

IT National Training Organization (2000) http://www.itito.org.uk

Keen, J. (1981) *Managing Systems Development.* John Wiley & Sons, Chichester.

Lorriman, J. (1997) *Continuing Professional Development – a practical approach.* Institute of Electrical Engineers, London.

Lotus (2000) Lotus Development Corporation, Cambridge MA, `http://www.lotus.com`

Microsoft (2000) Training and Services. Microsoft Corporation, Redmond WA, `http://www.microsoft.com`

Parkin, A. (1980) *Systems Management.* Edward Arnold, London.

Peppard, J. ed. (1993) *IT Strategy for Business.* Pitman Publishing, London.

Soat, D. M. (1996) *Managing Engineers and Technical Employees.* Artech House, Norwood MA.

Steed, C. (2000) The Five Best Sites for E-Learning, *IT Training*, April 2000.

Sun Microsystems (2000) Sun Microsystems, Inc, Palo Alto, CA, `http://www.sun.com`

Further Reading

The following publications, some of them already cited above, provide additional insight and suggestions for managers of technical people:

Honey, P. (1994) *101 ways to develop your people, without really trying!* Peter Honey Publications, Maidenhead.

Humphrey, W. S. (1997) *Managing Technical People.* Addison-Wesley Longman Inc, Reading, MA.

Lorriman, J. (1997) *Continuing Professional Development – a practical approach.* Institute of Electrical Engineers, London.

Soat, D. M. (1996) *Managing Engineers and Technical Employees.* Artech House, Norwood, MA.

The following publication provides an introduction to IT topics. It is suitable for business managers trying to see where IT fits in the business context, and for new entrants to IT from a business background:

Peppard, J., ed. (1993) *IT Strategy for Business.* Pitman Publishing, London.

Index

academic course, *see* higher
  education
academic year 56
accreditations 47–53
  assessment methods 50–51
  description 47
  main features 47–49
  purpose 49–50
  selection criteria 52
  when to use 51
  see also national vocational
    qualification
  see also professional
    qualification
  see also proprietary certification
action group 81–84
  entry-focused 82–83
  role-focused 82
  topic-focused 82
action plan 17–18
activist, *see* learning models
adaptability 134, 185
adult learning, *see* learning models
adventure course, *see* outward
  bound course
analytical ability 134
assessment 48, 50–51, 115–127
  examination 48, 50–51, 55–56, 117–118
  portfolio of evidence 48, 50, 53
  project 56, 59, 61
assessment centre 125–127
Association for Project Management
  (APM) 53
audio cassettes, *see* self-study

Barton, D. 144
behavioural competency, *see*
  competency
books, *see* self-study
briefing, *see* learner support
British Computer Society (BCS) 51, 108,
  113, 117–118
business analysis 83, 126–127, 162–163
business awareness 13, 42, 178–179, 185

C++ 14–18
career development 103–114
  defining job roles
    see role definition
  developing within a role 111–112
  experience as a training
    method 103–106
  moving between roles 109–111
  professional society support 112–114
coaching 32, 34, 35, 38, 41–42, 78–81, 111
  to support long-term study 81
  what to discuss 80
  when to coach 80
  who can coach 78–80
Cobol 98
commercial background 166
communication (as competency) 134
communication network 163, 172
communication skills 68–70, 75–78, 81
competency 107, 126
  definition 130–131
  examples, *see* individual
    competency
  room for improvement 133
  uses 131–133
computer fundamentals 166, 174
computer studies 54, 59, 60, 61–62
computer-based training,
  see self-study
conceptual thinking 134
conferences 111, 112
conscious competence, *see*
  learning models
Continuing Professional
  Development (CPD), *see*
    professional development
contract staff 7
corporate university, *see* higher
  education
cost centre management 35, 37
course, *see* training course
course feedback form, *see*
  evaluation
customer, *see* stakeholder
customer service 52, 121

database support 24, 97–98
day-release 53, 56–57, 60
debriefing
   see evaluation
   see learner support
degree course, *see* higher
   education
department structure 144–150
   hybrid 149–150
   impact on training 144–150
   matrix 147–149
   project-based 146–147
   traditional 144–145
developing others 131–132
development activities 108, 111–112
development centre
   125–126, 136
development review 9, 109
diploma course, *see* higher
   education
distance learning, *see* higher
   education

e-learning 27, 57–58
education 1
education course, *see* higher
   education
European Computer Driving
   Licence (ECDL) 118
evaluation 15, 22, 85–101
   long-term
      see performance appraisal
   medium-term 91–94
      post-experience questionnaire 91–92
   the need to evaluate 87
   remedies 98–100
   short-term 88–91
      course feedback form 89
      debriefing session as evaluation
         tool 90–91
      post-course questionnaire 88–90
   what evaluation is for 85–87
   when and how to evaluate
      88–98
   worth of 100–101
examination, *see* assessment

feedback 13, 22, 86, 93
future skills 177–185
   analysing 178–181
   does the future ever come 184–185
   planning 177–178
   support 183–184
   training for 181–183

handling conflict 83
higher education 53–62
   corporate university 62
   course structures 59
   description 53
   distance learning 53, 57–59
   main features 54–56
   modes of attendance 53, 56–58
   open learning 53, 57–59
   selection criteria 60–61
   teaching methods 58–59
   when to use 59–60
Honey, P. and Mumford, A. 3–4
Humphrey, W. 144

Industry Structure Model (ISM) 108, 113, 179
influencing skills 13–14, 18, 24, 47
Information Systems Examination
   Board (ISEB) 47, 51
initiative 134
Institute of IT Training (IITT) 23, 89
Institute for the Management of
   Information Systems (IDPM) 113
internet 20, 22
   as research tool 111
   for training delivery 27, 57–59
interpersonal skills, 26–27, 29, 42, 126
   see also soft skills
interviewing skills 127
IT department structure, *see* department
   structure
IT management 46
IT National Training Organization
   (ITNTO) 49

Java 31
JCL 35–36
job roles, *see* career development
   see role definition
joining instructions 23, 156–158

Kalinauckas, P. and King, H. 5
Keen, J. 144
keyboard skills 5
Kolb, D. 3

leadership 30–31, 111, 126, 138–139
learner support 6, 65–84, 136, 140–141,
   183–184
   briefing form 66–67
   briefing session 66–68
   coaching, *see* coaching

debriefing form 71–72
debriefing session, as support 71–74
post-training 71–78
pre-training 65–71
reinforcing the learning 74–75
learning by experience 2
  see also career development
  see also learning log
learning centre 27, 28
learning culture 8
learning cycle, see learning models
learning from mistakes 6, 8
learning log 104–106
learning models 3–5
  conscious competence 5
  learning cycle 3, 6, 8, 74
  learning styles 3–5, 12, 21, 22–23, 29, 60
    activist 3, 12, 22
    pragmatist 4
    reflector 4, 29, 61
    theorist 4, 29, 61
learning objectives 14–17, 22, 60,
  66, 90
learning points 8, 21, 22, 35, 74, 104
learning styles, see learning models
learning to learn 8
lessons learnt 71, 74, 105
library, see training library
Lotus Authorised Education
  Center 50
Lovell, R. 5

mentor 112
  choosing 44
  skill mentor 148–149
mentoring 41–47
  description 41–42
  main features 42–43
  schemes 45–46
  success factors 45
Microsoft Certified Network Engineer
  (MCNE) 52
Microsoft Certified Software Engineer
  (MCSE) 47
multi-skilling 163–164, 185

National Training Standards, see
  training, standards
National Vocational Qualification
  (NVQ) 47–52, 62
negotiating skills 137–138
new methodology (any) 97, 158–162
new technology, moving to 10, 11–12
nurturing 8, 44

objectives
  see learning objectives
  see training objectives
on-the-job training 32–40, 91
  activities 34
  description 32
  form 33
  planning 32–35
online university 59
open learning, see higher education
Open University 53, 54, 57, 61, 184
outward-bound course 140

Parkin, A. 144
partnership 6, 62, 162, 181–182
performance appraisal 9
  as an evaluation tool 94–95
  observations of performance 120–121
  for skill assessment 119–122
  viewpoints 119–120
performance review, see performance
  appraisal
portfolio of evidence, see assessment
post-course questionnaire, see
  evaluation
pragmatist, see learning models
presentation skills 14–18, 31–32, 35,
  38–40, 127, 130–131, 137
professional development 112–114
  Continuing Professional
    Development (CPD) 113
  Professional Development
    Scheme (PDS)113–114
  see also development activities
professional qualification 47–52
professional society 47, 49, 50, 51, 112–114
programming skills 172, 174
project
  in accreditations, see assessment
  in higher education, see assessment
project management 31, 53
proprietary certification 47–52
psychometric tests 122–125
  description 122–123
  reasoning skills 123–124
  room for improvement 124–125
  uses 124

quality of training, see training, quality
quality of work 11

Rapid Application Development
  (RAD) 68, 75, 80

reasoning skills, *see* psychometric
    tests
reflector, *see* learning models
remedies, *see* evaluation
REXX 71, 78, 104
role definition 106–109, 113, 131, 179
    role definition sheet 106–108
role model 44, 136–137, 139
role profile 179–180
    see also role definition

self-development 134
self-study 25–32, 163
    audio cassettes 30
    books 29
    computer-based training 25–28, 88
    description 25
    selection criteria 30
    training videos 29
short course, *see* training course
simulation 27, 28, 31, 53
skill 2, 5, 107, 130
    examples, *see* individual skill
    non-technical, *see* soft skills
    technical 115–116
skill assessment
    see assessment centre
    see performance appraisal
    see technical testing
    see psychometric tests
skill development 1, 5, 78, 86, 91, 95
skill gap 119, 180
skill set 5, 106–108, 130, 147, 179–181
skill test, *see* technical testing
smaller IT department, *see*
    training, in smaller IT department
Soat, D. 8
soft skills 129–141
    challenges 139–141
    developing 135–139
    what soft skills are 130–131
        see also competency
    which ones are important 133–135
software engineering 54
SQL (Structured Query
    Language) 30
stakeholder 5–7
    customer 6–7
    individual 5–6
    organization 6
    team 6
    team leader 6
    trainer 6
strategic vision 24–25, 178
stress management 13–14

structure of IT department, *see*
    department structure
styles
    see learning models
    see training styles
support, *see* learner support

taught course, *see* training course
teaching objectives, *see*
    training objectives
teaching styles, *see* training styles
team leader
    role in training 7–8
teamworking 138
technical testing 115–119
    methods 116–118
    uses 118–119
technical background 46
theorist, *see* learning models
time management 11, 24, 31
trainees 165–175
    encouraging 174–175
    graduate entrant 170–172
    how to develop 167–169
    mature entrant 172–174
    organizing training 169–170
    programme 169–170
    supporting 83–84, 170
    what they need to know 166–167
training 1
    budget 23, 25, 86–87, 147, 155–156
    evaluation form, *see* evaluation
    feedback form, *see* evaluation
    providers, *see* training suppliers
    quality 22, 88–90
    in smaller IT department 163–164
    standards 48–49
    venue 23, 155
    videos, *see* self-study
training accreditations 23
Training and Enterprise Councils
    (TECS, SCOTVECS in Scotland) 20, 50
training course 19–25, 88, 91
    description 19–20
    main features 20–21
    selection criteria 22–23
    suitable 21–22
    when to use 21–22
training evaluation, *see* evaluation
training evaluation form, *see*
    evaluation
training event 153–161
    checklist 155–156
    detailed requirements sheet 153–155
    details sheet 155–157

evaluation 158
  practical arrangements 155–158
  requirements 153–155
training feedback form, *see*
  evaluation
training library 28, 30, 163, 182, 184
training needs 9–17
  perceived 9–10
  real 10–14
  SMART objectives 14–17
training objectives 22, 66
training programme 28, 150–163,
  181–183
  description 150–153
  setting up 162–163
training style 21, 22–23

training suppliers 20, 85, 88, 99–100,
  153–155, 162
  preferred suppliers 22, 23

understanding the business, *see*
  business awareness

videos, *see* self-study
virtual university, *see* online university
Visual Basic 23–24

word processor 25
workbooks, *see* self-study, books

PRACTITIONER SERIES

Series Editor: *Ray Paul*
Editorial Board: *Frank Bott, Nic Holt,*
Kay Hughes, Elizabeth Hull,
Richard Nance, Russel Winder and Sion Wyn

These books are written
by practitioners for practitioners.

They offer thoroughly practical hands-on advice on how to tackle specific problems. So, if you are already a practitioner in the development, exploitation or management of IS/IT systems, or you need to acquire an awareness and knowledge of principles and current practice in an IT/IS topic fast then these are the books for you.

All books in this series will be clear, concise and problem solving and will cover a wide range of areas including:
- systems design techniques
- performance modelling
- cost and estimation control
- software maintenance
- quality assurance
- database design and administration
- HCI
- safety critical systems
- distributed computer systems
- internet and web applications
- communications, networks and security
- multimedia, hypermedia and digital libraries
- object technology
- client-server
- formal methods
- design approaches
- IT management

All books are, of course, available from all good booksellers (who can order them even if they are not in stock), but if you have difficulties you can contact the publishers direct, by telephoning +44 (0) 1483 418822 (in the UK & Europe), +1/212/4 60/15 00 (in the USA), or by emailing orders@svl.co.uk

www.springer.de www.springer-ny.com

Managing
Electronic Services
A Public Sector Perspective

PRACTITIONER SERIES

Åke Grönlund

Managing Electronic Services provides an easy to read and practical guide to portal-electronic services development in the public sector. This book takes an organisational perspective asking 'How do you make things work in your organisation and in relation to your customers or users?' By integrating the managerial, technical and economic issues, the authors can put them into context with the need to understand user requirements and expectations.

Contents

Introduction
Part I - The Story of The Dozen Challenges
Challenge 1: Start Up
Challenge 2: Thousands of Pages
Challenge 3: Messy Appearance
Challenge 4: Parallel Systems
Challenge 5: Choosing the Future Technical Platform
Challenge 6: Cross-Departmental Integration of Data Resources
Challenge 7: Staff Motivation
Challenge 8: Poor Usability
Challenge 9: Where is the Payoff?
Challenge 10: What is Our Role?
Challenge 11: Where Are the Users?
Challenge 12: Managing Administrative Tribes
Conclusions From the Dozen Challenges
Part II - Electronic Service Management
Introduction to Part II
Cities and the Local Information Society
Conclusions
References

268 pages
Softcover
ISBN 1-85233-281-6

Please see page 197 for ordering details